Pension Fund Governance

Pension Fund Governance

A Global Perspective on Financial Regulation

Edited by

John Evans

University of New South Wales, Australia

Michael Orszag

Watson Wyatt Ltd, UK

John Piggott

University of New South Wales, Australia

Edward Elgar

Cheltenham, UK • Northampton, MA, USA

Published by
Edward Elgar Publishing Limited
Glensanda House
Montpellier Parade
Cheltenham
Glos GL50 1UA
UK

Edward Elgar Publishing, Inc.
William Pratt House
9 Dewey Court
Northampton
Massachusetts 01060
USA

A catalogue record for this book
is available from the British Library

Library of Congress Control Number: 2008927681

ISBN 978 1 84720 485 1

Printed and bound in Great Britain by MPG Books Ltd, Bodmin, Cornwall

Contents

List of Figures	vii
List of Tables	ix
List of Contributors	xi
Acknowledgments	xiii

1. Introduction   1
   John Evans, Michael Orszag and John Piggott

PART I   FRAMEWORKS

2. Pension Fund Governance: Expertise and Organizational Form   9
   Gordon L. Clark
3. Pension and Corporate Governance Reforms: Are They Twins?   30
   Mario Catalán
4. Conflicted Super Structures: Are Australian Investors Being Short-changed?   61
   Anthony Asher

PART II   GLOBAL GOVERNANCE: PRACTICE AND EXPERIENCE

5. Pension Supervision: Understanding International Practice and Country Context   99
   Richard P. Hinz and Anca Mataoanu
6. Governance of Public Pension Plans: The Importance of Residual Claimants   139
   Gregorio Impavido
7. Benchmarking the Performance of Superannuation Funds   158
   Hazel Bateman and Robert J. Hill

PART III   COUNTRY STUDIES

8. Public Sector Pension Governance, Funding and Performance: A Longitudinal Appraisal   179
   Tongxuan (Stella) Yang and Olivia S. Mitchell

v

9. How Do Australian Superannuation Fund Trustees Perceive
    Their Role and Effectiveness?   200
    Vrinda Gupta, Henry Jin, Michael Orszag and John Piggott

PART IV   GOVERNMENT GUARANTEES

10. Pricing Defined Benefit Pension Insurance   223
    David McCarthy and Anthony Neuberger

References   247
Index   259

Figures

3.1	Endogenous Determination of the Share of External Funds Raised (x^*)	40
3.2	Endogenous Determination of the Level of Investor Protection (k^*)	44
3.3	The Effects of Reforms	49
4.1	Sources of Conflict of Interest and Duty	75
5.1	Intensity Scales for Pension Supervision Activities	109
5.2	Australia: Intensity of Supervisory Activities	111
5.3	United States: Intensity of Supervisory Activities	113
5.4	Ireland: Intensity of Supervisory Activities	114
5.5	Hungary: Intensity of Supervisory Activities	117
5.6	Mexico: Intensity of Supervisory Activities	120
5.7	Chile: Intensity of Supervisory Activities	121
5.8	Argentina: Intensity of Supervisory Activities	123
5.9	Hong Kong: Intensity of Supervisory Activities	124
5.10	Correlation among Primary Elements of Pension Supervision: Licensing, Analysis, Intervention and Correction	126
5.11	Correlation among Primary Elements of Pension Supervision: Communication and Monitoring	127
5.12	Primary Elements of Supervision and GDP per Capita	128
5.13	Primary Elements of Supervision and Financial Market Development	129
5.14	Rule of Law Index and Average Score of Intensity of Supervisory Activities	131
5.15	Primary Elements of Supervision and the Number of Privately Managed Pension Funds	132
5.16	Type of Retirement Income Provision System: Mandatory versus Voluntary	134
5.17	Intensity of Supervision	136
9.1	Mean Response of Australian and British Trustees to Industry Issues	216
10.1	Historical Default Rates of Global Bond Issuers, 1970–2003	231
10.2	Distribution of Claims in Worst One-year and Five-year Period in 30 Years	237

Tables

4.1	Australia: Main Types of Superannuation Fund	62
4.2	Australia: Manner of Investment of Fund Assets	65
4.3	Australia: Asset Allocation of Funds by Type of Fund	85
4.4	Australia: Funds' Costs as a Share of Their Assets by Type of Fund	86
4.5	Australia: Wealth Management and Insurance Industry Charges	87
A4.1	Australia: Aggregate Gross Returns of Funds by Type of Fund	93
6.1	Investment Mandates	149
6.2	Investment Policy Restrictions	149
6.3	Portfolio Allocation	150
6.4	Board Composition	152
7.1	Benchmarks Used by Funds for Typical Investment Options	161
8.1	United States: Public Plan Assets, Liabilities, Funding and Contribution Patterns, and Public Plan Investment Performance	181
8.2	United States: Summary of the Empirical Findings of Previous Research on Public Plan Funding	183
8.3	United States: Determinants of Public Pension Plan Funding Status and Investment Performance	192
8.4	United States: Estimated Responsiveness of Key Explanatory Variables	195
9.1	Australia: Distribution of Funds and Trustees	203
9.2	Australia: Background of Trustees	204
9.3	Australia: Expertise of Trustees	206
9.4	Australia: Beliefs, Attitudes and Working Relationships of Trustees	208
9.5	Logit Results: Quality of Meetings, Skill Mix and Responsibilities	210
9.6	Australia: Decision Making	212
9.7	Logit Results: Board Cohesion, Responsibilities and Time	214
9.8	Logit Results: Good Governance, Skill Mix and Awareness of Fiduciary Responsibilities	214

9.9   Logit Results: Time, Decision Making and Financial
        Proficiency   214
9.10   Australia: Industry Issues   215
A9.1   Breakdown of Trustees' Responses to Industry Issues   218
10.1   Premium and Average Claims with Structural Default   235
10.2   Simulation of Claims in Worst One-year and Five-year
        Period in 30 years   236
10.3   Five-year Ratings Transition Matrix (p_{ij}) and Distribution
        of UK Pension Schemes by Rating Category   243
10.4   Cross-subsidies under Different Premium Arrangements   244

Contributors

Anthony Asher, Visiting Associate, Department of Actuarial Studies, Macquarie University, Sydney

Hazel Bateman, Associate Professor, School of Economics, University of New South Wales, Sydney

Gordon L. Clark, FBA, Halford Mackinder Professor of Geography and Executive Director, Oxford University Centre for the Environment; and Senior Research Associate, Labor and Worklife Program, Harvard Law School, Harvard University, Cambridge MA

Mario Catalán, formerly Assistant Professor, School of Advanced International Studies, Department of Economics, Johns Hopkins University, Washington DC; currently Economist, International Monetary Fund Institute, Washington DC

John Evans, Associate Professor, University of New South Wales, Sydney

Vrinda Gupta, Economist, Watson Wyatt Worldwide, Delhi

Robert J. Hill, Professor, School of Economics, University of New South Wales, Sydney

Richard P. Hinz, Pension Policy Adviser, Human Development Network, World Bank, Washington DC

Gregorio Impavido, Senior Financial Economist, World Bank, Washington DC

Henry Jin, Research Associate, Centre for Pensions and Superannuation, University of New South Wales

Anca Mataoanu, Consultant, Human Development Network, World Bank, Washington DC

David McCarthy, Lecturer, Finance Group, Tanaka Business School, Imperial College, London

Olivia S. Mitchell, International Foundation of Employee Benefit Plans Professor of Insurance and Risk Management, Executive Director of the

Pension Research Council, and Director of the Boettner Center for Pensions and Retirement Research, Wharton School, University of Pennsylvania, Philadelphia PA

Anthony Neuberger, Professor of Finance, Warwick Business School, University of Warwick, Coventry

Michael Orszag, Head of Research, Watson Wyatt, London

John Piggott, Professor of Economics, Australian School of Business, University of New South Wales, Sydney

Tongxuan (Stella) Yang, Research Affiliate, Pension Research Council, Wharton School, University of Pennsylvania, Philadelphia PA

Acknowledgments

The authors would like to thank Watson Wyatt Ltd for their research support in the production of this volume.

1. Introduction

John Evans, Michael Orszag and John Piggott

Global pension fund assets amounted to over US$23 billion in 2007, and that is before the substantial amount of pension savings in insurance vehicles is taken into account. There are few markets across the major developed economies in which pension and life insurance assets combined do not represent more than half of all financial assets; in some countries they comprise more than four-fifths of all assets under management. Corporate and government pension funds often do not have assets on hand to meet all their liabilities, so asset-based measures potentially understate the importance of pensions and pension funds to economies.

Pension funds and long-term pension-related savings vehicles are key investors in financial markets and critical in providing retirement incomes. Good governance of pension funds is therefore crucial, not only in protecting the interests of contributors, but also in advancing good governance at the enterprise level. We need to keep in mind that for many large corporations, benefits and pension obligations are a significant fraction of their total overall obligations, and therefore an important component of corporate governance in their own right.

Yet there are plenty of disappointments in pension fund governance. Corporate pension funds rarely play an important role in advancing broader corporate governance agendas. Instead, most of the activist pension fund investors tend to be public investors such as the California Public Employees' Retirement System (CalPERS). But for every activist public pension fund with a strong corporate governance agenda, there are many others around the world that operate with multiple agendas, seeking to support local or national infrastructure at the expense of higher returns for members. Pension fund boards of trustees are often viewed as not having the appropriate level of expertise or as responding too conservatively to changes in market conditions. And governance and long-run incentives are often an afterthought in public policies on pensions.

There was a wave of interest in corporate governance following the collapse of Enron and WorldCom in 2002 and the subsequent passage of the

Sarbanes-Oxley legislation, designed to improve the governance and accounting standards of American companies. However, this has largely left pension funds and pension issues untouched. It is true that in the United Kingdom, the 2001 Myners review considered the pension trustee issue (HM Treasury 2001), and the subsequent Morris review examined a number of other pension-related questions (HM Treasury 2005). It is also the case that accounting standards for pension fund reporting in various countries have improved somewhat, although accounting standards have little to do with the major governance issues in pension funds.

Unlike corporate governance legislation, which has changed significantly in recent years, pension fund governance structures have been slow to evolve. A recent survey of multinationals by Watson Wyatt (2007) found that pension fund governance is a big issue for most multinationals because of the underlying risks. In fact most companies have made changes to their governance arrangements in the past three years. However, because of the complexity of governing global benefit plans, the desired centralization of governance has proven challenging to implement. About half of large US multinationals appear to lack centralized decision making, even with regard to benefit design. In practice, the information that central headquarters has about benefit structures and obligations in distant locations is sometimes very incomplete.

More attention needs to be given to the development of good pension fund governance structures. Legislation drawn up for corporations and other institutional investors may not be appropriate for pension funds. While governance structures vary considerably across countries, there is a general tendency for pension fund governance to involve more consensus and less emphasis on technical skills and other considerations than is the case for other forms of investment.

The OECD has played an important leadership role in drawing attention to the need for better pension plan governance standards. In July 2002 it approved a set of guidelines for pension fund governance (OECD 2002). This marked the first initiative by OECD countries to set international standards for the governance and oversight of pension funds. The guidelines set out specific standards for transparency, actuarial valuations, auditing, accountability and legal structures; they provide an important benchmark by which legislation and individual pension funds can be judged.

But in many respects devising the guidelines is not the hard part; the principles of good governance are clear enough, but implementation is another matter. Guidelines need to be translated into a practical, workable regulatory and supervisory framework. At the same time, private sector practice needs to develop in accordance with the guidelines. Overcoming the obstacles here is not simple, as there are major gaps in experience and capabilities both in government and in industry. The Sarbanes-Oxley legislation has shown the drawbacks of heavy-handed use of legislation to solve underlying governance problems. The potential implications of pension legislation are similarly worrying, because the levels of capability and expertise to develop and implement legislation are that much more limited.

Academics also have some way to go to develop their capabilities in pension fund governance. The academic literature on this topic is sparse. This volume aims to begin to fill some important gaps in the literature by bringing together original contributions from around the world on a number of subjects related to pension governance. Because this is the only collection to date of academic work on pension fund governance, we felt it was important to strike a balance between the various dimensions of the governance problem. We wanted to make sure that the theoretical frameworks were represented, but at the same time we wanted to leave space to report empirical work. We wanted to cover private pensions, while also acknowledging that public pension funds are extremely important actors. We wanted to cover most of the major markets of the world, but at the same time include articles on key countries. The structure of the book reflects these various interests.

THE ORGANIZATION OF THE BOOK

The book is divided into four parts. Part I lays out the main frameworks for pension fund governance. Part II examines global governance practice and experience. Part III contains country studies on pension funds in the United States and Australia. The final section discusses the role of government guarantees.

Part I: Frameworks

In Chapter 2, Gordon L. Clark looks at the structure and organizational form of corporate pension plans. He argues that codes of conduct are unlikely to be effective on their own in dealing with governance issues. Instead, he suggests that human capital factors such as the qualifications, expertise and judgment of pension fund trustees are likely to be more important.

Next, Mario Catalán looks at the need for reform of member protection as funds make the transition from pay-as-you-go to fully funded arrangements (Chapter 3). He also looks at the effects of such reform on capital markets.

In Chapter 4, Anthony Asher describes the conflicting relationships that exist in pension fund systems. He shows how these conflicts create the potential for significant problems and argues, in particular, that they lead to higher costs. He suggests a combination of pension simplification and governance reforms as an important step forward.

Part II: Global Governance: Practice and Experience

Richard P. Hinz and Anca Mataoanu begin the section on global governance by attempting to classify the supervisory practices in place around the world (Chapter 5). They find that a country's level of economic development, financial structures and legal framework all play an important role in determining the type of supervision in use.

Gregorio Impavido argues in Chapter 6 that there is a need for strong governance procedures in public pension plans to ensure adequate transparency and accountability.

In Chapter 7, Hazel Bateman and Robert J. Hill consider the appropriate construction of benchmarks for adequate measurement of the investment performance of pension funds.

Part III: Country Studies

This section begins with an article by Tongxuan (Stella) Yang and Olivia S. Mitchell (Chapter 8). They construct data on US public pension plan practices related to administration, benefits, contributions and membership. They then correlate this information with plan funding patterns and investment performance. Yang and Mitchell find that management practice and governance variables play a very important role in determining funding levels. They suggest particular governance reforms to improve the investment performance of public pension plans.

In Chapter 9, Vrinda Gupta, Henry Jin, Michael Orszag and John Piggott report the findings of a survey of governance in Australian superannuation funds. This survey, which covered over a quarter of the top 200 funds in Australia, found that trustees emphasize consensus over technical issues and that there is hostility to formal regulation. The results are strikingly similar to those of an earlier survey carried out in the United Kingdom (Robinson and Kakabadse 2002; Kakabadse, Kakabadse and Kouzmin 2003), even though the pension structures of the two countries are very different. This may be because, before the introduction of licensing in 2005, Australian structures for pension governance had been static for some time.

Part IV: Government Guarantees

The last section looks at guarantee funds. Guarantee funds such as exist in the United States and United Kingdom are a symptom of the lack of attention of policy makers to governance issues, rather than the cause of governance issues for pension plans.

In Chapter 10, David McCarthy and Anthony Neuberger examine the recent introduction of the Pension Protection Fund in the United Kingdom. They model the cost of providing pension insurance and argue that some form of cost smoothing and redistribution is inevitable in a social guarantee fund. They conclude that if all pricing were risk based, it would be so volatile as to be politically unacceptable.

We are the first to acknowledge that this collection of papers, while breaking new ground, leaves many questions unanswered. Although pension funds and pension savings are extremely important, research into pension fund governance is in the early stages relative to the corporate governance literature. At the same time, we believe that this book pulls together much that is valuable in pension governance research and will play a vital role in providing a foundation for further research.

PART I

FRAMEWORKS

2. Pension Fund Governance: Expertise and Organizational Form

Gordon L. Clark*

1. INTRODUCTION

Pension funds are remarkable institutions. In the Anglo-American world, public and private pension funds provide employer-sponsored pension benefits, including defined benefit, defined contribution and hybrid schemes. These are vital supplementary institutions given the modest value of most countries' social security benefits (Emmerson 2003; Munnell 2003). Charged with the responsibility of protecting and, in some cases, insuring beneficiaries' promised retirement income, pension funds are institutions that must be governed.[1] Golden rules such as the exclusive benefit rule do not always resolve the dilemmas, conflicts of interest and reasonable doubts over the proper course of action facing pension funds (Clark 2006). Those who are knowledgeable about pension funds and related institutions will readily acknowledge this as a fact of life;[2] those more removed from the practice of decision making in trust institutions and drawn to parsimonious recipes of institutional form in economic theory may find the argument contentious (see, for example, Jensen 2000).

Historically, trustees have had considerable discretion (in the scope of decision making) when exercising their responsibilities (protecting the welfare of beneficiaries). Given the covenant or mandate of each fund when established, and given the presumption in favour of supervision as opposed to direct regulation, trustees have wide-ranging powers consistent with the English common-law trust institution (Langbein 1997). Discretion with responsibility provides an opportunity for plan-specific, efficient and equitable solutions to retirement income provision, perhaps more so than if the state were to regulate plan decisions directly. Over the twentieth century, however, legislation became more intrusive with regard to trustee responsibilities, and the scope of discretion was narrowed with respect to ensuring the public interest in pension security and equity (Blake 2003). But the scope of discretion foreshadows the principal–agent problem, just as trustee responsibility can be understood in terms of the moral hazard problem.[3] The governance of trustee decision making is a crucial issue for the integrity of private pensions and the provision of pension benefits, whether defined benefit, defined contribution or some hybrid version of these (Clark 2003a).

Much is expected of pension funds, in part because of their importance as institutional investors in national and global financial markets. In the aftermath of the dot-com boom, bubble and bust, academic and policy commentators raised doubts about the skills and expertise of pension fund trustees. Shiller (2002), for example, suggested that the herd behaviour of institutional investors, combined with the use of benchmarks measuring the relative performance of pension funds, contributed to the escalation of the speculative bubble. He contended that if pension fund trustees had exercised appropriate judgment in a timely fashion, the bubble could have been contained. In a related vein, the Myners report on the decision making of British institutional investors and pension fund trustees suggested that the latter lacked the expertise necessary to make independent judgments in the face of the influence of consultants and the financial services industry (HM Treasury 2001). And yet, throughout the industry, an often heard lament is the risk aversion of fund trustees. Sophisticated risk management strategies are often eschewed in favour of convention. Inertia seems commonplace.

In this chapter I explore the problem of pension fund governance. Given the scope of trustee discretion and responsibility, I focus on the internal governance of pension funds. Implied by discretion is a supposition that trustees have considerable expertise, whereas the reality is a world characterized at best by trustee competence and at worst by amateurish confusion. Absent trustee expertise, governments may be tempted to regulate the actions of plan officials in ever finer and more comprehensive detail. I suggest that the tension between discretion and regulation is actually a dispute about the nature of decision making in general and the prospects for trustee expertise in the context of financial risk and uncertainty. As is apparent from recent work (Clark, Caerlewy-Smith and Marshall 2006, 2007), I argue that trustee competence is more likely than trustee expertise in these circumstances; expertise suggests a quality of decision making rarely achieved by most people.

In sections 2 and 3 of the chapter, I look at the form and functions of pension funds and their codes of conduct. As intimated above, the pension fund is unusual when compared with the institutions that exist in much of continental Europe. Its functions follow its historical form, with due regard to its evolution over the twentieth century. I look more closely at the relative status of competence and expertise in section 4 before moving on to consider Rawls' (1954) classic paper on rule-based decision making in section 5. This allows me to reconsider the virtues or otherwise of procedural as opposed to substantive measures of trustee decision making. To sustain my argument, I refer briefly to the path-breaking work of Gigerenzer et al. (1999) and his colleagues on heuristics and shortcuts. In the penultimate section of the chapter, I look once again at the governance of contractual relationships, arguing that pension funds must develop an institutional form and expertise consistent with their reliance on consultants and the fund management industry. Unfortunately, recent commentators on the topic have tended to rely on idealized models of the trust institution and trustee decision making; in the end, I argue that better governance demands a different institutional form than that inherited from the nineteenth century.

This chapter develops these arguments with respect to internal governance (the principal–agent problem). In a related paper (Clark 2006), I have examined the regulation of plan governance (the moral hazard problem), noting the evolution and development of the various regulatory regimes used to manage the issue. Together, this and my previous paper provide a critical perspective on the problems of pension fund governance relevant to the Anglo-American world of public and private pension systems.

2. PENSION FUND FORM AND FUNCTIONS

For F.W. Maitland, one of the leading legal historians of the nineteenth century, the trust institution had a unique place in English law and statute.[4] Historically, it provided private agents with considerable discretion away from the direct scrutiny and tax powers of the Crown. It separated the interests of beneficiaries from the interests of those charged with administering the trust, allowing for the preservation of wealth and its transfer between generations. In fact, Maitland suggested that the perpetual nature of the trust and its reliance on a functional model of trustee responsibility encouraged economic and financial innovation. He cited a number of examples, including the creation of Lloyd's of London and the London Stock Exchange. He observed that by the end of the nineteenth century, the combination of trustee discretion and responsibility had facilitated the liberalization of what counted as an investment asset and the transfer of wealth between the landed gentry and the emerging urban industrial elites. He noted, moreover, that the trust relationship was neither a contractual relationship nor a strictly commercial relationship; it was (and is) a form of obligation.[5]

Pension funds inherited their governance procedures from English common law and the trust institution. Much has been written about this institution, its significance for Anglo-American commercial and financial systems (Langbein 1997) and its significance for the evolution of private retirement income systems over the last 50 years or so (Hawley and Williams 1999). Although now just one element in a comprehensive web of nation-state statutory and market regulation, it remains an important reference point in setting the roles and responsibilities of pension fund trustees (Ellison 2002). It provides justification for trustee discretion in the interest of beneficiaries' welfare, subject to the public interest in the equitable treatment of beneficiaries. At the same time, the trust institution has no equivalent in much of continental Europe; it requires a stretch of the imagination to equate trustees' responsibilities for beneficiaries' welfare to the responsibilities of fathers for the welfare of their families (as in France). In fact, the trust institution is an important element in observed systemic differences between whole countries' legal and financial systems.[6]

At the same time, as I have shown elsewhere (Clark 2007), pension funds are hardly transparent organizations governed without fault or favour by trust and statute. There remain systemic problems of asymmetrical information that work against the efficacy of fund governance (cf. Jensen 2000). Trustees' motivations are difficult to observe; the interests of plan administrators and service providers are not always apparent; and the costs of market failure are too often borne by those who should otherwise benefit from pension fund decision making. In this respect, pension funds are like other organizations in having shortfalls in governance and regulation that make them vulnerable to the principal–agent problem and the moral hazard problem.[7] As a consequence, there is a significant premium associated with the proper internal governance of pension funds; that premium can be priced as beneficiaries' welfare, but it can also be priced as the value of innovation in the design of pension benefit systems and the investment of pension fund assets.

The trust institution provides pension funds with a generic form. But as we know, there are all kinds of pension funds—some governed by a single trustee; some governed by sponsor-nominated trustees; some governed by a mix of sponsor and beneficiary representatives; and some including independent and professional trustees. There are also public and private funds; funds sponsored by single or multiple employers; and craft, union and industry-sponsored funds. As well, funds vary according to the nature of the benefits offered: final salary (defined benefit), accumulation (defined contribution) and related hybrid versions of these (including cash balance schemes). Few defined benefit plans hold elections for trustee boards; most trustees are nominated and appointed by the plan sponsor. On the other hand, larger defined contribution plans tend to seek nominations from, and hold elections for, member representatives. There are systemic differences between countries in terms of the dominant type of fund, just as there are differences within countries. For example, the United States has a number of very large, public defined benefit funds governed and administered by a single trustee, as well as many thousands of small defined contribution schemes governed by trustees appointed by the plan sponsor.

Whatever their differences, pension funds have a number of commonalities. Most funds perform three functions, most of which can be outsourced to industry service providers: (1) administration; (2) determination of benefit eligibility and value; and (3) asset management. Administrative functions include the collection, tagging and protection of pension contributions. In a mature fund, administrative procedures may be dominated by the valuation and distribution of benefits to retirees. At issue is the cost efficiency of carrying out these functions, especially if a fund is small relative to the provision of such services by third-party agents. Benefit adjudication functions may include the determination of eligibility against plan criteria, the resolution of difficult cases and the enforcement of procedures regarding the separate interests of plan sponsors and beneficiaries. Asset management functions may include asset–liability matching and asset allocation (in defined benefit plans) or the evaluation of investment product providers and the provision of advice on investment options and policies for plan participants (in defined contribution plans).

Whatever the functional performance of funds, it is apparent that funds have considerable discretion and responsibility in executing these functions. Plan participants are, more often than not, participants by virtue of their employment contract; in most cases, plan participation is a condition of employment.[8] In the few countries where a market exists for pension participants to switch between plan providers, it is not clear that switching decisions are consistent with the time horizon over which the relative virtues of competing plans should be considered. It is also apparent that plan participants rarely if ever play an active role either in the governance of pension funds or in the scrutiny of administrative and trustee decision making. Even when plan participants are adversely affected by specific actions and policies, few appeal. When they do appeal, the relevant procedures are obscure, cumbersome and overwhelmed by the language of the plan covenant. Third-party appeal procedures are similarly problematic and time consuming. Finally, it is clear that collective action by plan participants with respect to plan governance has proven very problematic. The costs of such action are prohibitive. As a consequence, prior membership of an employee representative group (such as a union) is an important way of mobilizing plan participants and beneficiaries.

Exit, voice and loyalty—the conventional mechanisms used to govern the principal–agent relationship—are rarely if ever directly available to plan participants. Trustees may be 'representative' of plan participants, but they are not directly accountable in the sense we associate with representative democracy. Indeed, Maitland argued that the trust institution was conceived as it was precisely to avoid the need for ongoing close scrutiny and regulation of agent decision making.[9]

3. CODES OF CONDUCT

Given pension funds' lack of direct accountability, it is not surprising that the regulation of their tasks and functions is an important issue. Elsewhere, I look at the 'external' regulation of funds, emphasizing moral imperatives, legislation and market mechanisms (Clark 2006). But there is a different model of regulation, one focused on internal governance procedures and the nature and quality of trustee decision making. In this section I consider codes of conduct. Recently, governments have sought to strengthen corporate codes of conduct in the aftermath of accounting and financial scandals in companies such as Enron and WorldCom (in the United States) and Ahold and Parmalat (in Europe). At the same time, the interventions of public sector pension funds in issues related to corporate governance and global standards of behaviour have prompted industry commentators to raise exactly the same questions about the governance of pension funds, and especially the role of political appointees to trustee boards (Clark and Hebb 2004).

Unlike in the corporate arena, however, it is very difficult to design and implement a single code of conduct for pension funds; as noted above, funds come in many different shapes and sizes, recognizing, no doubt, the historical legacy of English common law, employer interests and nation-state development. The trust institution has been important precisely because of the multiplicity of possible formations, as noted by Maitland. However, the debates over the pension fund directive, the financial services directive and the development of a single European capital market have all served to underline the importance of common expectations, if not a common history, for such institutions. In this regard, the OECD's (2002) guidelines for pension fund governance, designed for 'autonomous, collective and group pension funds that support private occupational pension plans', stand as an important reference point. The guidelines deliberately and explicitly exclude individual pension funds and insurance systems, but recognize trusts, foundations and corporate entities as pension plan sponsors.

It should be recognized that the OECD's (2002) guidelines have a form and logic consistent with the OECD's (2004) principles of corporate governance. One way or another, the implied relationship and apparent overlap between these two types of regulatory instrument suggest a common concern for the financial performance and stability of both types of institution. However, common concern does not exhaust the interests of the constituencies served by these different types of regulatory regime. Indeed, given the debate in Europe over the proper role and status of private pension funds, the OECD guidelines can be seen as part of a larger agenda aimed at encouraging European pension 'reform' and institutional innovation.[10]

In large part, the OECD guidelines have a significant normative quality in that they focus on the proper organizational form of pension funds and their accountability. While not expressed as such, we can identify three core principles underpinning the guidelines. In the first instance, they are conceived to ensure that pension fund decision making is *consistent* with the terms and conditions of the pension plan covenant or mandate. Here, there is a concern for the interests of the plan sponsor and beneficiaries. In the second instance, the guidelines encourage the design and implementation of *coherent* internal rules and procedures. Here, there is a concern that the formal structure of decision making implies logic and order rather than arbitrariness. In the third instance, the guidelines suggest that the organization of pension funds must be *compatible* with high standards of behaviour. Probity and professional standards are the issues in this regard. These three principles—consistency, coherence and compatibility—are at base all about ensuring that pension funds are managed and organized according to recognized standards of behaviour.

Looking at the detail, the OECD guidelines recommend that pension funds be governed by recognized statutes, bylaws, rules and regulations that provide (among other functions) for the monitoring and oversight of administrative decision making. They also recommend high standards of behaviour, indicating that those in positions of responsibility should as far as possible be fully informed about the nature and consequences of their decisions, consistent with their responsibilities. The guidelines recognize the need for high levels of professionalism and expertise and suggest that pension funds seek appropriate external advice. Reporting should be accurate, timely and clear in a manner consistent with full disclosure to plan stakeholders. The guidelines recommend the appointment of external auditors, actuaries and custodians such that there are independent checks on plan solvency, financial integrity and pension benefit security. In sum, they suggest that pension funds should be organized rationally, rather than being subject to the whims of plan officers or the faith of plan sponsors.[11]

Three basic questions may be raised about the comprehensiveness of the OECD guidelines. Most importantly, there is an ambiguity at the very heart of the guidelines: recognizing that private pension plans have sponsors and beneficiaries, the guidelines are silent about their respective powers and responsibilities. Furthermore, the guidelines are all about establishing and maintaining pension funds as whole organizations protected from the pernicious interests of insiders and outsiders. Again, if this is to be the case, what are the powers of pension funds in relation to their sponsors and beneficiaries? This issue comes into play most obviously with regard to plans that offer defined benefit pensions. In this case, plan sponsors may pay a high price indeed for their separation from pension fund decision making in the interest of sustaining coherence and compatibility. In other cases where beneficiaries carry the risk of benefit value—as in defined contribution plans—the beneficiaries may pay the price for coherence and compatibility.

Implied by the guidelines, moreover, is an assumption that the formal organization of a pension plan according to the principles of consistency, coherence and compatibility is sufficient to drive its functional performance.

On the face of it, this is a remarkable assumption.[12] It may be true if functional performance is measured in terms of the cost effectiveness of administrative and service-related tasks measured against industry standards. Cost efficiency is a very important criterion by which to judge performance, even if comparable data are difficult to obtain (especially in a world where industry providers bundle services together). If apparently self-evident in terms of the economic theory of institutions (see Jensen 2000), it ignores the reality of transaction costs, multiple and inconsistent objectives, and a lack of clarity in large organizations between the means and ends for any particular task or function. Of course, greater efficiency is possible and desirable. But organizational form is just one component among many in determining institutional performance (March 1994).

At the same time, the guidelines are clear about the need for responsible plan officials to obtain, where necessary, the expert advice needed to make better decisions. Like many codes of conduct governing corporate boards of directors, the OECD guidelines recognize that pension fund officials and board members may not have the specialist skills or expertise available in the financial services industry. This is more true of some functions than others; investment management, including strategic and tactical asset allocation, requires a level of expertise and experience that is in very short supply in the academic world and industry, let alone private pension funds (Campbell and Viceira 2002). It is clear, moreover, that the connection between fund governance and investment decision making in the context of risk and uncertainty is quite problematic. The OECD guidelines are properly vague about this particular issue, notwithstanding the fact that investment decision making is as important for fund sponsors and beneficiaries as cost effectiveness in the provision of member services.

4. TRUSTEE EXPERTISE AND COMPETENCE

In the previous two sections, I analysed plan officers' discretion and responsibility in managing pension plans. The presumption in favour of plan officers means that a great deal is expected of their decision-making capabilities. I suggest in this section that there are two rather different views on this matter. Before proceeding, however, we should be clear about the assumptions we might make about rationality—a core concept in social science theory and a crucial behavioural anchor in studies of the performance and structure of financial markets (Houthakker and Williamson 1996; Litterman et al. 2003).

Williamson (1996) assumed economic agents to be *intentionally rational*, rather than *ipso facto* rational in the strong sense associated with much of neoclassical economic theory (cf. Jensen 2000). This definition, which Williamson owed to Herbert Simon (1982), suggests that rationality is a social practice subject to cognitive limits and the vagaries of the environment in which decision making takes place, rather than a universal, once-and-for-all state of mind. Moreover, emphasis on intentionality implies deliberate planning and the possibility that decision making may improve over time.[13]

For policy makers, the Myners report makes this connection clear. It was sponsored by the UK Treasury to determine

> the extent to which institutions' approaches to investment decisions are:
> * rational;
> * well-informed;
> * subject to the correct incentives; and
> * as far as possible, undistorted (HM Treasury 2001: 4).

After commenting briefly on the significance of UK institutional investors in terms of the volume of assets they own and their significance for equity markets, the report identifies occupational pension funds as the most important group of institutional investors; it is their decision making that is the focus of the report itself. The report notes that a survey of about 250 trustees conducted for the review indicated that 'many trustees are not especially expert in investment'. For example, a majority had no professional qualifications in finance or investment; had little initial training; did not attend training courses during the first 12 months of appointment; and spent very little time during the week preparing for pension fund investment decisions.[14]

If being an expert is so important, what is meant by the terms 'expert' and 'expertise'? The Myners report is not entirely clear on this point. But in discussions with UK industry insiders, policy makers and pension fund representatives, it has been suggested that experts should have four qualities: (1) high levels of formal education; (2) professional qualifications; (3) task-specific training; and (4) significant levels of experience. These four qualities are generic in that they are particular neither to the pension fund sector nor to the investment services industry—they are the qualities of an expert whatever that person's occupation or industry. None of these qualities are acquired quickly; in combination, they require time, effort and resources. Becoming an expert also requires continuity of occupation, the incremental accumulation of relevant knowledge and the application of that knowledge to related problems and issues over a long period of time. Troublingly, it would seem that few people are truly experts, and that very few people under the age of 40 *could* be experts. Not surprisingly, in many cases formal education and professional qualifications may be deemed sufficient to compensate for the lack of experience.[15]

Being an expert need not translate directly into expertise, however. Wagner (2002) suggests that expertise is performance related with respect to problem solving in specific settings. Summarizing the literature, he suggests that expertise has four cognitive attributes:

1. Experts spend proportionally more time assessing the problem and less time solving it, compared to novices who do just the opposite.
2. Experts recognize and categorize problems on the basis of deeper principles, whereas novices recognize and categorize problems on the basis of surface features.
3. Experts are able to perceive large patterns of information quickly.
4. Experts have superior memory, both short- and long-term, for problem-relevant information (Wagner 2002: 57).

In essence, a person's problem-solving ability can be measured, assessed and evaluated over time against accepted benchmarks of performance. As with solving crossword puzzles, a person can practise, improve on and hone each attribute to perfection. We can judge who is, and who is not, good at problem solving in specific contexts. Expertise combines cognitive attributes with cost effectiveness and consistency over time, assuming that deeper principles and calibrated experience allow individuals to adapt quickly and efficiently to changing circumstances and new situations.

Are plan trustees experts if judged against the model of expertise presented above? Myners and many in the Anglo-American financial services industry have no doubt about the answer to that question: too few, given the importance of their tasks and responsibilities. At the same time, there are many plan tasks and functions that do not demand the statistical and pattern recognition skills associated with investment management (Bunt, Winterbotham and Williams 1998); experience in personnel management, dispute resolution and rule interpretation may well be just as important. In this respect, there are often significant differences between trustees in terms of the qualities and attributes of their expertise. In a survey of recently appointed pension plan trustees undertaking training with the UK National Association of Pension Funds, it was found that some trustees had the first two qualities of an expert and were familiar in their own professional lives with some of the attributes associated with effective problem solving. But many trustees were not so accomplished, although by virtue of their experience they may have been familiar with the problems of personnel management. Few trustees had the substantive knowledge or experience industry observers claim are so important in developing expertise (Clark, Caerlewy-Smith and Marshall 2006, 2007).

The available evidence would suggest that trustees are less skilled than their peers (advisers, plan administrators, service providers and perhaps even some regulators). The fact that plan administrators are paid substantially less than those who perform similar functions in large financial services companies suggests that, even here, there is an unequal distribution of analytical and financial skills across the industry. And the fact that pension fund trustees are hardly ever compensated in proportion to their responsibilities suggests that their motives are quite different from those of industry service providers. Considering that pension fund trustees are rarely appointed for their expert qualifications and attributes in pension fund management and investment, it would appear that few plan officers would qualify as experts. Only in the largest corporate pension funds dominated by sponsor-nominated trustees employing the knowledge and skills of corporate treasury departments might such expertise be realized. Short of replacing nominated trustees with a cadre of independent professionals appropriately compensated for their responsibilities, the model remains an abstract ideal (cf. Horack, Martin and Young 2003).

The alternative model for pension fund governance is a 'competency' model associated with the market for financial services, which combines the available skills of administrators and trustees with well-defined rules and procedures for decision making. In this model, funds take advantage of the mix of skills available within the institution, recognizing the different skills needed for the effective performance of the various functions of the fund and the need to locate responsibility with well-managed subcommittees. Fund performance would depend in part on the extent to which internal competence allowed for the recruitment of expert advice from industry consultants and financial service providers, subject to appropriate safeguards on conflicts of interest and independence. At the limit, the competency model puts the weight of governance on the governance of contractual relationships, and implies that a crucial test of fund competence is the ability to hire and fire industry service providers according to independent standards of performance. The competency model of pension fund governance implies that plan officers are best seen as consumers, rather than the locus, of expertise. At the same time, the demand for expertise provides plan officers with a set of criteria by which to judge those offering their services.

At one level, the competency model is a version of what often happens in the industry (Clark 2000). At the same time, the model makes four presumptions: (1) that plan officers should be chosen in part for their skills in relation to a mix of functional responsibilities; (2) that internal rules and procedures should be well conceived with respect to the execution of the management of tasks and functions; (3) that, wherever possible, tasks and functions should be outsourced to industry providers according to independent, competitive standards of performance; and (4) that the purchase of external services should be governed by selection criteria and assessment procedures based on high standards of expertise.

5. DECISION MAKING: RULES AND PROCEDURES

Considering the importance of rules and procedures for pension fund decision making, we should be clear about their nature and significance. Our lives are governed by rules. Most obviously, there are rules for driving a car, but more subtly, there are rules for conducting economic and social relationships. Some rules are formal and are codified in law. Others are informal and are part of customary practice learnt over time through context-specific experience. In many ways, the rules governing everyday life are rarely if ever considered explicitly; more often than not, they are fully integrated into behaviour and are considered only if, for some reason, they fail to work. On the other hand, the rules and procedures governing the decision making of pension funds and their relationships with external service providers have a deliberate or explicit quality to them such that their design and implementation is (or should be) monitored continuously.

One (strong) theory of rules would have it that their design and implementation are determined by the expected value of desired outcomes. By this logic, one rule or one set of rules may be judged better than others by virtue of the consequences. Following Rawls (1954), a number of implications follow from such a theory. In the first instance, it is supposed that we make each and every decision on its merits, applying the available skills and experience in such a way as to maximize the results of our actions. In the second instance, it is commonly supposed that people with similar skills and experience sharing similar goals would decide issues in much the same way. So if, for example, pension fund boards are comprised of trustees with the same expert qualities and attributes, and are similarly committed to maximizing beneficiary welfare, then decision making should be unproblematic at least with respect to the shared criteria used to make decisions. Thus, it is arguable that rules develop over time such that, as each issue is confronted, it is simultaneously *placed* according to past decisions, and decisions made in past cases are applied as rules to current cases.

In this theory of decision making, expertise is crucial. The four attributes of expertise identified above have an important role to play in locating each and every issue with respect to inherited rules; assessing the problem, categorizing the problem, placing the problem in relation to recognized patterns and processes, and using knowledge of the past to adjust the decision-making process are all important for the integrity of rules. Over time, with a sequence of issues that is more or less the same, it is supposed that the classification of issues becomes quicker and the application of rules to those cases more or less automatic. We would expect that both the speed of decision making and its efficiency would improve over time as the rules themselves become more coherent and better defined with respect to one another. Even so, it should be recognized that rules are only valuable with respect to their utility. If new cases or issues come along that do not fit with the rules, then the rules would have to be adjusted and refined. Ultimately, each and every issue becomes a test of the inherited rules; the rules themselves have no virtue other than the substantive value of their results.

This is a most demanding theory of rules. Consider the following objections, relevant to the issue of pension fund decision making. Underpinning the logic of the argument is an assumption of homogeneity with respect to both the skills and expertise of trustees and their commitment to a single objective function (maximizing beneficiary welfare). While such an assumption may be necessary for the logic of governance, it seems quite unlikely given the nature and composition of many pension boards. As well, the importance of information processing with respect to case recognition in relation to *a priori* defined patterns presupposes that trustees have the knowledge, time and resources to undertake such analysis. More likely, the only groups with the requisite knowledge, time and resources are the external service providers. Even expert pension fund trustees are likely to depend on others for this kind of analysis—hence the necessity of governing the principal–agent relationship. Furthermore, the formation of rules out of cases presupposes the stability of the underlying processes. Uncertainty may cloud judgment, introducing doubt about the placement of cases against pre-existing patterns and, ultimately, the allocation of issues to their relevant rules. Cases and rules may be lost in ambiguity, conflict or doubt.[16]

Most importantly, the strong theory of rules verges on the super-rational. In allocating cases to rules, in revising and adapting rules in relation to new cases and in judging the utility of rule-based behaviour against its consequences, remarkable assumptions have to be made about the robust rationality of trustees and their agents. Implied is a process of comprehensive and continuous assessment of each and every issue, ignoring resource constraints, cognitive limits and the need for timely decision making. In this idealized world, there are no systemic psychological biases (for example, risk aversion) or cognitive traps (for example, herd instinct or market speculation). Against all the psychological evidence to the contrary, trustees are assumed to follow issues in all their complexity through to conclusion; the real world of decision making is largely ignored (Gigerenzer et al. 1999). It is a theory of rule making that would disqualify most trustees from the decision-making process; indeed, it would seem to disqualify almost anyone from serving on a board of trustees. In the end, this theory of rule-based decision making is as profoundly paternalistic as it is idealistic.

A rather different view of the nature and significance of rules and procedures would have it that they are social assets, embedded in institutions and driven by the need to economize on resources and time. By this logic, rules and procedures are task related and develop as institutions develop in an incremental fashion around the execution of tasks and functions. More often than not, economic agents do not take the time to design or remake inherited rules; at most, they adapt or adjust existing rules within the constraints of their organizations. Where rules and procedures are imposed on institutions, as is often the case with statute-based rules and regulations, economic agents may have to deal with overlapping and even conflicting sets of rules that are neither coherent with respect to one another nor unambiguous as to their ultimate objectives. At the limit, rules and procedures are a bureaucratic skeleton resistant to the kind of rule-rationality sketched above but nevertheless valuable for the ways in which they define expected practice.[17]

As in the strong theory of rule making, I assume that the utility of rules has to do with their consequences. At the same time, if we assume that economic agents in general and pension plan trustees in particular have limited knowledge, time and resources, then rules allow economic agents to take short-cuts—to economize on the costs of decision making by providing an *a priori* reference point for issues as they arise. They are used, more often than not, as automatic filters for classifying the significance or otherwise of those issues. This is despite the fact that the consequences of such shortcuts may be seen, in a larger context, as less than optimal. In fact, this suggests that the social value of rules and procedures is to be found, not in their precise utility on a case-by-case basis, but in their generality. Being 80 per cent right may be sufficient for economic agents to hold to a set of rules, recognizing that evaluating exceptions is a time-consuming process. Only when exceptions accumulate and a pattern is revealed in those exceptions *might* those that rely on rules look to revising the rules themselves.

Of course, the reform and revision of rules is more problematic than the strong theory of rules would seem to suggest. In many cases, rules and procedures are social practices shared among institutions on the basis of their common problems and overlapping legislative frameworks. Rules and procedures may be both informal and formal, and their interpretation and application to specific cases are likely to be guided in part by the expectations of the relevant community (as noted by Shiller 2002). This suggests that institution-specific revisions to inherited rules and procedures may fall foul of community expectations notwithstanding their theoretical virtues. Moreover, in view of the widely shared nature of such rules and procedures, it may be difficult for any institution to claim authority in establishing new rules and procedures. Expertise may warrant such innovations; even so, rules and procedures have a life of their own outside of their immediate consequences. This is surely the reality experienced by many in pension fund management.

Most importantly, working by inherited rules and procedures may be a refuge for pension plan officers who can best be characterized as competent rather than expert in their fields. The challenge, in this context, is to design a set of rules and procedures in the public domain that requires pension plan officers to interrogate the efficacy of their decision-making practices while at the same time being sufficiently flexible to accommodate local innovations that go beyond common practice. More often than not, rules and procedures establish minimum standards of competence; however, they must also be able to accommodate changing circumstances that demand expert qualities and attributes. Too often public rules and procedures only penalize non-compliance, when they should also reward innovation outside the inherited framework of rules and procedures.

6. GOVERNANCE THROUGH CONTRACT

Rules are often effective but they may also promote less than optimal results. As well, the main object of such governance instruments continues to be defined benefit plans, despite the growth in popularity of defined contribution schemes. This is most apparent in the Myners report, where Treasury concerns about officers' lack of expertise in areas such as asset allocation and private equity partnerships are given a great deal of weight. But of course, the number of UK participants in defined contribution plans is growing quickly, and the rate of closure of defined benefit plans appears to be increasing, notwithstanding the continuing significance of defined benefit plan assets (Clark 2003a). Embedded in the defined contribution world is a model of plan governance that relies more on contract in the market for financial services than on plan expertise and the internal provision of tasks and functions. In this respect, contract buttressed by fiduciary duty represents an alternative model of plan governance.[18] Moreover, given the problems apparent in many pension plans with regard to competence as opposed to expertise, one option is simply to transfer to consultants and then to service providers the shortfall in requisite expertise.

There is a massive literature on contract, governance and organizational form.[19] I do not intend to rehearse the well-known claims and counterclaims about the virtues of contract for the design of institutions. Rather, I look at a simple and conventional view of governance through contracts and then suggest how that view might be modified in the light of the particular circumstances of many pension funds. As is well appreciated, the neoclassical theory of contract assumes that there are many buyers and sellers in the marketplace, that full information is available to market agents, that transaction costs are negligible and that there is nothing that would lock parties into second-order contracts. In effect, this is a world of discrete exchange that can be executed and revised (indeed revoked) without cost should better opportunities become available. There is considerable debate about the empirical and logical plausibility of this model.[20] For our purposes, it represents a conceptual reference point, if not exactly current practice.

Less discussed in the literature is the competence of contracting parties. There has been considerable discussion about the fairness of contracts, where one party is deemed less competent by virtue of the asymmetrical distribution of information (Cartwright 1991). Similarly, there is a long history of state intervention designed to protect parties to contracts against the costs of coercion, collusion and exploitation (Atiyah 1979). But while these issues may be important on a case-by-case basis, in relation to pension fund governance, it should be apparent that pension fund trustees must often defer to the expertise of other parties. Even if service providers are bound by fiduciary duty, in many cases pension fund trustees do not have the expertise necessary to question the expert judgment of the service providers; the only option available to many of them is to question the efficacy and efficiency of the procedures whereby service providers fulfil their tasks. In this respect, consultants have a vital role in representing trustees' best interests at the nexus of contracts. This is the most important contract, and it is characterized by continuity (over many cases) and longevity (over time) given the specificity of plan circumstances and interests.[21]

In these circumstances, any contract between a pension plan and its consultants must be sensitive to the costs and benefits of long-term commitment, and to the inability of trustees to observe the relationships between plan consultants and financial service providers. There is a subtle and difficult-to-calibrate trade-off between discounting the value of a contract given its long-term nature against the unknown opportunities for immediate reward offered by the financial services industry for specific deals. Indeed, to reap the benefits of the contract as a system of pension plan governance, it would seem necessary to have different types of contracts—some relational and some discrete—and to use the prospect of switching between providers and varying the terms of contract as a mechanism for disciplining potential and actual service providers. One response to these problems of governance may be to introduce third-party auditors and advisers. But as we have seen with recent corporate governance scandals, there is no guarantee that auditors will pick up conflicts of interest if secrecy between conspiring partners is the organizing principle. Transparency is an essential ingredient in governing such relationships (Hebb 2006).

At the core of this model of pension fund governance is the management of contract. This requires comprehensive and detailed systems of oversight and assessment. There is, however, an alternative. Instead of governing external contracts, pension funds may wish to keep their tasks and functions internal, governing their own employees through personnel contracts and the like. A variety of arguments may be made in favour of this approach. One is that internal contracts may be cheaper, because employees may be willing to take lower salaries in return for tenure of employment. It is apparent that the high cost of industry service providers is due, in part, to the cost of employees, recognizing that most employees trade off high current salaries against limited job tenure. Of course, there are dangers in such compensation strategies, including the selection bias implied regarding the risk-adverse nature of some employees in different organizations.

Another argument in favour of such an approach would invoke the mission of pension funds: unlike many industry service providers, pension funds have a beneficial ethical or moral mandate. This may allow for the coexistence of internal (less expensive) contracts with external (more expensive) contracts, since the moral mandate is a form of self-governance shared by employees (Clark 2006).

Here, of course, there is an issue of scale: few pension funds have a large enough asset base to be able to provide both routine and highly specialized tasks and functions at a competitive, performance-related price. Given the fact that the overwhelming majority of pension funds—whether defined benefit or defined contribution—are very small, this option is in practice irrelevant for most funds. Only in circumstances where funds amalgamate and form their own service-providing organizations may small funds be able to take advantage of their moral mandate. This is, of course, precisely the option favoured in a number of countries, including Australia and the Netherlands.[22] Even if these larger organizations do not internalize all tasks and functions, their larger size allows them to employ and retain highly qualified and experienced plan officials, thus evening out the distribution of expertise among funds, consultants and service providers (Clark 2003b). Missing in the United Kingdom and the United States, it seems, are adequate incentives for fund amalgamation and collective governance.

7. CONCLUSIONS

Maitland's history of the trust institution stretches back over many centuries. When comparing it to Germanic legal traditions, Maitland emphasized the uniqueness of the trust and the special place it occupied relative to the Crown and corporation. For Maitland, the trust had many beneficial features, not least of which was the separation of trustees' and beneficiaries' interests. He also suggested that it was a site of innovation, especially with respect to financial institutions and instruments. Similarly, legal scholars such as Langbein (1997) have argued that the trust institution is crucial in differentiating Anglo-American financial systems from their European cousins. These ideas find common cause among those advocating the relevance of trust-based pension fund institutions for European private pension and retirement income systems over the coming decades. It is arguable that idealization is a necessary element of any comparative analysis of nation-state economic and financial institutions (Allen and Gale 2000). But in this case, there are increasing doubts about the capacity of pension funds to operate as equal players in the market for financial services.

Doubts have been raised about the internal structure and management of pension funds; notwithstanding some widely recognized cases of outstanding pension fund management, it would appear that the vast majority of such funds are poorly organized relative to beneficiaries' welfare. In any event, to the extent to which they rely on external service providers for the execution of many of their tasks and functions, it would seem that the overwhelming majority of pension fund trustees defer to the expertise of service providers. In both cases, Maitland's nineteenth-century ideal has been overtaken by the increased complexity of funds' tasks and functions, and the astonishing growth of the financial services industry and its instruments over the past 50 years. In the United Kingdom, the Myners report argues that if funds are to fulfil their obligations to beneficiaries and take an active role in the financial services industry commensurate with their significance in terms of total assets, then the governance of pension funds must improve along with the knowledge and expertise of pension fund trustees. As is widely appreciated in the industry, many pension funds lack a rudimentary knowledge of advanced financial instruments.

In this respect, moves to 'reform' pension fund governance have taken a variety of forms. Most obviously, codes of practice have encouraged the development of management systems that are more consistent with pension plan tasks and functions. Such codes have added a level of specificity to governance not apparent in the generic qualities attributed to trust institutions. I have suggested that codes of practice are valuable both for their contribution to the cost efficiency and consistency of decision making and for their value as benchmarks in evaluating the functional performance of plans. Arguably just as important is that the quality of internal decision making distinguish between the expertise and competence of trustees. This is most obvious when considering the investment management functions of pension funds, but can be extended to any issue involving judgment about beneficiaries' welfare. One response has been to invest a great deal in internal rules and procedures, invoking tests of efficacy and efficiency. But, as noted, rules and procedures are more than instruments for promoting economic welfare (in general) and beneficiaries' welfare (in particular)—they play a vital social role in helping institutions cope with limited resources in the context of risk and uncertainty.

But too many 'solutions' do not confront the most important issue: the relative power of pension funds and their officers in the market for financial services. In that regard, I would suggest that the only real solution to the apparent problems of governance and lack of expertise within pension funds is their transformation into organizations that have sufficient internal resources to allow them to employ professional managers and advisers. This suggests that pension fund governance is as much an issue of size and scale as it is one of proper rules and procedures, competence and expertise. One of the lessons to be learnt from the Australian and Dutch experience is that large, industry-based pension funds are better able to compete in the marketplace for tasks and functions than smaller, single-sponsor pension funds. This does not mean that large multi-employer pension funds ought to be financial institutions in their own right; size and scale give pension fund trustees a choice about the nature of their organizational form, recognizing the costs and benefits of internal provision as opposed to being at the nexus of contracts with external providers.

Poor organizational systems combined with a palpable lack of expertise make many pension funds a soft target for unscrupulous financial service providers. Furthermore, at a time when large public-sector pension funds have played a significant role in promoting reform of corporate governance, the prospect of other large financial institutions being formed to occupy a similar position in the market for financial services will surely not be welcomed by entrenched corporate management. And yet this is exactly what is implied by government rules and regulations that require pension funds and related institutions to vote their proxies. At present, the small size and lack of expertise that characterize most pension funds mean that this policy is likely to remain the terrain of only the biggest funds. Only if governments promote the formation of larger, multi-employer pension funds will the apparent deficit in pension fund expertise be addressed in a manner consistent with the conscientious exercise of funds' responsibilities. And only this solution is consistent with the interest of the financial services industry in promoting financial innovation.

NOTES

*   This chapter is based on Clark (2004) and is part of a project on the governance and regulation of pension funds. It was funded in part by the National Association of Pension Funds. My thanks go to my colleagues Tessa Hebb, John C. Marshall and Emiko Caerlewy-Smith for their insights and inspiration. I also wish to record my appreciation for the interest shown in this work by John Evans, Christine Farnish, Simon Ford, Giles Keating, Roger Urwin, Michael Orszag and Ann Robinson. None of the above should be held responsible for any errors or omissions, or for that matter my inability to take into account their well-conceived comments and criticisms.

1.   In this chapter, the term 'governance' is used to refer to the formal mechanisms by which an institution makes decisions, is held accountable to its stakeholders and beneficiaries, and acts in accordance with public and private standards.

2.   See, for example, the essays on pension fund governance published by AMP, a leading Australian financial services company, in its *Insights* magazine (www.amp.com.au). In a brief editorial, John Evans suggests that the current interest in pension fund governance reflects growing unease about the responsiveness of pension fund officials to stakeholder interests (*Insights*, June 2003: 3).

3.   As Williamson (1996: 56) has observed, in theory the principal–agent problem and the moral hazard problem are closely related (when we combine self-interest with the asymmetrical distribution of information). Even so, in reality they are separable in that the scope of discretion depends on the governance of the principal–agent relationship, while the costs of trustee decision making are borne, more often than not, by beneficiaries. There are many agents in financial markets, both inside and outside pension funds. At the same time, it is not always

clear precisely who the principals are—plan sponsors, trustees, and plan beneficiaries and retirees can all claim to be heard in this respect (Black 1992).

4. Here, I refer to his essays on trust, the state and the corporation. Published in the first decade of the twentieth century, these have been collected and edited by Runciman and Ryan (2003).

5. 'Obligation' refers to a social claim on private agents to act properly—a normative imperative that may be defined by law but could be just a moral standard. Whether private agents act in accordance with an obligation is open to scrutiny and, at the limit, may be enforced by sanctions. I do not believe that an obligation is necessarily defined by its sanctions, however. Like Johnson (1991: 134–5), I would argue that:

> ... among the characteristic features of obligation is the idea that the performance of obligation is conceived to be a matter of legitimate interest and concern of others, whether they be members of some immediate group or community, or of humanity generally.

6. See La Porta et al. (1997, 1998) on the global map of financial systems and their rather different regulatory regimes.

7. See Clark (2000, 2003b) on the scope and significance of these issues for Anglo-American and continental European circumstances.

8. Mandatory plan participation is often encouraged by government regulation and tax benefits (Bateman, Kingston and Piggott 2001). In some countries, however, employees are given the option to opt out to another pension benefit provider at the time of engagement. In the United Kingdom, it is not obvious that the opt-out option has been beneficial to those that have taken it; plan participation is often more cost effective than any similar benefits available in the private insurance market. In any event, stability of plan membership is one condition for minimizing administrative costs.

9. This is evident in a number of ways. For example, plan administrators and trustees are only liable for wrongful decisions; any appeal against their actions must in some way show that those actions violated either the terms of the plan covenant or natural justice. Even if their decisions may result in adverse outcomes for plan beneficiaries, it is presumed that administrators and trustees act in the best interests of beneficiaries. Poor decisions are not the same as wrongful decisions. See Coleman (1992) for a theoretical exposition of this point and the related judicial decision (*Harvard College v. Amory* 26 Mass. 446 (1830)).

10. An example is the blueprint for pan-European pension institutions published by the European Federation for Retirement Provision (EFRP 2003).

11. In the United Kingdom, in the wake of the inquiry into Robert Maxwell's diversion of the Mirror Group's pension assets, the Pensions Act of 1995 went some way towards requiring rules and procedures that sustained the integrity of the trustee decision-making process.

12. This is most apparent when considering the failure of formal mechanisms of corporate governance and the related external audit agents used by institutional investors during the 1990s to assess corporate risk. See Coffee (2006) on the limits of such 'gatekeepers' in relation to the Enron debacle. He notes that, notwithstanding their reputational capital, professional gatekeepers acquiesced to managerial fraud.

13. Much of economic theory implies that the rational decision maker is an expert. At the same time, economic theory recognizes that there is a wide distribution of agent skills and knowledge. It is not assumed that all decision makers are the same; rather, there is a supposition that, where it matters, only expert decision makers will survive market arbitrage and competition. Survival of the fittest is the mantra (see Alchian 1950).

14. This confirms qualitative evidence presented by Bunt, Winterbotham and Williams (1998) and Thomas et al. (2000).

15. This is certainly common in the investment management industry, where there has been a proliferation of professional certificates and accreditation boards. See, for example, the website of the UK Society of Investment Professionals, which is a member of the Chartered Financial Analyst (CFA) Institute (http://www.uksip.org). These institutes oversee 'the CFA qualification, a globally recognized professional qualification'.

16. In these circumstances, conflict between those deemed responsible may become endemic to the trust institution, prompting the invention of rules and the arbitrary allocation of cases in

order to sustain the social if not economic process of decision making. See Clark (2000) on the collegial logic of collective decision making.

17. See Rawls (1954: 24) on the value of rules. He says in part:

> ... practices are set up for various reasons, but one of them is that in many areas of conduct each person's deciding what to do on utilitarian grounds case by case leads to confusion, and that the attempt to coordinate behaviour by trying to foresee how others will act is bound to fail.

A more recent development of the notions of practice and behaviour is to be found in the work of Bourdieu (1990).

18. Herein lies a most important difference between the regulatory systems of the United States and the United Kingdom. In the United States those involved in the management of pension fund assets must observe the principles of fiduciary duty, whereas in the United Kingdom this level of commitment is reserved for trustees and plan officials.

19. See generally Masten (1996) and Williamson (1985).

20. See Epstein (1999) and compare with Trebilcock (1993, 1999).

21. Klein (1996) provides a useful case study of the significance and possible consequences of institutional specificity for the formation of contracts. Most importantly, specificity may result in the vertical integration of financial functions and the formation of long-term contractual relationships that effectively capture those on either side of the contractual divide.

22. See Buckley (1999: 306), who notes, in relation to the conceptual niceties of current theoretical debate, that 'an ounce of comparative law is worth a pound of theory'.

3. Pension and Corporate Governance Reforms: Are They Twins?

Mario Catalán*

1. INTRODUCTION

In the last two decades, an impressive wave of pension reforms involving transitions from pay-as-you-go to partially or fully funded schemes has occurred in many developing countries, especially in Latin America.[1] The Latin American pension reforms have two characteristics: first, they were followed by legal reforms aimed at improving investor protection in capital markets; and second, governments restricted pension funds to holding mainly domestic securities. These characteristics motivate the questions addressed in this chapter: why do pension and corporate governance reforms occur together, and why do governments restrict pension funds to holding domestic securities only?[2] I argue that pension reforms must be followed by improvements in investor protection and provide a rationalization for the existence of portfolio restrictions aimed at preventing the international diversification of pension funds' assets.

In short, the complementarity of pension and corporate governance reforms results from the fact that policy making is influenced by special interest groups that have the political power to block the reforms.[3] Publicly traded firms in developing countries are typically owned by a handful of powerful groups that are able to influence the government and determine the level of investor protection in capital markets according to their interests. Workers and labour unions may also be powerful enough to block pension reforms. In such an environment, reforms can only occur if the relevant interest groups benefit from them. This chapter extends the 'crime and punishment' framework of corporate finance developed by Shleifer and Wolfenzon (2002) for a small open economy—a model that is consistent with the cross-country stylized facts of investor protection and capital market development—to determine the conditions that give rise to pension and corporate governance reforms.

The move from a pay-as-you-go pension system to a funded system in which investments are restricted to domestic securities creates a captive source of low-cost funds that gives domestic public firms the incentive to offer a more costly, higher level of investor protection. Workers, on the other hand, are willing to accept the change from a pay-as-you-go system that pays low-risk retirement benefits to a funded system that allocates their contributions to higher-risk domestic public firms only if a corporate governance reform reduces the expropriative activities of the public firms' insiders. Thus, simultaneous pension and corporate governance reforms are the outcome of a mutually beneficial agreement among interest groups.[4]

More specifically, influenced by the insiders or controllers of public firms, the government defines and protects investors' rights within the legal system. The law reflects public firms' choice of the optimal level of investor protection, and the role of the government is simply to detect violations and enforce the law. Given the atomistic structure of outside investors and the associated free-rider problem, crime detection and law enforcement require that the government monitor the public firms through supervisory agencies. Naturally, the cost of supervision and the level of investor protection will increase as the intensity of supervision increases. If the government makes public firms internalize the cost of supervision through a specific tax, firms choose the level of investor protection optimally by weighing the marginal benefit against the marginal cost of more protection. The marginal benefit of more investor protection is associated with the additional funds that firms can raise when they offer more protection to outsiders; the marginal cost is the increased tax associated with the greater enforcement costs incurred to create more investor protection. In this environment, publicly traded firms are willing to improve investor protection and pay the higher cost of legal enforcement if by doing so they can raise funds at a lower cost. The pension reform, combined with the portfolio restrictions on pension funds, creates the captive source of low-cost funds that makes the corporate governance reform feasible.

On the other hand, the pension reform must be acceptable to workers. If the pay-as-you-go system is non-compulsory—that is, as long as the returns on voluntary pay-as-you-go contributions are greater than the returns on international and domestic investments net of capital market participation costs (intermediation fees)—then workers are willing to accept the change from a pay-as-you-go to a funded system only if the latter offers a higher return on contributions. A corporate governance reform that improves investor protection makes this possible through two channels. First, it raises the return on domestic securities by reducing the probability of expropriation. Second, it develops domestic capital markets, and therefore reduces intermediation fees.

In this fashion, the corporate governance reform is necessary to make the pension reform acceptable to workers. However, public firms are not willing to offer more investor protection unless they can reduce their cost of funds. This can happen only if public firms are able to internalize part of the intermediation cost reduction that is caused by the corporate governance reform and the development of domestic capital markets. If there were no intermediation cost reduction, or if firms were unable to internalize it, then the corporate governance reform would not be feasible.[5]

Notice that the portfolio restrictions on international diversification are unnecessary (non-binding) if the corporate governance reform reduces the individual's intermediation fees in domestic markets but leaves the participation cost in international markets unchanged. However, the development of domestic capital markets may also reduce the individual's cost of participation in international capital markets. If this effect is sufficiently strong that unconstrained pension funds would only hold international assets, then the portfolio restrictions must be imposed to create the captive source of low-cost funds for domestic public firms that makes the corporate governance reform feasible in the first place.

If the pay-as-you-go system is compulsory, two other possibilities arise. First, a pension reform that allows pension funds to diversify their investments internationally is feasible and is the best outcome for workers. Second, if financial incumbents can impose their political might, they may be able to benefit from the fact that workers are willing to accept the pension reform, and from the portfolio restrictions aimed at creating a captive source of low-cost funds, without this requiring an improvement in investor protection. The pension reform without the corporate governance reform may benefit both workers and public firms. Thus, if the pay-as-you-go system is compulsory, no corporate governance reform occurs.

Finally, the analysis suggests that the lower the rate of return on pay-as-you-go contributions, the more likely it is that the twin reforms can be implemented. This seems consistent with the fact that the Latin American pension reforms occurred after periods of poor performance of their pay-as-you-go systems. If the returns on pay-as-you-go contributions fall steadily over the years, the incentive for interest groups to lobby for the twin reforms arises when the pay-as-you-go system is still voluntary and before the returns on contributions fall so low that the system becomes compulsory.

The previous arguments rest on the idea that improvements in investor protection help develop domestic capital markets, an effect that has been solidly documented in the literature. For example, La Porta et al. (1998, 2000) show that differences in the ownership structure of publicly traded firms across countries can be explained by the extent to which the law protects outside investors from expropriation by the insiders. In those countries where the rights of investors are protected by law and effectively enforced, firms raise more external finance, ownership is more diffuse and capital markets are more developed than in those countries where expropriative activity is punished only mildly by law.

The rest of the chapter is organized as follows. Section 2 briefly reviews the nature and effects of pension reforms and pro-investor legal reforms in Chile and Argentina, to illustrate the interaction between the two. Section 3 presents the author's model of pension and corporate governance reforms in a small open economy and analyses the results. Section 4 summarizes the main conclusions.

2. HISTORICAL BACKGROUND

This section briefly reviews the dynamic interaction between the pension reforms and the pro-investor legal reforms in Argentina and Chile since the 1980s. A corporate governance reform is defined as any change in the legislation or in the practical enforcement of the law that reduces the intensity of the expropriative activities of insiders.[6] Given the focus of this section on legislation rather than enforcement, the question arises as to whether the enactment of pro-investor laws *per se* improves corporate governance. I justify the exclusive focus on legislation on the following grounds. Before pro-investor laws are enacted, investors' rights are nonexistent, and therefore unenforceable. Upon the enactment of the laws, insiders and investors are uncertain as to whether the legislation will be enforced in the future. As long as they believe that there is a probability that enforcement will occur, the mere approval of pro-investor laws must discourage expropriation by insiders and make investors more willing to participate in domestic capital markets.[7]

In 1993, Argentina introduced legislation to change its pension system from a government-sponsored pay-as-you-go scheme to a private fully funded scheme (Law 24,241).[8] Pension funds were required to invest retirement contributions in financial assets, subject to some portfolio restrictions. Notably, they were restricted to holding no more than 10 per cent of their portfolios in foreign shares and government bonds. Even though Argentina already had basic legislation on capital markets dating from 1968, it introduced substantial new pro-investor legislation in the 1990s.

Chile changed its pension system from a government-sponsored pay-as-you-go scheme to a private fully funded scheme in 1980. Even though some pro-investor legislation had been introduced before then,[9] the country experienced a striking sequence of pro-investor legal reforms after the pension reform was launched.[10] The new pension funds were restricted to holding only domestic securities until 1992, when they were allowed to invest a maximum of 9 per cent of their total assets abroad.

It is possible to identify two stages in the dynamic interaction between pension reforms and investor protection in Argentina and Chile. In the first stage, pension reforms were followed immediately by pro-investor legislation. This first round of corporate governance reforms provided the minimum standards of protection and transparency necessary to make the pension reform acceptable to the population at large, whose retirement savings were to be allocated to domestic capital markets. In the second stage, pension funds became significant creditors and shareholders of a large number of publicly traded firms. They began to monitor the activities of these firms and initiate actions to defend minority shareholders against expropriation from the controllers.[11] The importance of pension funds in capital markets motivated, and provided the political impulse for, continual improvements in investor protection.

The laws improving investor protection in Argentina and Chile required, among other things, the independence of auditors, the risk rating of publicly traded securities and the public disclosure of transactions involving majority shareholders. They also regulated the use of privileged information and transactions between insiders and related parties. The new legislation gave minority shareholders more rights to sue boards and created pre-emptive rights to new issues. The text of recent legislation[12] in Argentina explicitly acknowledges that the predominance of pension funds in capital markets has motivated the new rules, while the post-pension reform legislation in both Argentina and Chile explicitly mandates the fiduciary duty of insiders towards minority shareholders. Thus, the new laws are aimed at moving both countries away from their civil law traditions, towards the practices of countries with a common law tradition.[13] Appendix A3.1 provides a more detailed account of the reforms, and of pension fund activism in Argentina and Chile.

3. MODEL

This section is organized as follows. The first subsection presents a general description of the economy that is the basis of the model, reviews some of the results obtained by Shleifer and Wolfenzon (2002), characterizes the optimal decisions of a risk-neutral individual with generic entrepreneurial skills g and shows how the level of investor protection is determined endogenously. The second subsection describes the heterogeneity in the demographic structure of the economy and characterizes the decisions of different groups under a pay-as-you-go pension system. The third subsection analyses the effect of a pension reform. The proofs to the propositions discussed in each of these subsections may be obtained from the author on request.

Description of the Economy and Decisions of a Risk-neutral Individual

Consider a small open economy populated by individuals endowed with productive or entrepreneurial skills g and initial wealth W_1. There is a single investment/consumption good. Each individual can invest her wealth in international markets and/or set up a domestic public firm and raise funds in the world capital markets to produce domestically. The entrepreneurial skills of an individual determine her (constant) productivity. Thus, the individual's productive project returns $1+g$ units of the good per unit invested. We assume that the rest of the world is populated by some risk-neutral investors who are willing to finance any project with an expected rate of return that is equal to the risk-free international interest rate i.

The model has two dates. Once an individual is born at date 1, she chooses whether to set up a public firm or participate in capital markets as an investor.

Due to their political influence, public firms jointly choose the level of legal protection of outside investors, $k \in [0,1]$. The role of the government is to supervise public firms and enforce the law. The government makes public firms internalize the costs of supervision and legal enforcement through a specific tax. The *total* cost of legal enforcement $C(k)$ is an increasing function of the investor protection level k, and is paid by public firms on a pro rata basis through the specific tax. Henceforth, we will also refer to this tax, which is equal to the legal enforcement cost per public firm, as the firm's cost of going public.

Denote by W the net wealth of an investor who sets up a firm; that is, W equals W_1 minus the cost of going public. First, the entrepreneur contributes an amount $R_E \leq W$ from her wealth to the firm and invests the remaining wealth $W - R_E$ in the market. Second, the entrepreneur raises an amount R_M from the market by selling a fraction

$$x = \frac{R_M}{R_M + R_E}$$

of the firm's cashflow rights to outsiders. Like Shleifer and Wolfenzon (2002), we assume that the entrepreneur retains control of the firm regardless of the fraction of cashflow rights sold. However, in contrast to Shleifer and Wolfenzon, we assume that the entrepreneur is restricted to selling cashflow rights that are equal to the fraction of the funds contributed by outsiders. In other words, if outsiders contribute a fraction x of the total initial amount invested at date 1, then they are entitled to receive a fraction x of the cashflow of the firm at date 2. Thus, all shares give rise to identical cashflow rights. The funds raised, $R_M + R_E$, are then invested in the project. Denote by I the scale of the investment project, $I = R_E + R_M$.

The individual can also opt to participate in capital markets as an *investor*, which is costly. The individual's participation cost can be interpreted as financial intermediation fees. Participation in international markets costs c_{int} per unit of investment and provides perfect risk diversification; that is, the investor earns a net risk-free rate of return equal to $i - c_{int}$. Participation in domestic capital markets consists of buying the shares of domestic public firms, and costs c_{dom} per unit of investment. The returns on domestic investments involve the non-diversifiable risk of expropriation by the firm's insiders.

Optimal decisions if the cost of going public is sunk

Suppose that the entrepreneur has already paid the cost of going public. Let us determine the optimal decisions of the entrepreneur.

At date 2, revenue Π is realized. After observing the revenue of the firm, the controlling entrepreneur chooses to divert fraction d of the revenue. The level of investor protection k is equal to the probability that she is caught diverting the revenue of the firm. If the entrepreneur is caught, she is forced to return the diverted amount to the firm and pay a fine $f(d)\,\Pi$ to the authorities. In this case, the entire revenue of the firm is distributed as dividends; that is, outside investors receive $x\,\Pi$ and the entrepreneur receives $(1-x)\,\Pi$. On the other hand, if the entrepreneur is not caught, she discloses a total revenue equal to $(1-d)\,\Pi$ to the markets, stealing the amount $d\,\Pi$. The disclosed revenue is then distributed as dividends to outsiders, $x(1-d)\,\Pi$, and to the entrepreneur, $(1-x)(1-d)\,\Pi$. The entrepreneur then consumes the appropriated net revenue.

The revenue of the firm, Π, and the entrepreneur's expected pay-off at date 2, U, are given by:

$$\Pi = (1+g)I, \tag{1}$$

$$U = (1-x)[1-(1-k)d]\Pi + (1-k)d\Pi - kf(d)\Pi + (1+i)(W - R_E). \tag{2}$$

At date 2, the entrepreneur chooses the level of diversion that maximizes her pay-off. The first-order condition is given by:

$$kf'(d^*) = (1-k)x, \tag{3}$$

where $d^*(x,k)$ is the optimal diversion level. The condition equates the marginal expected cost to the marginal expected benefit of diversion. The former is the marginal fine multiplied by the probability of detection. The latter is the extra revenue stolen from outsiders multiplied by the probability of keeping it.

Assumption 1: The function $f(d)$ satisfies:

a. $f(0) = 0$;
b. $f'(0) = 0$;
c. $f''(d) > 0$,
d. $f'''(d) > 0$;
e. $1 > \dfrac{f'}{f'' \cdot d} > \dfrac{\partial}{\partial d}\left(\dfrac{f'}{f''}\right) > 0$;
f. $\dfrac{\partial^2}{(\partial d)^2}\left[\dfrac{f'}{f''}\right] < -\dfrac{f'}{f''} \cdot \dfrac{\partial}{\partial d}\left(\dfrac{f'}{f''}\right) \cdot \left[\dfrac{\partial}{\partial d}\left(\dfrac{f'}{f''}\right) + 1\right].$

Shleifer and Wolfenzon assume that assumptions (1a) to (1c) and $\dfrac{\partial}{\partial d}\left(\dfrac{f'}{f''}\right) > 0$ in assumption (1e) hold, and obtain the following results.

- The optimal diversion level is zero when the entrepreneur does not raise outside funds, that is, $d^*(0,k)=0$.
- The optimal diversion level is increasing in the fraction of cashflow rights sold to outsiders for a given level of investor protection, that is, $d_1^*(x,k)>0$.
- The optimal diversion level is decreasing in the level of investor protection for a given fraction of outsiders' cashflow rights, that is, $d_2^*(x,k)<0$.
- The sensitivity of the optimal diversion level to changes in the fraction of outsiders' cashflow rights is decreasing in the level of investor protection, that is, $d_{12}^*(x,k)<0$.
- The expected fine is larger in countries with poorer investor protection for a given level of outsiders' cashflow rights, that is, $\left(\dfrac{\partial}{\partial k}kf(d^*(x,k))\right)_x<0$.
- The optimal diversion level is decreasing in the level of investor protection if and only if the condition $\dfrac{\partial}{\partial k}\left(\dfrac{1-k}{k}\cdot x^*\right)<0$ is satisfied.

As I show below, $1>\dfrac{f'}{f''\cdot d}$ in assumption (1e) guarantees that the indirect utility of an entrepreneur who goes public is increasing with respect to the level of investor protection. Assumption (1f) guarantees that the expected fine decreases at an increasing rate as the level of investor protection increases. This result, combined with assumption (1d) and $\dfrac{f'}{f''\cdot d}>\dfrac{\partial}{\partial d}\left(\dfrac{f'}{f''}\right)>0$ in assumption (1e), guarantees that the marginal pay-off of an entrepreneur who goes public is increasing with respect to the level of investor protection.

At date 1, the entrepreneur chooses the size of the project, I, the amount of funds that she contributes to the firm, R_E, and the amount of funds raised in international markets, R_M. Risk-neutral international investors are willing to invest in the project as long as the expected rate of return is equal to the international interest rate i. Thus, the following participation constraint must be satisfied:

$$R_M(1+i)\le x\left[1-(1-k)d^*\right]\Pi \quad \text{if} \quad R_M>0. \tag{4}$$

The entrepreneur solves the following problem:

$$U(k,g,i,W)=\underset{I,R_E,R_M}{Max}\left\{(1-x)\left[1-(1-k)d^*\right]+(1-k)d^*-kf(d^*)\right\}\Pi$$

$$+(1+i)(W-R_E)$$

$$s.t. \ (3.1), (3.4), \ 0\le R_E\le W, \ 0\le R_M, \ I=R_E+R_M, \ x=\dfrac{R_M}{R_E+R_M}. \tag{5}$$

According to problem (5), the entrepreneur maximizes her pay-off by choosing the size of the investment project and the financial structure of the firm subject to the participation constraint of outside investors and the restriction that the cashflow rights per unit share owned by insiders and outsiders must be equal.

From equation (1), $I = R_E + R_M$ and $x = \dfrac{R_M}{R_E + R_M}$, we can express the participation constraint of international investors in equation (4) as follows:

$$d^*(1-k) \le \frac{g-i}{1+g} \quad \text{if} \quad R_M > 0. \tag{6}$$

Now, we can rewrite the entrepreneur's optimization problem in (5) as follows:

$$
\begin{aligned}
\frac{U(k,g,i,W)}{1+g} = \underset{R_E, R_M}{Max} & \left\{ \frac{g-i}{1+g} - (1-k)d^* \right\} \cdot R_E \\
& + \left\{ (1-k)d^* - kf(d^*) \right\} \cdot (R_E + R_M) + W\left(\frac{1+i}{1+g} \right)
\end{aligned}
$$

$$s.t. \quad (3.6), \ 0 \le R_E \le W, \ 0 \le R_M. \tag{7}$$

Proposition 1: The solution to problem (7) is as follows.

a. If $g < i$, the entrepreneur sets $R_M^* = 0$ and $R_E^* = 0$. Thus, the entrepreneur does not raise external funds and invests all her wealth in the market.

b. If $g = i$, the entrepreneur sets $R_M^* = 0$ and $R_E^* \in [0, W]$. Thus, the entrepreneur does not raise external funds and is indifferent between investing all her wealth in the market and investing any fraction of her wealth in her project without raising external funds.

c. If $g > i$, the entrepreneur sets $R_E^* = W$ and raises the maximum amount of external funds $R_M^* = \left(\dfrac{x^*}{1-x^*} \right) \cdot W > 0$, where x^* satisfies the participation constraint with strict equality:

$$(1-k) \cdot d^*(x^*, k) = \frac{g-i}{1+g}.$$

If $g > i$, the entrepreneur invests all her wealth and raises the maximum possible amount of external funds. Intuitively, once the entrepreneur has invested all her wealth in her own project, the marginal benefit of raising external funds is given by the expected diversion per unit of investment $(1+g) \cdot (1-k) \cdot d^*$ and the marginal cost is given by the expected fine per unit of investment $(1+g) \cdot k \cdot f(d^*)$. The difference, $(1+g) \cdot \left\{ (1-k) \cdot d^* - k \cdot f(d^*) \right\}$, is the entrepreneur's marginal utility of raising external funds, which is strictly increasing in x and R_M. Hence, the entrepreneur raises the maximum possible amount of external funds, and the international investors' participation constraint holds with equality. The (binding) investors' participation constraint determines the optimal share of external funds, $x^*(k,g,i)$.

Proposition 2: The optimal share of external funds $x^*(k,g,i)$ has the following properties.

a. It is strictly increasing in the level of investor protection, that is, $\dfrac{\partial x^*}{\partial k} > 0$.

b. It is strictly increasing in the entrepreneur's productivity, that is, $\dfrac{\partial x^*}{\partial g} > 0$.

c. It is strictly decreasing in the interest rate, that is, $\dfrac{\partial x^*}{\partial i} < 0$.

The message from propositions 1 and 2 is shown in Figure 3.1. The graphs depict the marginal benefit and marginal cost (per unit of revenue) of raising external funds against the share of external funds x. As the marginal benefit is always greater than the marginal cost when the international investors' participation constraint does not bind, the entrepreneur optimally chooses the maximum level of external finance. The binding participation constraint defines the optimal share of external funds, $x^*(k,g,i)$.

Figure 3.1a shows that an increase in the level of investor protection from k_0 to k_1 increases the share of external funds raised by the entrepreneur from x_0^* to x_1^*.[14] Figure 3.1b shows that an increase in the entrepreneur's productivity from g_0 to g_1 increases the optimal share of external funds from x_0^* to x_1^*. Figure 3.1c shows that a reduction in the international interest rate from i_0 to i_1 increases the share of external funds raised by the entrepreneur from x_0^* to x_1^*.

The properties of the optimal amount of external funds function, $R_M^*(k,g,i,W)$, follow directly from the properties of $x^*(k,g,i)$. Notice that an increase in the entrepreneur's wealth W has no effect on the optimal share of external funds x^*, but it increases the optimal amount of external funds R_M^*. The following corollary summarizes these properties.

Corollary 1: The optimal amount of external funds function $R_M^*(k,g,i,W)$ has the following properties.

a. It is strictly increasing in the level of investor protection, that is, $\dfrac{\partial R_M^*}{\partial k} > 0$.

b. It is strictly increasing in the entrepreneur's productivity, that is, $\dfrac{\partial R_M^*}{\partial g} > 0$.

c. It is strictly decreasing in the international interest rate, that is, $\dfrac{\partial R_M^*}{\partial i} < 0$.

d. It is strictly increasing in the entrepreneur's wealth, that is, $\dfrac{\partial R_M^*}{\partial W} > 0$.

Figure 3.1   *Endogenous Determination of the Share of External Funds
Raised (x*)*

(a) An increase in the level of investor protection
increases the share of external funds raised

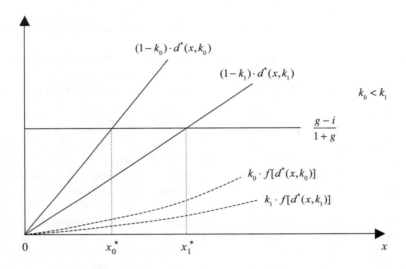

(b) An increase in the entrepreneur's productivity
increases the share of external funds raised

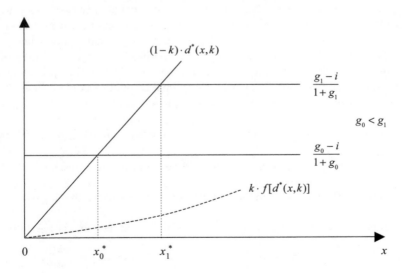

(c) A reduction in the interest rate increases the share of external funds raised

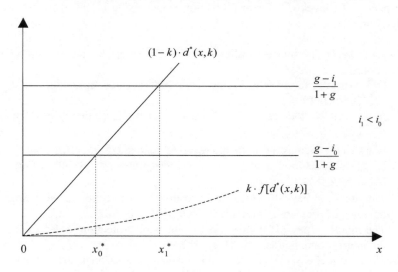

We now analyse the indirect utility function of the entrepreneur and study the response of the entrepreneur's pay-off to changes in the level of investor protection. The knowledge of this relationship will allow us to compare the costs and benefits of legal enforcement and select the optimal level of investor protection.

The indirect utility function of the entrepreneur is:

$$U(k,g,i,W) = \begin{cases} W(1+i) & \text{if } g \leq i \\ \left\{ g - i - (1+g) \cdot kf\left[\dfrac{g-i}{(1+g)\cdot(1-k)} \right] \right\} \cdot \left(\dfrac{W}{1-x^*} \right) + W(1+i) \\ \quad \text{if } g > i, \text{ where } x^* = x^*(k,g,i). \end{cases} \tag{8}$$

The following lemma and proposition state the properties of the indirect utility function and its derivatives, given that $g > i$.

Lemma 1:

a. $-2 \cdot d_{12}^* + (1-k) \cdot d_{122}^* < 0$. Thus, $\left(\dfrac{\partial^2 kf\left[d^*(x,k) \right]}{\partial k^2} \right)_x < 0$;

b. $\dfrac{\partial}{\partial x} \left(\dfrac{\partial kf}{\partial k} \right)_x < 0$.

Lemma (1a) states that, for a given fraction of outside funds x, the expected fine decreases at an increasing rate as the level of investor protection increases.

Lemma (1b) states that the (negative) sensitivity of the expected fine with respect to the level of investor protection is increasing in the fraction of outside funds x.

Proposition 3: The indirect utility function $U^{g>i}(k,g,i,W)$ has the following properties.

a. It is strictly increasing in the level of investor protection, that is, $U^{g>i}_k(k,g,i,W) > 0$.
b. It is strictly increasing in the entrepreneur's productivity, that is, $U^{g>i}_g(k,g,i,W) > 0$.
c. It is strictly decreasing in the interest rate, that is, $U^{g>i}_i(k,g,i,W) < 0$.
d. It is strictly increasing in the entrepreneur's wealth, that is, $U^{g>i}_W(k,g,i,W) > 0$.
e. The marginal pay-off with respect to investor protection is increasing in the level of protection, that is, $U^{g>i}_{kk}(k,g,i,W) > 0$.
f. The marginal pay-off with respect to investor protection is decreasing in the interest rate, that is, $U^{g>i}_{ki}(k,g,i,W) < 0$.
g. The marginal pay-off with respect to investor protection is increasing in the entrepreneur's productivity, that is, $U^{g>i}_{kg}(k,g,i,W) > 0$.
h. The marginal pay-off with respect to investor protection is increasing in the entrepreneur's wealth, that is, $U^{g>i}_{kW}(k,g,i,W) > 0$.

Optimal investor protection

We now go one step back and consider the problem of an individual who must decide whether to pay the cost of going public and set up a firm or participate in the market as an investor. Having introduced a cost of legal enforcement, we must determine the individual's optimal decisions in the new environment. Those individuals who set up firms and go public must optimally choose the level of investor protection.

The cost of legal protection $C(k)$ satisfies the following assumption.

Assumption 2:

a. $C(k)$ is continuous and differentiable;
b. $C(k) \geq 0$ for all $k \in [0,1]$ and $C(0) = 0$;
c. $C'(k) > 0$;
d. $C''(k) > 0$;
e. $\lim_{k \to 0} C'(k) = 0$ and $\lim_{k \to 0} C'(k) = \infty$.

Assumption 2 says that total and marginal costs are increasing in the level of investor protection ((2c) and (2d)). A system of perfect injustice is costless (2e). As the probability of crime detection and punishment approaches one, the marginal cost of enforcement approaches infinity (2e). Assuming that there are N individuals with skills level g, that each one must pay $\frac{C(k)}{N}$ to set up a public firm and that $\frac{C(k)}{N} > W \cdot c_{\text{dom}}$, the following result holds.

Proposition 4: Conditional on the level of investor protection k, $k > 0$, an individual sets up a firm if and only if $g \geq \underline{g}$, $\underline{g} > i$. An individual who sets up a firm raises funds in the market, that is, sets $R_M^* > 0$ and $R_E^* = W$.

The pro rata cost of investor protection alters the results of Shleifer and Wolfenzon (2002) in the following way. In the costless case, individuals with skills $g = i$ are just indifferent between setting up firms and investing in the market. However, if the cost of setting up a firm outweighs the cost of market participation as an investor, then individuals with skills $g = i$ strictly prefer to participate as investors. Because the indirect utility function is increasing in the skills level g, it follows that there exists some minimum level of skills $\underline{g} > i$ such that the individual is indifferent between setting up the firm and investing in the market. Moreover, only an individual who is planning to raise external funds will find it worthwhile to pay the legal enforcement tax.

Proposition 5: If there are some individuals with entrepreneurial skills $g \geq \underline{g} > i$ who set up public firms in the economy, then there exists one (interior) level of investor protection $k^* \in (0,1)$ that is optimally chosen by those firms. The comparative statics for the optimal level of investor protection $k^*(g,i,W)$ is as follows.

a. The optimal level of investor protection is increasing in the entrepreneur's productive skills g, that is, $\frac{\partial k^*}{\partial g} > 0$.

b. The optimal level of investor protection is decreasing in the international interest rate i, that is, $\frac{\partial k^*}{\partial i} < 0$.

c. The optimal level of investor protection is increasing in the entrepreneur's wealth, that is, $\frac{\partial k^*}{\partial W} > 0$.

Figure 3.2 shows the endogenous determination of the level of investor protection and its comparative statics. Figure 3.2a shows how the level of protection is determined by the intersection of the marginal cost and the pay-off schedules. Figure 3.2b shows that an increase in the entrepreneur's productivity shifts the marginal pay-off curve upwards and increases the level of investor protection. Figure 3.2c shows that a reduction in the interest rate shifts the marginal benefit schedule upwards and increases the optimal level of protection. Figure 3.2d shows that an increase in the entrepreneur's wealth shifts the marginal benefit schedule upwards and increases the optimal level of investor protection. Figure 3.2e shows the effect of an increase in the number of

*Figure 3.2   Endogenous Determination of the Level of Investor
              Protection (k*)*

(a) Initial equilibrium

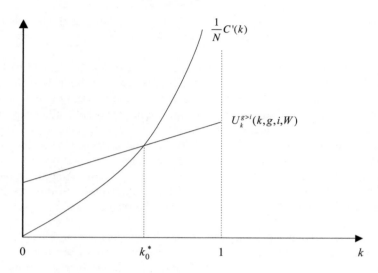

(b) An increase in the entrepreneur's productivity
increases the optimal level of investor protection

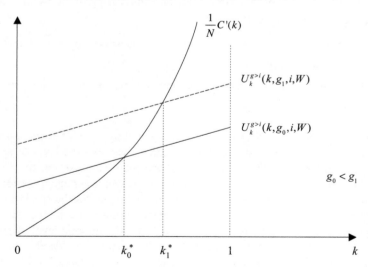

(c) A reduction in the interest rate increases the optimal level of investor protection

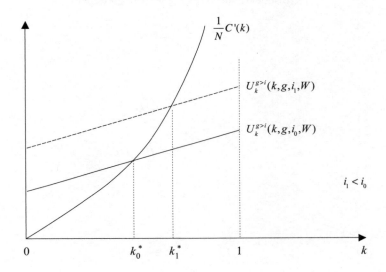

(d) An increase in the entrepreneur's wealth increases the optimal level of investor protection

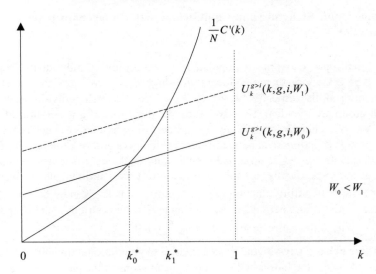

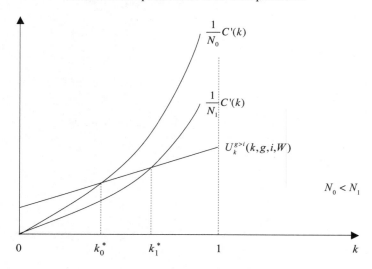

(e) An increase in the number of public firms
or a reduction in the marginal cost of enforcement
increases the optimal level of investor protection

domestic public firms. As the number of entrepreneurs who go public increases, the marginal cost schedule shifts downwards and increases the optimal level of investor protection.

Demographic Structure and Equilibrium with Endogenous Investor Protection

The small open economy is populated by two groups of individuals. Type 1 and type 2 individuals are endowed with high g_1 and low g_2 levels of entrepreneurial skills respectively, where $g_2 < i < \underline{g} < g_1$. All individuals within each group are identical. Here we study the decisions of a generation of size $N = N_1 + N_2$, where N_1 and N_2 are the numbers of individuals of each type. The two groups of individuals have different preferences and risk tolerances. Type 1 individuals are risk neutral and type 2 individuals are either risk neutral or risk averse. Specifically, the utility function of type 1 individuals is given by $U^1 = Z^1$ and the utility function of type 2 individuals is given by $U^2 = U^2(Z^2)$, where Z^1 and Z^2 are period 2 consumption levels. U^2 is strictly increasing, that is, $\dfrac{\partial U^2}{\partial Z^2} > 0$, and weakly concave, that is, $\dfrac{\partial U^2}{\partial Z^2} \leq 0$.

There exists a pay-as-you-go system of intergenerational transfers. Per unit invested during the individual's youth, contributions to the pay-as-you-go system return $1 + n$ units of the good when the individual is old. Assume that retirement contributions are risk free, that it is common knowledge that the rate of return on contributions per period n is lower than the international interest rate, that is, $n < i$, and that all individuals are endowed with an identical initial wealth W_1.

We consider two alternatives based on whether participation in the pay-as-you-go retirement system is compulsory or voluntary. Besides the pay-as-you-go system, an individual faces the following options. First, she can set up a firm, as explained previously. Second, she can invest in a risk-free international portfolio. Third, she can invest in a non-diversified, risky portfolio of domestic assets. Consider the following two cases.

Case 1: $c_{int} = c_{dom} = 0$; that is, there is free participation in both domestic and international markets.

Case 2: $c_{int} \geq c_{dom} \geq 0$ and $\dfrac{C(k)}{N_1} > W \cdot c_{dom}$; that is, participation in markets is costly and the cost of going public domestically is greater than the cost of domestic participation as an investor.

Voluntary pay-as-you-go system
Denote by r_f^i the riskless rate of return that gives a type 2 individual a utility level that is equal to the expected utility of investing in domestic public firms when the domestic market participation cost is zero. Call this interest rate the risk-free equivalent rate r_f^i. At the pre-pension reform stage, domestic firms pay to investors an expected rate of return that is equal to the international interest rate i. Obviously, if type 2 individuals are risk neutral, then $r_f^i = i$. Otherwise, the risk of expropriation reduces their expected utility $r_f^i < i$, and each individual is willing to pay a premium rate equal to $i - r_f^i$ for full insurance against the expropriation risk. The following proposition holds.

Proposition 6:
a. In case 1 (free participation in domestic and international markets), type 1 individuals go public and do not make contributions to the pay-as-you-go system. Type 2 individuals invest all their wealth in international markets if they are risk averse, and are indifferent between investing their wealth in international markets and in domestic public firms if they are risk neutral. The pay-as-you-go system receives no contributions.
b. In case 2 (costly market participation), type 1 individuals go public and do not make contributions to the pay-as-you-go system. A voluntary pay-as-you-go system exists if and only if $n \geq \max[i - c_{int}, r_f^i - c_{dom}]$.

In case 1, proposition 6 leads to the results directly. Even if type 2 individuals are risk neutral, they do not set up firms. Therefore, if they are risk averse, they are even less willing to do so. International investments dominate the pay-as-you-go alternative, because they offer a risk-free return that is strictly greater than the return on pay-as-you-go contributions. The domestic risk of expropriation implies that risk-averse type 2 individuals strictly prefer international investments over domestic ones.

In case 2 and according to proposition 6, a type 1 individual prefers to pay the legal enforcement cost and set up a firm even if the alternatives are costless. Because market participation as an investor is costly, the type 1 individual's surplus of going public is even greater. Thus, a voluntary pay-as-you-go system can only exist if type 2 individuals are willing to make the contributions. The choices of type 2 individuals are as follows. If $n \geq \max[i - c_{int}, r_f^i - c_{dom}]$, then type 2 individuals invest all their wealth in the pay-as-you-go system. If $i - c_{int} > \max[n, r_f^i - c_{dom}]$, then type 2 individuals invest all their wealth in international markets. If $r_f^i - c_{dom} > \max[i - c_{int}, n]$, then type 2 individuals participate in domestic capital markets, buy only domestic shares and take the risk of being expropriated by insiders. In order for a voluntary pay-as-you-go system to exist, the return on pay-as-you-go contributions must weakly dominate the other two alternatives. Thus, a necessary and sufficient condition for the existence of a voluntary pay-as-you-go system is that $n \geq \max[i - c_{int}, r_f^i - c_{dom}]$.

Compulsory pay-as-you-go system
We say that the retirement system is compulsory if (at least) some individuals are forced to contribute part of their initial wealth to the pay-as-you-go system, even though they might prefer to allocate their wealth to some alternative if they were free to do so.

This system always imposes an implicit tax on type 1 individuals, that is, those with high entrepreneurial skills. If the rate of return on pay-as-you-go contributions n is less than $\max[i - c_{int}, r_f^i - c_{dom}]$, then the pay-as-you-go system imposes a burden on type 2 individuals as well. After making the required pay-as-you-go contributions, type 2 individuals invest their remaining wealth internationally if $i - c_{int} > r_f^i - c_{dom}$ and domestically if $r_f^i - c_{dom} > i - c_{int}$.

The Effect of a Pension Reform

Figure 3.3a shows the utility of a risk-neutral type 2 individual as a function of her period 2 consumption. Point A indicates the utility level that the individual attains when she contributes all her wealth to the pay-as-you-go retirement system and obtains the riskless return $W(1 + n)$ at point A'. On the other hand, if the individual invests all her wealth in domestic firms, she faces the risk of being expropriated by insiders, who can divert a fraction d^* of the revenue. If the crime of revenue diversion is detected, then the individual receives a high dividend, Z_H^2. Otherwise, the individual receives a low dividend, $(1 - d^*) \cdot Z_H^2$.

Figure 3.3   The Effects of Reforms

(a) Type 2 individual choices

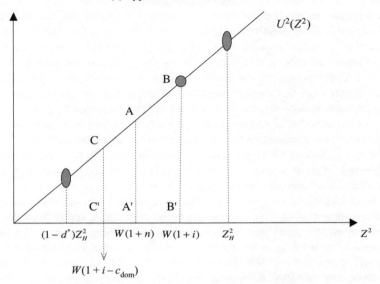

(b) Type 2 individual choices and the twin reforms

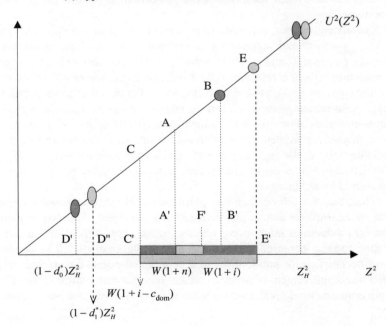

At the pre-pension reform stage, the expected return from domestic investment is equal to $W(1 + i)$ at point B'. Thus, because the individual is risk neutral and $r_f^i = i$, point B shows the individual's expected utility of investing
in domestic public firms if the participation in domestic markets is costless.
However, if the domestic market participation is costly, then the net expected
return is at point C' and the expected utility is at point C. Observe that Figure
3.3a shows the case of a voluntary pay-as-you-go system, because C' is to the
left of A', that is, $c_{dom} \geq i - n$. In other words, the domestic participation cost is
sufficiently high that the pay-as-you-go return dominates the net return from
investments in domestic public firms and international markets.

As explained below, a corporate governance reform is an increase in the
level of investor protection that reduces the extent of revenue diversion d^*, and
leaves Z_H^2 unchanged. Thus, a corporate governance reform increases both the
expected return that investors can appropriate from investments in domestic
firms and the expected cost that firms must pay to raise funds.

Consider the case $c_{dom} \leq i - n$. In this case, the net expected return on domestic investment (point C') is somewhere between points A' and B' in Figure 3.3a.
The pay-as-you-go system is compulsory and the change from it to a funded
scheme does not require a corporate governance reform. The individual is better off if she receives the net risky return $W(1 + i - c_{dom})$ under the funded
scheme instead of the riskless return $W(1 + n)$ under the pay-as-you-go system. Thus, type 2 individuals accept the pension reform without demanding
an improvement in the level of investor protection. Therefore, the reforms are
not twins.

Consider again the voluntary pay-as-you-go case that is shown in Figure
3.3a, $c_{dom} \geq i - n$, and suppose that the reforms have no effect on market participation costs c_{dom} and c_{int}. In this case, a pension reform without a corporate
governance reform is rejected. Type 2 individuals are worse off if they switch
from the pay-as-you-go to the funded scheme. On the other hand, public firms
reject a corporate governance reform because it raises the expected cost of
domestic funds above the international interest rate i; that is, an increase in
d^* increases the expected cost of funds and the expected return to outsiders
to some point to the right of point B'. The reforms are not twins in this case
either, because the pension reform requires a corporate governance reform that
is rejected by public firms.

Thus, the twin reforms can take place only if market participation costs fall
and public firms are able to internalize a substantial part of the cost reductions.
The cost reductions might occur because of the improvement in investor protection and the increased scale of domestic capital markets.[15] Two conditions
must be satisfied for public firms to accept the corporate governance reform.
First, the improvement in investor protection must allow firms to raise funds
from domestic markets at an expected cost (net of internalized cost reductions)

that is lower than the international interest rate. Second, the benefits associated with the lower cost of funds must outweigh the increased costs of legal enforcement. If those two (sufficient) conditions are satisfied, then the corporate governance reform is feasible.

On the other hand, type 2 individuals accept the change from the pay-as-you-go to a funded scheme if and only if the return on contributions to the funded system is greater than the return on pay-as-you-go contributions.

Figure 3.3b shows the effect of the reforms. At the pre-pension reform stage, the type 2 individual receives her pay-as-you-go return at point A', and the expected cost of funds for firms is at point B'. Point C' is the net expected return that the individual would obtain if she invested her wealth in domestic public firms. Thus, the domestic market participation cost accounts for the distance between points B' and C'.

Consider a corporate governance reform that increases the individual's net expected return from domestic investment from C' to A', when no market participation cost reduction occurs; that is, the reform improves investor protection to the point where the individual is just indifferent between investing her wealth in the pay-as-you-go system and in domestic firms. This corporate governance reform reduces the fraction of revenue diverted by insiders from d_0^* to d_1^*, and leaves Z_H^2 unchanged. The low outcome of the lottery shifts from D' to D", and the expected value of the new lottery is now at point E'. It follows immediately that public firms must be able to internalize a cost reduction of the individual's market participation cost that is at least as large as the distance between points E' and B' in order to reduce their net cost of funds and accept the corporate governance reform.

In general, only a market participation cost reduction that is appropriately shared between firms and individuals can provide type 2 individuals with an expected return at least as great as $W(1 + n)$, that is, at some point to the right of A', and enable firms to reduce the cost of external funds to some point to the left of B'. The grey boxes in Figure 3.3b give an example of such cost reduction. The improvement in investor protection allows type 2 individuals to appropriate the segment C'A', and firms appropriate the full market participation cost reduction F'E'. In this example, the post-reform individual participation cost in domestic markets is given by the segment A'F'.

It remains to be shown that the dividend paid by domestic public firms to the type 2 individual, Z_H^2, is insensitive to the reforms. The lottery that the individual investor faces by investing in domestic public firms is the following. The type 2 individual receives revenue $x_2 \cdot \Pi_{\text{Total}}$ from domestic firms with probability k, and receives revenue $x_2 \cdot \Pi_{\text{Total}} \cdot (1 - d^*)$ with probability $1 - k$, where x_2 is the fraction of the individual's cashflow rights on the revenue and Π_{Total} is the total revenue of domestic publicly traded firms. Because there are N_1 domestic public firms and N_2 type 2 individuals in the domestic economy,

$\Pi_{\text{Total}} = (1 + g_1) \cdot [N_1 \cdot R^*_{\text{int}} + N_1 \cdot W + N_2 \cdot W]$, where R^*_{int} are the external funds that each public firm raises from international investors. Thus,

$$N_2 \cdot x_2 = \frac{W \cdot N_2}{W \cdot N_2 + W \cdot N_1 + N_1 \cdot R^*_{\text{int}}}$$

and $N_2 \cdot x_2 \cdot \Pi_{\text{Total}} = W \cdot N_2 \cdot (1 + g_1)$. Therefore, $Z^2_H = x_2 \cdot \Pi_{\text{Total}} = W \cdot (1 + g_1)$. Thus, Z^2_H is a constant, and this is directly implied by the assumption that all shares give rise to identical cashflow rights to insiders and outsiders. Finally, observe that the corporate governance reform reduces the diversion of revenue d^* only if the condition $\frac{\partial}{\partial k} \left(\frac{1-k}{k} \cdot x^* \right) < 0$ is satisfied.

A similar analysis for the case of risk-averse type 2 individuals leads to similar conclusions. Twin reforms can occur only if the cost of participation in domestic markets falls and both individuals and public firms can appropriate part of the cost reduction.

The portfolio restrictions imposed on pension funds to prevent the international diversification of assets are unnecessary (non-binding) if the corporate governance reform reduces the participation cost in domestic markets but leaves the participation cost in international markets unchanged. This is because of the assumption that $c_{\text{int}} \geq c_{\text{dom}}$. However, the development of domestic capital markets may also reduce the individual's cost of participation in international capital markets. If this is the case, then portfolio restrictions may be necessary to create the captive source of cheap funds for domestic public firms that makes the corporate governance reform feasible in the first place. To illustrate this point, consider the reforms shown in Figure 3.3b, and suppose that $c_{\text{int}} = c_{\text{dom}}$ before and after the twin reforms are implemented, that is, that the domestic and international market participation cost reductions are equal. The post-reform market participation costs are measured by the segment A'F'. It follows that unconstrained pension funds would allocate all their assets to international markets, because the return on international assets (point B' minus the segment A'F') dominates the return on domestic investments (point A'). Thus, the portfolio restrictions are necessary if the corporate governance reform causes a large reduction in the individual's participation cost in international markets.

Finally, the previous analysis provides us with an interesting insight on the timing of the twin reforms. If the performance of the pay-as-you-go system deteriorates over time, that is, if the returns on pay-as-you-go contributions fall steadily over the years, and if the sufficient conditions are ever satisfied, then the twin reforms take place when the pay-as-you-go system is still voluntary and before the returns on contributions fall so low that the system becomes compulsory. This seems consistent with the fact that the Latin American pension reforms occurred after periods of poor performance of their pay-as-you-go systems. Figure 3.3b illustrates this point. If the return on pay-as-you-go contributions is high (say $n = i$ at point B'), then no reform takes place. Once the return on pay-as-you-go contributions falls enough, say to point A', the twin reforms take place. As the performance of the pay-as-you-go system deteriorates, the twin reforms occur before point A' falls to the left of point C'.

4. CONCLUSION

This chapter has shown that pension and corporate governance reforms are mutually consistent if some conditions are satisfied. Specifically, the reforms must cause a substantial reduction in the individual's market participation cost and domestic public firms must internalize part of this cost reduction. Public firms must be able to shift away from expensive international sources of funds to cheaper domestic ones. The reduction in the net cost of domestic funds for public firms can be associated either with a reduction in the individual's participation cost in domestic markets that leaves the international participation cost unchanged, or with a reduction in both the domestic and international participation costs that is combined with portfolio restrictions to prevent the international diversification of pension funds' assets. If the performance of the pay-as-you-go system deteriorates over time, the twin reforms occur when the pay-as-you-go system is still voluntary.

There is an interesting variation of the model described above that could be developed. A key feature of Shleifer and Wolfenzon's (2002) framework is that even though the production technology of entrepreneurs is deterministic, the investment return is risky from the outside investor's standpoint. It is the nature of the legal system that gives rise to the randomness of the investor's return profile, because the system detects the crime of revenue diversion with some positive probability. In this environment, an increase in investor protection increases the expected cost of funds for domestic public firms, and makes the market participation cost reduction necessary. Thus, the deterministic nature of the productive technology and the specific definition of the corporate crime lead to the conditions identified in this chapter. Alternatively, we could imagine a framework characterized by stochastic productive technologies, where insiders choose the riskiness of the investment projects and where the crime is defined in terms of excessive risk taking by insiders against outside investors' interests. In this environment, a corporate governance reform would reduce the variability of the pay-offs to outside investors. Risk-averse investors would be willing to trade off a lower expected return for less variability. Thus, more investor protection would be associated with a lower expected cost of funds. My conjecture is that the market participation cost reduction is not necessary for the twin reforms to occur in this alternative framework. In practice, whether corporate governance reforms discourage the diversion of deterministic revenue or excessive risk taking remains an open question. This chapter has demonstrated the conditions that give rise to the twin reforms in the former case.

APPENDIX A3.1: PRO-INVESTOR LEGAL REFORMS IN ARGENTINA AND CHILE

Argentina

Argentina has had basic legislation on capital markets and investor protection since 1968. The Securities Law, which empowers the National Securities Commission (CNV) to supervise and regulate securities markets, was approved in 1968, and the Corporations Law was approved in 1972. With this basic framework in place, Argentina made substantial progress on investor protection in the 1990s.

The first round of pro-investor legal reforms took place in the period 1992–96. Decree 656 (1992) and Resolution 200 of the Ministry of Economy and Public Services (MEyOSP-1992) together with Decree 2,019 (1993) require the risk rating of public securities. Resolution 204 (MEyOSP-1992) requires the disclosure of transactions that involve the majority shareholders of public firms. Resolution 214 (MEyOSP-1992) requires foreign firms listed in domestic markets to provide daily information on the prices and traded volumes of their securities in foreign markets. Decree 1,073 (1993) regulates the public issuance of debt instruments by small and medium firms. Resolution 215 (CNV-1992) standardizes the public offering procedure. Resolution 227 (CNV-1993) mandates the disclosure of relevant events and regulates the use of privileged information. Resolution 239 (CNV-1993) establishes that risk-rating agencies must disclose their rating methodologies. Resolution 242 (CNV-1994) defines and regulates mutual funds. Resolution 244 (CNV-1994) authorizes pension funds to act as depository institutions of the Caja de Valores (the body responsible for securities custody at the Buenos Aires Stock Exchange).[16] Resolution 250 (CNV-1994) authorizes the Caja de Valores to recognize the Superintendency of Pension Funds as the principal institution overseeing pension funds. Law 24,522 (1995) reforms bankruptcy procedures. Law 24,441 (1995) aims to promote the securitization of mortgages and Decree 304 (1995) requires the risk rating of mortgage-backed securities. Law 24,552 allows mutual funds to invest in real as well as financial assets. Resolution 262 (CNV-1995) regulates the acquisition of a public company's own stock to guarantee transparency. Resolution 276 (CNV-1995) allows pension funds to invest in the public debt instruments issued by small and medium firms. Resolution 721 of the Superintendency of Pension Funds allows pension funds to invest in mutual funds (or, more precisely, *fideicomisos financieros*). Decree 340 (1996) defines the concept of 'market maker' for public debt instruments.

A second round of pro-investor legal reforms is contained in Decree-Law 677 of 2001 on Capital Market Transparency and Best Practices. The law is explicitly motivated by the role of pension funds in the domestic financial system, stating that 'this goal is especially important for the public interest of the Republic of Argentina, as the largest investments in the domestic market are made by pension funds, which manage the retirement savings of a large proportion of the population'. The law mandates more disclosure of information, includes secrecy provisions and regulates the use of privileged information. It also enhances the transparency of the market for corporate control and regulates the independence of auditors.

The law specifically protects minority shareholders in the following ways.

- Managers of publicly traded companies are mandated to pursue 'the common interest of all shareholders', which is interpreted as being 'the creation of value for shareholders'.
- A residual stake acquisition system grants minority shareholders the right to purchase or sell, at a fair price, their stakes in companies that have lost their 'open' nature.
- Transactions involving parties related to the issuer are regulated by the guidelines of the Principles of Corporate Governance of the American Law Institute.
- The law imposes regulations on publicly traded companies characterized by concentrated ownership structures, to enhance market liquidity.

Chile

The first round of pro-investor legal reforms in Chile was contained in the Law of Superintendency of Securities and Insurance (SVS) (December 1980), the Corporations Law (October 1981) and the Securities Law (October 1981). The SVS creates the institution that regulates and oversees the issuers of publicly offered securities as well as brokers, dealers, stock exchanges, insurance companies and rating agencies. These laws and Regulation 30 of the SVS (1989) improve the disclosure of relevant information in the following ways.

- They require public companies to file detailed quarterly and annual reports, and issue press releases when certain events occur.
- The Corporations Law renders directors and officers jointly and severally liable for violations of disclosure obligations.
- The Securities Law prohibits false statements and transactions, and trading in securities for the purpose of stabilizing, fixing or causing artificial fluctuations in market price. Those violating the law are subject to criminal liability.

The Corporations Law and the Securities Law establish the fiduciary duty of insiders to minority shareholders in the following ways.

- The Corporations Law and its regulations give minority shareholders appraisal rights: 'a minority shareholder who opposes a resolution adopted through a shareholders' meeting is entitled to exercise appraisal rights whereby the dissenting shareholder's stock in the company must be bought by the company (at a fair price)' (Stetson, Stolper and Hill 1999: 1–25).
- The Corporations Law and its regulations give minority shareholders pre-emptive rights: a company's shareholders have the right to maintain their equity interest, that is, avoid dilution, when a company decides to issue shares, convertible bonds or any other security that confers stock rights on the holder.
- The Corporations Law enables shareholders to participate in annual share-holder meetings through proxies.
- Shareholders may petition the board of directors to call an extraordinary meeting of shareholders, provided that at least 10 per cent of the company's shareholders support the initiative.
- The Corporations Law regulates and provides defences against hostile take-overs.
- A number of rules impede the takeover of a company without prior disclosure of the intent to take control to the target's shareholders and the SVS.
- The Corporations Law requires the merger of a corporation or the sale of all or substantially all of a corporation's assets to be approved at a sharehold-ers' meeting by an affirmative vote of at least two-thirds of the outstanding voting shares, with any dissenting shareholder entitled to appraisal rights. It also mandates the disclosure of shareholder agreements that limit the trans-ferability of registered shares, thereby limiting undisclosed control agree-ments.

Initially pension funds were not allowed to invest in stocks. Legislation introduced in January 1985 and between December 1985 and March 1986 allowed pension funds to participate in stock markets. In January 1985, Law 18,398 amended Decree-Law 3,500 of 1980 to create a risk-rating commis-sion. Risk rating was required for all the instruments in which pension funds were allowed to invest but, remarkably, the decisions made by the commission were initially based on studies conducted by the pension funds themselves. In October 1987, Law 18,660 created a private system of risk rating that gave rise to specialized risk-rating agencies. The ratings are currently publicly available and are used to determine the investment limits of pension funds for different types of instrument. Circular 574 SVS (December 1985) defines the concept of related parties and requires the disclosure of transactions between related parties. This facilitates the exposure of insider trading.

The second round of pro-investor legal reforms was characterized by pen-sion fund activism. Iglesias (2000) argues that pension funds protect the rights of minority shareholders, firstly because the law requires the funds to exercise their voting rights, participate in elections of board members and monitor the firms in which they invest, and secondly because Chilean markets are relatively illiquid, which prevents pension funds from using exit (selling out) strategies when they disagree with management decisions. However, the law restricts the monitoring activities of pension funds. Collusive conduct by pension funds is forbidden. They are not allowed to elect persons related to majority shareholders to the board, or to express publicly their opinions about the management of the companies in which they invest. Thus, pension funds can only protect minority shareholders' rights by calling and participating in shareholder meetings or by initiating legal actions against the controllers.

According to Iglesias (2000), given the concentrated ownership structure of public firms in Chile (Majluf et al. 1998; Lefort and Walker 2000), the role of pension funds in electing independent board members helps to prevent the expropriation of outsiders by controllers. Pension funds have also been known to initiate legal action in defence of minority shareholders. Agosin and Pastén (2001) describe two legal suits in which pension funds played a key role. In one case, pension funds managed to overturn a public tender offer that would have given rise to enormous profits for the controllers of the firm in which they had invested, and that imposed unfavourable conditions on minority shareholders.[17] In the other case, they sued controllers for alleged losses from the sale of assets to another firm in which the controllers had a large stake.

The second round of corporate governance reforms regulated and defined the use of privileged information and the conflicts of interests between controllers and outsiders; it is contained in Law 19,301 (1994), which amends the Securities Law (Stetson, Stolper and Hill 1999). Finally, pension fund activism led to the enactment in December 2000 of the Tender Offers and Corporate Governance Law 19,705, which protects the rights of minority shareholders and enhances the transparency of takeover procedures.

NOTES

*   I am grateful to Carlos Végh, Gordon Bodnar, Arnold Harberger, Amartya Lahiri, Aaron Tornell, Anders Sorensen and Robert Palacios for helpful comments and suggestions. All errors are my own.

1.   The sequence of pension reforms in Latin America was Chile (in 1981), Peru (1991), Argentina (1994), Colombia (1994), Uruguay (1996), Bolivia (1997), Mexico (1997) and Costa Rica (1998).

2.   For instance, pension funds in Argentina were allowed to invest a maximum of 10 per cent of their portfolios in foreign assets, while pension funds in Chile were allowed to invest up to 9 per cent of their total assets in such assets after 1992. These portfolio restrictions are puzzling, because in practice governments insure the retirement income of the population, explicitly or otherwise. Thus, it should be in their interest to encourage rather than prevent the cross-country diversification of pension funds' assets.

3. The fundamental idea that special interest groups can prevent financial development has been put forward in a comprehensive and integrated way by Rajan and Zingales (2003).
4. Edwards' (1998) account of the political difficulties of approving the pension reform in Chile shows why a lack of transparency or accountability would have made the political obstacles insurmountable. He says:

    > From a political point of view, the launching of the reforms faced some difficulties. First, many interest groups—including public sector workers, teachers, and workers in the health sector—firmly opposed any changes. ... Jose Piñera, the father of the reforms, has pointed out that, owing to stiff opposition, the implementation of the reform had to be postponed for almost a full year. ... As a way to increase the appeal of the new system and reduce political opposition, the architects of the plan determined the new contribution rates so as to increase net take-home pay for those joining the new system. On average, those who transferred to the privately run capitalization system experienced an 11 per cent increase in after-tax pay (Iglesias and Vittas 1992, cited in Edwards 1998: 39).

5. If there are intermediation cost reductions, then financial incumbents are able to lower their cost of funds in two ways. First, the cost reductions may allow for a simultaneous increase in the return on retirement contributions and reduction in the required rate of return on securities issued by public firms. The other possibility is that public firms internalize part of the cost reductions through the ownership of pension funds. In this case, even though the corporate governance reform increases the rate of return on domestic securities, the net cost of funds for public firms falls, because the firms internalize the cost reductions and the profits of pension funds. In Latin America, financial incumbents positioned themselves as significant players in the pension fund business as soon as the pension reforms were launched.
6. Corporate governance is a multi-dimensional concept. For instance, La Porta et al. (1998) propose six measures of investor protection:

    1. whether proxy voting (by mail) is allowed, making it easier for minority shareholders to exercise their voting rights;
    2. whether shares can be blocked prior to a general meeting of shareholders, making it difficult for minority shareholders to vote;
    3. whether cumulative voting is allowed (if minority shareholders can vote cumulatively, they have a better chance of electing at least one director of their choice);
    4. whether there is a right to sue the board, allowing minority shareholders to seek redress for harm caused by a board's decisions (in some countries this takes the form of class action suits);
    5. whether there is a pre-emptive right to new issues, to protect minority shareholders from dilution by the controlling shareholders; and
    6. whether there is a right to call an extraordinary meeting of shareholders (minority shareholders are more protected when relatively few shares are required to call such a meeting).

    Public disclosure of relevant information and accounting standards could also be added to this list.
7. A seemingly alternative view was advanced by Bhattacharya and Daouk (2002), who found that the cost of equity in a country does not change significantly (in a statistical sense) after the introduction of insider trading laws, but decreases significantly after the first prosecution. These findings might suggest that investors consider the enactment of insider trading legislation to be completely irrelevant until they observe evidence of enforcement. However, the authors' empirical analysis is based on a large pool of both developed and developing countries, and is confined to insider trading laws, which are only a minor part of the broader concept of corporate governance.
8. The new scheme also had a public pay-as-you-go component, but most people are enrolled in the private scheme. For a comprehensive description of the Argentinean pension reforms, see FIEL and ASAP (1998).
9. For instance, the government developed a plan to modernize stock markets in 1978, and in the late 1970s the liberalization of stockbrokers' commissions reduced transaction costs substantially (Valdés Prieto 1992).

10. According to Arrau (1994: 21), 'The imminent financial crisis of 1982 and the need to provide a solid capital market for the effective functioning of the new private pension system triggered a hectic pace of legislative activity aimed at strengthening the financial system'.

11. In the literature, this is known as pension fund activism. Del Guercio and Hawkins (1999) survey the evidence on pension fund activism in the United States.

12. Decree-Law 677 of 2001 on Capital Market Transparency and Best Practices.

13. Beim and Calomiris (2001: 163) make the point that the concept of insiders' fiduciary duty to minority shareholders does not exist in civil law countries: 'Many such practices (tunneling practices) can be attacked in common law jurisdictions as a violation of the insiders' fiduciary duty to minority shareholders, but there is no such concept in the civil law countries'.

14. In Figure 3.1a, a downward shift in the marginal cost (per unit of revenue) schedule is implied by the result

$$\left(\frac{\partial}{\partial k} kf(d^*(x,k)) \right)_x < 0 \, .$$

15. Financial markets are typically characterized by increasing returns to scale.

16. Before Resolution 244 was passed, pension funds were required to deposit their securities with the Caja de Valores, which imposed high transaction costs on pension funds due to their frequent trading activities. A similar reform took place in Chile in 1995.

17. In 1997, ENERSIS, Chile's largest holding company in the utilities sector, was sold to ENDESA, a Spanish multinational. ENERSIS had two classes of shareholders: Class A shareholders, mainly employees and pension funds, who had dividend rights but no voting rights; and Class B shareholders, who were the controllers of the company. The price that ENDESA offered for a Class B share was 840 times higher than the price for a Class A share. Even though the value of Class A shares had increased several times, providing large gains to small shareholders, pension funds argued that the benefits were unevenly distributed between controllers and outsiders. They succeeded in having the tender offer declared void in the courts.

4. Conflicted Super Structures: Are Australian Investors Being Short-changed?

Anthony Asher*

Are members of superannuation (pension) funds in Australia being short-changed? Different types of superannuation fund do charge significantly different fees. Some of the difference clearly arises from the quality and scope of the service offered, but there are other, less innocent, explanations for the high level of fees. Of particular concern are the conflicts of interest in some organizational structures.

The first section of this chapter identifies the various types of fund. The second describes the main kinds of regulatory protection provided to members, some of which give rise to additional expenses. The third section examines the role of market or regulatory failures in explaining the apparently excessive level of charges of some funds. The fourth section looks at the functions performed by fund trustees, and identifies potential conflicts of interest as an alternative explanation of additional charges. The fifth section looks at the charges associated with the different types of fund and identifies the main drivers of expense. The final section suggests some topics for additional research and addresses some policy questions.

1. TYPES OF SUPERANNUATION FUND

Australian superannuation funds are classified in a variety of ways in legislation and in the industry statistics published by the Australian Prudential Regulation Authority (APRA).[1] There are inconsistencies in the definitions depending on the purpose for which they are used, but the main classifications are summarized in Table 4.1.

In this chapter, we are concerned only with complying funds.[2] Complying funds qualify for favourable tax treatment of investment income, and contribu-

Table 4.1   Australia: Main Types of Superannuation Fund[a]

APRA Classification	Is Employer Sponsored	Operates in the Public Sector	Operates in the Private Sector
Funds with 1–4 members			
Small APRA funds	Possibly	No	Yes
Self-managed superannuation funds	Possibly	No	Yes
Approved deposit funds with 1–4 members	No	No	Yes
Funds with 5+ members			
Corporate funds	Yes	No	Yes
Public sector funds	Yes	Yes	No
Industry funds	Possibly	Possibly	Possibly
Retail funds	Possibly	No	Yes
Special purpose funds			
Pooled superannuation trusts	No	Possibly	Possibly
Approved deposit funds with 5+ members	No	Possibly	Possibly
Eligible rollover funds	Possibly	Possibly	Possibly

a   'Possibly' indicates that the fund may in some cases have the characteristic given in the column heading.

Source: Author's mapping of the APRA statistical publications and SIS legislation.

tions to such funds may be tax deductible. These funds can be classified in four ways: by trustee, by contractual party, by benefit structure and by manner of investment.

By Trustee

With the exception of retirement savings accounts, all superannuation funds must be managed by a trustee. The trustee is generally a corporate body with its own board of directors but in some circumstances may refer to a group of natural persons. I mean both types when referring to trustees in this chapter. There are currently three classes of trustee licence: the non-public-offer entity licence; the public offer entity licence; and an extended public offer entity licence[3] for trustees of a public offer fund who also operate other funds.

By Contractual Party

Superannuation funds can also be classified according to the party that initiates the contract of membership.

Employer-sponsored funds
A fund is a standard employer-sponsored fund[4] if all contributions to the fund are made as a result of an arrangement between the employer and the trustees, and just an employer-sponsored fund if the contributions are made as a result of an arrangement between the members and their employer. APRA's statistical collections sort employer-sponsored funds into three types: corporate funds, public sector funds and industry funds. Corporate funds are sponsored by a single employer or group of employers in the private sector. Public sector funds are sponsored by the government or its agencies.[5] Industry funds are sponsored by a diverse group of employers in the same or a related industry, in either the public or the private sector, where the common link and driving force is often a representative union. Legislation passed in 2005 allows most members to choose their funds.[6]

Public offer funds
Public offer funds[7] are open to individuals, self-employed or otherwise, who then have a direct arrangement with the trustees to which the employer may or may not be party. Some are employer-sponsored funds, especially industry funds, that have opened their doors to the public. But most are commercial companies that initially catered to individuals, but later also to groups of employees. They are the retail funds of the APRA statistics.

Approved deposit funds[8] are public offer funds whose operations are restricted to receiving a transfer of benefits from other funds or certain payments from the Australian Taxation Office (ATO).

A pooled superannuation trust[9] is a unit trust whose only investors are other superannuation entities. Life insurance companies may invest in a pooled superannuation trust, designate a portion of their assets as a virtual pooled superannuation trust or place the assets backing annuity products in a pooled superannuation trust of their own. The assets backing life insurers' annuity products are shown in the APRA statistics as the 'balance of statutory funds'. Pooled superannuation trusts are not counted in the statistical returns, as this would result in double counting of superannuation assets. No statistics are collected for virtual pooled superannuation trusts.

Retirement savings accounts[10] are open to applications from individuals and operate like bank deposits. They are intended for people with small balances in their superannuation funds and for those who wish, for short periods, to make use of the capital guarantee they offer. They do not have registered trustees and are not defined as public offer funds. Members have a contractual relationship with the bank or life insurance company offering the account; the institution may then be seen as having a fiduciary responsibility towards its account holders.

Member-initiated funds

There are two types of small member-initiated funds. The first are the self-managed funds, in which each trustee is also a member of the fund.[11] They are regulated by the ATO rather than APRA because no prudential risk is involved. The second are the small APRA funds.[12] Established by members, their operations are delegated to a separate trustee. They are regulated by APRA because of the prudential risk involved.

Eligible rollover funds

Trustees face various restrictions[13] in the amounts they can charge in administration fees. If they believe that a member's account is too small to be managed economically, they are allowed to transfer that person's benefit into an eligible rollover fund (without first obtaining the permission of the member).[14] Eligible rollover funds are intended to provide low-cost services for small accounts, and so are restricted in what they can charge.

By Benefit Structure

Defined benefit funds are defined variously in the SIS Act as funds that have at least one member with a prospective benefit related to salary, or taking a fixed pension.[15] Accumulation funds[16] are defined as those funds that are not defined benefit funds. The APRA statistical returns add an intermediate category of hybrid funds that have both defined benefit and accumulation members. However, because trustees are allowed to categorize funds subjectively, some retail funds with defined benefit members have defined themselves as accumulation funds for statistical purposes.

APRA statistics show that over two-thirds of the assets in Australian funds are in accumulation funds, with over 90 per cent of the balance residing in funds defining themselves as hybrid funds. The accumulation funds can be divided further into those that offer choice of investment type and those that go further to offer choice of investment manager. The latter are often called master trusts, although there appears to be no legal definition of this term.

By Manner of Investment

The underlying assets of a fund can be held directly, or through a range of alternative vehicles. Table 4.2 shows how the manner in which APRA classifies fund investment is related to the type of investment held and the tax consequences of each type.

Table 4.2   Australia: Manner of Investment of Fund Assets

APRA Classification	Assets Held by the Fund	Tax on Investment Earnings
Directly invested	Shares, property, fixed interest etc. managed internally	Paid by fund on direct income
Placed with investment manager	Shares etc. managed under a specialist mandate	Paid by fund on direct income
	Wholesale or retail unit and property trusts	Paid by fund on income that is passed on by the manager
	Pooled superannuation trusts	Paid by pooled superannuation trust
Held through life insurance companies	Life insurance policies	Paid by life insurance company

Source: Author's mapping of APRA (2003) and taxation legislation.

2. MAIN FORMS OF REGULATORY PROTECTION

This section discusses the main forms of regulatory protection provided to fund members. Some regulations can be expected to limit the costs associated with superannuation; others may increase them. The discussion focuses mainly on the APRA-regulated funds (that is, those managed by people other than the members), and on accumulation funds.

Fiduciary Responsibility

The commercial law framework for Australian superannuation funds is based on the law of trusts. It is set out, *inter alia*, by Glover (2002):

> Investors, and more particularly members of superannuation funds, enjoy significant protection from the common (or general) law. Corporate officers and advisers with whom we are concerned are disciplined at general law as 'fiduciaries'. The term refers to the law's code for the maintenance of the honesty and integrity of persons in positions of ascendancy and trust. Its centrepiece is an 'inflexible rule' which prohibits fiduciaries, such as corporate officers and advisers, from putting themselves in positions where their interest and duty conflict.[17]

'Interest' refers to the personal financial interests of fiduciaries, 'duty' to their duty to members or perhaps shareholders. Glover goes on to identify conflicts of duty where a director may owe different duties to different groups of shareholders. He points out that the traditional formulation of the rule is strict: 'Possibility of a conflict is enough to attract the rule. … Exposure of one's self to temptation is made wrongful. Directors, as it were, are not given the chance to be dishonest' (Glover 2002). He describes a failure in this area as fraud.

The prohibition on exposing oneself to conflicts of interest is common in the rest of the world, where it is also sometimes included in the basic law of agency. Civil law jurisdictions, which do not recognize trusts, incorporate the provision in other law governing fiduciaries.

The responsibilities of a fiduciary also include a requirement to be prudent, and a duty of care.

Main Legislation

Superannuation funds are subject to various, largely concessionary, tax provisions set out in the Income Tax (Assessment) Act 1936 and the Income Tax (Assessment) Act 1997. The confusingly named Superannuation Guarantee (Administration) Act 1992 requires employers to make superannuation contributions on behalf of employees, currently set at 9 per cent of remuneration. The 'guarantee' arises from the obligation placed on employers to guarantee that they have made the required contributions. The government takes on no financial obligations and there are no investment guarantees. The Superannuation Industry (Supervision) Act 1993 (the SIS Act) and its accompanying set of regulations—the Superannuation Industry (Supervision) Regulations 1994 (the SIS Regulations)—provide for compliance with tax, guarantee and other policy issues, and for prudential supervision. They can be seen as codifying, adapting and extending the provisions in the general law.[18]

Equal Representation on the Board

The boards of trustees of retail funds normally consist of individuals with varying degrees of commercial connection with the shareholders. Other boards of trustees may consist of member representatives, employer representatives and independent trustees. The SIS Act requires half the trustees of a standard employer-sponsored fund to be member representatives,[19] who may be elected directly or appointed by a representative union. Employer representatives may also be appointed by an organization representative of the employer's interests. While employer-appointed trustees can be expected to have greater technical knowledge of issues related to superannuation, member-appointed representatives are likely to be better at communicating with members. The duty of trustees to place members' interests first is reinforced by this diversity in the right to elect or appoint trustees. Public offer funds that have standard employer-sponsored members are only required to have policy committees on which members must be represented. The latter have no rights beyond the right to be consulted. Pensioners are not entitled to representation on fund boards.

Fitness of Trustees

APRA has the power to disqualify inappropriate persons from acting as trustees, actuaries or auditors.[20] The skill level required of a trustee in trust law is that of 'an ordinary prudent person'[21] without any particular skills in the management of superannuation. However, recent regulations[22] require the trustees of a fund to have 'skills relevant to the duties of a trustee', and APRA's fit-and-proper guidance note suggests that the trustees as a whole should have 'sufficient knowledge' to make 'informed decisions'. APRA therefore appears to require somewhat higher standards of knowledge and skill than the law.

Investment Choice

The protection of the general trust law against conflicts of interest in the area of investment choice is overridden in at least two sections of the SIS Act. First, the act makes specific provision to permit investments made at less than arm's length.[23] The protection given is that the price must be determined on an arm's-length basis. APRA says of investments made on an arm's-length basis: 'The test to apply is to consider whether a prudent person acting with due regard to their own commercial interests would have made such an investment'.[24] Second, the SIS Act contains complicated provisions that expressly permit in-house investments in related parties, including the employer sponsor, under some circumstances.[25] The requirement in trust law to invest prudently is made explicit, and the trustee is required to develop a strategy that considers investment risk, diversification, liquidity and the ability to meet liabilities.[26]

Accounting Procedures

Trustees are required to keep the assets of the fund separated from their own; prepare minutes, records and annual accounts; and make them and any other relevant information available to members.

Risk Management Planning

The SIS Regulations require trustees to submit a formal risk management strategy and business plan to APRA. The business plan must specifically address all the risks faced by the trustees and the fund, including:

* governance-related risk (definition, delegation and segregation of responsibilities, outsourcing, fraud);

- operational risk (information systems and records, strategy);
- investment-related risk (market, credit or liquidity); and
- risk mitigation through insurance.

Waiver of Charges on Small Accounts

Some accounts of less than A$1,000 are given member protection to ensure that the administrative charges on the accounts do not exceed their investment earnings.[27] This is a rather wasteful element of the system given the minuscule value of the long-term benefits; after all, A$1,000 represents less than a year's contributions for those on the minimum wage. In the meantime, uneconomic small accounts are proliferating—there are over 25 million accounts but fewer than 10 million workers. A high proportion of the uneconomic accounts belong to young, part-time and casual workers with low wages and high turnover. They would be much better off if they had the money to repay their debts.[28] In other instances members should be encouraged to consolidate their accounts rather than be given this trivial protection. The member protection rules do, however, establish the principle that charges can be capped.

3. MARKET, REGULATORY AND INSTITUTIONAL FAILURE

The puzzle that this chapter addresses is the difference in costs between retail and industry public offer funds. Retail funds charge members 1–4 per cent of the account balance per annum in fees, in addition to upfront deductions of up to 5 per cent of the contributions. Industry funds offer a similar if not identical service for charges of not much more than 1 per cent per annum, normally with no entry charge, despite having much smaller account balances on average. It is sometimes held that the apparently excessive costs of the retail funds are due to some form of market or regulatory failure. This section briefly analyses this possibility.

Market Failures

The standard economic explanations for market failures of this sort are monopolistic practices and information asymmetries.

Monopolistic practices

There are at least a dozen large institutions competing in the public offer market, as well as many smaller players. Given the relative ease of entry and the numerous participants, one might expect a high level of competition and a low level of fees in the industry. The Productivity Commission (2001), which specifically investigated the effect of legislation on competition and barriers to entry, found no evidence of a lack of competition in the industry. Partly as a consequence, it recommended additional restrictions to entry in the form of compulsory licensing of all trustees, with a view to giving members additional regulatory protection.

In studies undertaken for industry bodies, both Clare (2001) and Rice and McEwin (2002) concluded that the charges of funds largely reflected a competitive industry. In 1998, in a more detailed study of the consequences of a proposed merger between two large players in the funds industry, the Australian Competition and Consumer Commission (ACCC) also found no evidence of a lack of competition in the industry.[29] Thus, if fees are too high, it would appear to be necessary to look elsewhere for an explanation.

Information asymmetries
It has been argued that funds are able to charge excessively high fees because members, or their employers, are kept poorly informed about the full extent and level of the fees being charged. This possibility has led to considerable debate about the adequacy of product disclosure, especially the need for improved comparability of fee structures across funds, and for the disclosure of commission earnings by intermediaries.[30]

The Australian Securities and Investment Commission (ASIC) is responsible for regulating the behaviour of all financial market participants, including the trustees of public offer funds. It also regulates financial advisers. Legislative changes in the past five years[31] have set new standards for the disclosure of information, including requiring the licensing of financial advisers by ASIC.

There can be no doubt that the fee structures of superannuation funds are complex, but not insuperably so for a reasonable person prepared to devote time to the subject. A report by ASIC (2004a) provides a basis for determining a standard approach to disclosure. It lists eight different types of fee and makes some suggestions for uniformity. Further regulatory developments in this area seem inevitable.

The investment management component of superannuation charges is particularly transparent and subject to competition in master trusts, which offer a wide choice of investment manager. As discussed below, however, the fees of master trusts do not appear to be particularly competitive.

Again, it seems that information asymmetry does not offer a sufficient explanation for the high fees charged by some funds, suggesting that other factors must be at work.

Regulatory or Legal Failures

Fiduciary responsibility

The inflexible prohibition of trust law against conflicts of interest and duty is not always obeyed, or enforced. It is often argued that it is inconsistent with modern commercial practices—mainly those of directors with many interests or of large commercial firms providing advice to a large number of clients.[32]

'Everybody is doing it' is, however, a poor argument. It is easily rebutted by 'but that does not make it right'. The requirement to avoid conflicts of interest and duty is an ancient legal doctrine that provides one of the foundations of the division of labour that allows for our current economic prosperity. It follows from the recognition of human frailty in the face of temptation. Undermining it may risk undermining all contracts of agency, all delegation, all trusteeship, all professionalism.

The concept of fiduciary responsibility is particularly important in long-term contracts such as superannuation. It is difficult if not impossible for some employees to change funds. In such circumstances, competition and symmetrical information at the point of sale are of little value; the essential point is to ensure that the fund continues to be managed on behalf of members. Of course, the need to attract new members and retain those that have the option to move provides an ongoing competitive discipline, but this is not necessarily enough.

Eliot Spitzer, the New York attorney-general from 1998 to 2006, has stated that conflicts of interest have become institutionalized in many parts of the financial services industry (O'Brien 2004). His efforts to prosecute a number of financial firms for succumbing to conflicts of interest led to apparently reputable organizations in the United States paying billions of dollars in fines and compensation. This scandal was similar in many respects to the mis-selling problems of the UK life insurance industry in the 1990s.

It appears that, *prima facie*, conflicts of interest cannot be ruled out as an explanation for excessive fees in the Australian superannuation industry.

Agency risks

Agency risks have been investigated in the economics literature over the past three decades, although, perhaps surprisingly, they are not often mentioned in the context of market failure. The cure suggested in the literature is greater monitoring of agents and better alignment of the incentives of agents and principals.[33] The increased disclosure that has thus far been the major regulatory tool in Australia perhaps arises from this economists' perspective. But an alternative, more legal, view, expressed below, is that the key to the management of agency risks lies in a more appropriate application of the law of agency.

Specific prohibitions

The essential prohibitions in the law of agency are as follows.

- An agent or trustee is entitled to remuneration but should not make a secret profit. The level of remuneration should not only be disclosed, but should be agreed to by (in this case) the member or sponsoring employer.
- An individual should not enter into any contract both as a principal and as an agent or trustee of another person.
- The agent or trustee should not make a profit, disclosed or otherwise, that might be seen as influencing the agent's decision to the possible detriment of the principals or (in this case) members.

These issues—including the last, more debatable, point—are examined in more detail in section 4 of this chapter, where I look at the functions of trustees in greater detail. Before doing so, however, it may be helpful to look at some of the insights of institutional economics.

Institutional Factors

Keneley (2004) makes reference to some of the relevant literature in the field of institutional economics. This literature focuses on issues relating to the structure of firms and of markets, and the way that these have evolved to deal with transaction and information costs. Both within firms and in the market, unwritten 'rules of the game' can govern behaviour—with both positive and negative effects.

Regulatory capture
Of some interest in this context is the theory of collective action, which predicts that small organized groups will be able to influence regulation and capture benefits from the rest of society. It is recognized, for example, that large organizations are able, intentionally or otherwise, to influence regulation to make it more difficult for small organizations to flourish.

The tax, disclosure and prudential regulations surrounding Australian superannuation have reached what is perhaps an incomparable level of complexity. The main superannuation acts and regulations run to over 800 pages; the 2001 financial sector reforms added 150,000 words to this legislation. Advisers must understand not only the difficult provisions of the two income tax acts but also the rules for social security benefit payments. These complexities cannot but entrench the position of large firms that can afford the necessary specialists, thus making it more difficult for smaller firms to compete, and driving up the price of administration. This point was recognized but dismissed by the Productivity Commission (2001). It should perhaps be revisited.

Rules of the game: investment 'cults'
Given the common and not entirely unfair references to the 'cult of the equity', some consideration may be given here to the belief system surrounding invest-

ment markets. The belief that it is possible to beat the market appears to be more widespread than is justified by the research. Investment managers, operating on behalf of fund members, fulfil the important additional economic function of allocating savings to where they are most productive. If the investment managers are successful in their task, the expected return on all assets, after adjustment for risk, will be the same for all managers. Put differently, no manager will be able to outperform any other manager when considered *ex ante*. The intervention of random events does mean, however, that the returns produced by different managers will differ *ex post*—even in an efficient market.

It is difficult to discern whether the market is efficient and whether the *ex post* difference results from skill or is random. Behavioural economists have found that people are prone to recognize patterns in random events where none exist. Ferson, Saskissian and Simin (2002) found that this problem extended even to experts using sophisticated statistical tools. Blake and Timmermann (2004) reported findings showing that UK investors were influenced excessively by good past performance in spite of its possible lack of meaning.

The question as to whether the investment performance of managers persists over time has been researched intensively. In a finding that remains largely unchallenged, Carhart (1997) showed that it does—but only in the case of underperforming funds. He found weak evidence of persistent outperformance among funds that were able in some way quickly to capture new evidence in the market. On the other hand, he found strong evidence of persistent underperformance by other funds. Part of the underperformance could be explained by excessive trading; the rest must come from the purchase or sale of investments at uneconomic prices. One possibility is that managers are trading at an uneconomic price for some personal benefit, at the expense of fund members. Blake and Timmermann (2004) conclude that information on past performance should be made available to members so that they are able to avoid underperforming funds.

Coleman, Esho and Wong (2003) found some evidence of persistent underperformance by retail funds in Australia. This requires further investigation; a starting point would be to establish whether conflicts of interest can explain the transactions concerned.

In spite of the difficulties outlined above, there is some assistance available to help retail investors choose the best managers. Some such sources are the specialist media, including the financial sections of most newspapers; financial advisers to individuals, including fee-for-service financial advisers (whose numbers are increasing); investment consultancies that collect and analyse data; asset consultants, who largely advise companies; and managers of managers, who work for master trusts. At this stage there appears to be no evidence one way or the other that any of these are successful in distinguishing between the investment performance of two apparently competent managers. They may, however, be able to help investors avoid the less reputable managers.

Why does the funds management industry not focus more intently on what appear to be excessive expenses? In spite of the advances in computers, which should have reduced costs over the past 30 years, charges for investment management can be two or three times what they were in the 1960s. Moreover, they are two or three times higher than the costs actually reported.[34] This represents a real puzzle given the competition within master trusts referred to earlier.

Taleb (2001), who provides an insider's view of the funds management industry, repeatedly makes the point that completely random results will lead to wide differences in the performance of investment managers. Random differences are the result of luck, not good judgment, but people (and he includes himself in this) are not really able to distinguish between the two. The consequence appears to be that we are too easily persuaded to pay too much for investment management.

This position may be overstated. The excessive investment charges (if they exist) are a small percentage of assets, and make little difference when accounts are small. It is justifiable, in some instances, to ignore them. But as funds mature and their average account balances increase, the amounts involved become considerable. It may be that members do not adequately appreciate the difference, which is why greater disclosure and more investor education are needed. This education should focus mainly on teaching investors that past performance does not govern future returns—except perhaps in the case of underperforming managers, who are likely to continue to perform poorly—and that fees make more of a difference to returns in the long run.

Rules of the game: commissions

The early 1990s saw growing dissatisfaction with traditional front-end-loaded insurance and superannuation savings contracts, under which as much as the entire first year's premium on a new policy was often allocated to commission and other selling expenses. The apparent excesses of the front-end-loaded commission system led to a move to a new system involving much smaller front-end charges on savings contracts but the addition of trail commissions. The effect of this change was to reduce the initial cost of taking out a policy, but to increase it over the term of the policy, as explained in Appendix A4.1. Even a 0.5 per cent annual trail will be worth 30 per cent of a person's annual contribution after 30 years. It may be that the long-term effects of the new system were not initially evident, and that changes will be made as the larger trails begin to bite. Many people are already making their own changes, as can be seen from the growth in self-managed funds, which are more cost effective once the value of an account exceeds about A$100,000.

Social relationships

Another perspective is given by two sociologists. In a two-year study of the culture and behaviour of nine large pension funds in the United States, O'Barr and Conley (1992: 70) confirm the author's experience of 'surprising and sometimes disturbing' evidence of 'an unsystematic approach' to investment decisions. They observe that 'relationships are often more important than managing the bottom line in evaluating and deciding whether to retain managers'.

4. THE FUNCTIONS OF TRUSTEES AND POTENTIAL CONFLICTS OF INTEREST

We now turn to the ways in which conflicts of interest may lead to excessive costs. Figure 4.1 shows the main cashflows in the superannuation relationships, and highlights flows that may arise from potential conflicts of interest. The discussion that follows is grouped around the main functions of trustees: distribution, administration and investment.

Distribution

Something must bring members to a fund initially. Trustees must then find ways of persuading members or their employers to continue to contribute to the fund, and of attracting new members. This could also be called the marketing function.

Non-public-offer employer-sponsored funds
The trustees of corporate and public sector funds deal directly with employers and members, thus avoiding direct distribution costs. However, they still need to justify the fund's ongoing existence, and to market its benefits. Trustees wear two hats if they are also directors or managers of the employer. This creates a potential conflict of interest when discretionary benefits are discussed: as trustees, managers are supposed to put the interests of members first, but as managers, they have an interest in reducing the employer's contributions.

The equal representation rules provide some balance in this respect. They can also be expected to create a certain competitive tension between employer and member representatives on the board of trustees, although there is some debate about the productivity of this tension. It has been suggested that union directors are valuable board members because they are able to provide information that might not otherwise be available, and because they often have more time to devote to the board than other outside directors (Anonymous 1982). But Williamson (1984: 1,206) worries about the appointment of union directors 'deflecting strategic decision makers from their main purposes ... by forcing them to address operating level complaints' and, more seriously, about 'the problem of opportunism that inclusion of partisan constituencies on the board invites'.

Figure 4.1   Sources of Conflict of Interest and Duty

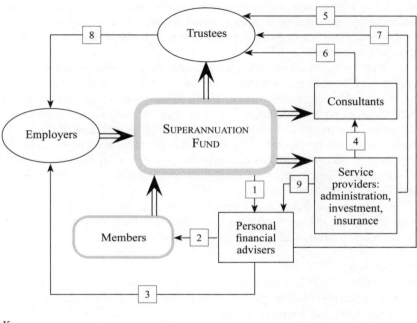

Key:
Essential cashflows ⟹   Potentially conflicted cashflows ⟶

Flows causing potential conflict of interest and duty (certainly if profits are secret):

1   Adviser owes principal duty to member but is paid by fund, trustee or life company—sometimes in soft dollars that are dependent on volumes.

2   Adviser passes on cost of additional commission and rebates to member, so reducing the member's superannuation account.

3, 8   Adviser, trustee or related-group company rebates commission or provides other benefits to employer.

4   Service provider makes discretionary or soft dollar payments to consultant.

5, 6, 7 Trustee or group makes profit from holding in or payments from adviser group, service provider or consultant.

9   Financial adviser receives payment from service provider.

Public offer industry funds

Industry funds with direct links to sponsoring employers are also able to avoid direct distribution costs and enjoy the 'benefits' of any tension between member and employer-appointed trustees. In cases where trustees are not members of the fund, there is an agency risk that they will pursue their own interests at the cost of members.

The non-profit nature of industry funds also sets up a tension between them and the retail funds that is identical to the tension between mutual and for-profit insurance companies. The non-profit industry funds and mutuals do not face the same conflicts of interest between members and shareholders as the for-profit retail funds and insurance companies. It is widely held, however, that their trustees or directors are not subject to the same level of discipline by members or policy holders as that imposed on the elected directors of retail funds and insurance companies by company shareholders (see, for example, HM Treasury 2004).

In developing a distribution channel, industry funds rely on direct contact with employers; union pressure on employers to persuade them to join; and, more recently, advertising to attract individual members.

Retail funds

Retail funds do not have the inherent links to members of the funds just discussed, and so must market themselves actively if they are to attract and retain members. The retail funds are mainly invested in life insurance policies,[35] and have in large measure inherited their distribution systems from the life insurers that initiated them. While superannuation may be distinguished from life insurance, it is probably unhelpful to make the distinction in this context. Many funds pay for life and disability insurance for members. The remuneration of the sales channel will include commissions from insurance sold to the same clients for insurance that is both inside and outside the superannuation fund.

The life insurance sales system can be classified as having four channels. The first is the traditional high-pressure channel, paid purely on commission. It is peopled by agents, normally in some dealer group, who sell only one company's products, and by brokers who sell the products of more than one company. They have been described as the archetypal salespersons. A scholarly analysis of their social status, and the extreme moral and financial pressure placed on them, is given by Guy Oakes in a book reviewed by Smith (1991: 287):

> The general thesis of this book is that these salesmen ... are subject to two inherently conflicting principles: a commercial idiom that stresses sales at all costs and a service idiom that stresses concern and sensitivity for the needs of clients. ... [T]he author reviews the five essential steps of selling insurance: prospecting, approaching, interviewing, closing (making the sale) and providing service to clients. ... After presenting both idioms, he offers a brief discussion of the major antimonies of the profession, namely, sacralization and manipulation, opportunism and pro-

fessionalism, toughness and sensitivity, sincerity and dissimulation. The book ends with an analysis of the ways in which most salesmen succeed in remaining ignorant of their own conflictual situation.

Given the unpleasantness and costs of this system, it may be asked why it perseveres. Zultowski (1979) surveys research on the widespread belief that life insurance 'is sold and not bought' that provides some justification for the high-pressure approach. The agents reported that less than 20 per cent of sales were initiated by policy holders, but the policy holders felt that the statistic was closer to 50 per cent. There appears to have been no formal research into the matter since then, but there is also little evidence that the position has changed.

In Australia, where superannuation contributions are compulsory, this argument cannot be said to hold. It may be argued, however, that high-pressure sales forces actively seek out small businesses and the self-employed and persuade them to contribute to superannuation, thus contributing towards greater compliance with the law.

Berger, Cummins and Weiss (1997), who investigated the coexistence of insurance distribution systems with widely differing fee structures, found that higher charges did not translate into higher profits, although they did seem to be related to a better-quality service. It would be an exercise beyond the scope of this chapter to determine whether any of the participants in the industry earned monopoly-type profits. What is clear is that the additional costs of the distribution system of retail funds accounts for a significant proportion of the difference in charges between them and the industry funds. An open and perhaps more pressing question is whether the extra costs are justified.

A conflict of interest occurs when commission-remunerated salespeople purport to be 'financial advisers'—a conflict that is aggravated if they claim to be independent. A strict interpretation of the law on conflicts would prohibit salespeople from purporting to give 'advice', and then receiving a commission from a third party that depended on the nature of that advice. However, the compensation given to those who had been mis-sold life insurance in the United Kingdom was not based on this strict interpretation of the law, but rather on legislation that required advisers to demonstrate they had given the 'best advice'.

In the Australian context, it would seem that members of corporate and industry funds receive less expensive advice than those in retail funds. On either a best advice rule or a strict interpretation of the law, this might seem to expose some retail funds to similar demands for compensation. However, the SIS Act and the Corporations Act (2001) expressly permit the payment of commissions to advisers, thus undermining a strict interpretation of the general law.

The second main channel for life insurance sales is also commission based, but is less pressured. In this channel, the incomes of the salespeople are not entirely dependent on life insurance or superannuation sales; they may also broker general insurance, occasionally recommend a product in their role as professional accountants or lawyers, or be based in bank branches where they also serve customers' other needs. Their business can be said to come to them; they are described as the 'farmers' of the life insurance business, against the 'hunters' of the first channel who have to go out and find their customers. For brokers, bank branches that generate leads can be twice as efficient as having to prospect for clients. To the extent that they are commission remunerated, they face the same conflicts as the salespeople in the first channel. But to the extent that they cannot justify their commissions in terms of the need to find clients, they may face a greater burden in justifying high commissions. Some members of this channel charge fees for their advice and deduct their commissions from these. In such cases, there is no conflict of interest.

In the case of both channels, a problem develops when a company pays overriding (additional) commissions to apparently independent brokers if they place larger volumes of business with it. This practice was investigated by ASIC (2004b). While widely accepted previously, it is now discouraged.

The third channel for life insurance sales is the bank branches where employees are paid regular salaries and bonuses rather than by commission. Here it would seem to be the bank that faces the conflict of interest. Glover (1995) suggests that banks may in some circumstances owe a fiduciary duty to their customers. To the extent that a bank, and not its employees, receives the commissions paid by a retail superannuation fund, and thus makes a secret profit, there is a conflict of interest between it and its customers. Determining this profit is not easy. Australian banks report relatively small profits from superannuation business, even though the estimates given in the next section suggest that superannuation and investment management charges make up perhaps half of their consolidated fee income from all sources, or 25 per cent of their total revenue. The actual contribution to profit depends on a relatively subjective allocation of overheads, so cannot easily be determined.

The final channel is direct distribution of life insurance products by mail or internet. There is unlikely to be a conflict of interest if the charges are adequately disclosed, although a problem may arise if a bank or other apparently reputable organization endorses an overpriced product. A bank that endorsed a product priced at several times the going market rate might well be exposing itself to subsequent claims for damages.

The role of employers
Employers are compelled by law to contribute to superannuation on behalf of their employees. Employers who are not governed by an award would appear to owe a common law duty of care and good faith to their employees when selecting an appropriate superannuation fund.

It is clear from the decline in the number of corporate superannuation schemes over the past few years that there are advantages for employers in merging their funds into larger industry and retail funds. APRA data on fund transfers show that it is the retail funds that have benefited most from this trend, even though they charge considerably more than the industry funds, and often because of the commissions that are paid to the intermediaries who initiate such a move.

A significant factor in this trend has been the willingness of retail funds to tackle the costs and other difficulties associated with administering residual defined benefits. Although defined benefit funds do not need to do as much data processing as accumulation funds, and so ought to be cheaper to run, their greater need for actuarial services creates a significant overhead. As a result, the smaller defined benefit funds, which often suffer from poor systems and controls, can be considerably more expensive to run than accumulation funds. While the retail funds define themselves as accumulation funds in the APRA statistics, some have been active in acquiring hybrid schemes—a market that appears of less interest to the industry funds. Retail funds have apparently also been more flexible in accommodating other idiosyncrasies in the fund rules.

These factors may explain the success of retail funds in acquiring defined benefit and hybrid funds, but they do not explain why they have been able to acquire so many accumulation funds. Is it because employers are reacting against union domination of the industry funds? Are the retail funds so very much more efficient administratively? Is it that the industry funds do not give enough support and advice?

Or one could be more suspicious. Do employers receive benefits from dealing with commissioned advisers in addition to the advice they receive on the superannuation fund? Is it possible that employers' duties to employees are being compromised by pressure from bank managers? The latter possibility is suggested by the market share gained by the life insurance companies attached to the four large banks. The growth in their assets over and above that of other life insurers during the years 1998–2003 suggests that the four large banking groups captured over 70 per cent of the flows out of corporate funds in that period, despite having an overall market share of only 40 per cent.

Administration

Trustees have to collect contributions and keep records of all member details. They must pay benefits to members or arrange for members' assets to be transferred into other funds. Other administrative tasks include the payment of taxes and levies, ensuring fund compliance with legislation and regulations, and amending the trust deed where necessary. In this context, the provision of life and disability insurance can also be regarded as an administrative service.

Trustees need to be aware that some of their duties may give rise to conflicts of interest.

Outsourcing

If trustees pay for the costs of outsourcing out of their own fees, paid to them by members, a conflict of interest does not arise. But if instead they use the fund's money to pay for an outsourced service, then a conflict may arise if the supplier is linked in some way to the trustee. Trustees face a conflict between their duty to members and their interest in, or duty to, suppliers, if they exercise their own discretion when choosing and paying an outsourced supplier. This problem is particularly relevant in the retail fund sector, where trustees and service suppliers frequently form part of the same group of companies, and in industry funds, where union-appointed directors often have links with union-owned suppliers.

A second area of conflict arises when the consultants to a fund recommend an outsourced service provider, and in consequence receive a commission from that service provider. An egregious example would be for consultants to recommend unnecessary or expensive insurance on which they are paid a commission.

Delegation

Not many trustees are experts on superannuation. They are therefore reliant on the help of experts in the administration of their funds and the investment of assets. Some trustees may be tempted to abdicate and yield power to the professionals, but an argument can be made that members are best represented by lay (non-expert) trustees who control the professional service providers. It needs to be emphasized that this system requires some diligence on the part of lay trustees if they are to preserve the balance of power. Professional service providers will always face the temptation to usurp power, for reasons of efficiency as well as commercial interest.

Two of the trends currently observable in the retirement funds industry illustrate the dangers of giving greater power to the professionals. The first is the tendency to devolve the power of choice of investment manager from trustees to members, even though the members are in a weaker position than the trustees when it comes to monitoring the value of investment management services. This surely explains some of the increase in costs that has inexorably accompanied the introduction of choice. The second is the suggestion that paid professional trustees sit on the board, as recommended, for instance, by Myners in his review of institutional investment in the United Kingdom (HM Treasury 2001). This again has apparent advantages, but clearly weakens the position of lay trustees on the board. If trustees want independent advice, they would be better advised to contract for it rather than surrender some of their powers.

Trustee discretion over benefits

Another potential area of conflict arises when trustees who are also members of the fund amend the trust deed or exercise their discretion in the governing rules to increase the benefits payable to one or more classes of beneficiary. This often involves the application of reserve funds.[36] It seems impractical to prevent members from being trustees. Nevertheless, they do need to be conscious of when their interests are affected; ensure that those interests are appropriately disclosed; and absent themselves from votes on such matters.

Investment

The money collected from members has to be invested with a view to providing the best possible mix of risk and return. Trustees normally delegate the choice of assets to a professional investment manager. The assets themselves are normally held by a custodian who buys and sells on instruction from the investment manager. Outsourcing this function to organizations linked to the trustees potentially creates the same kinds of conflicts described above for the outsourcing of administration. Giving members a choice of investment manager removes this problem so long as the choice is unfettered and members are given unbiased advice.

Stockbroking and shelf fees

The investment industry has its own peculiar, institutionalized conflicts in the soft commissions paid by stockbrokers to investment managers and, occasionally, other investment advisers. These normally take the form of research services and terminals that are provided free if the stockbroker earns sufficient commissions from the investment manager. That the commissions paid by stockbrokers are seldom disclosed separately in the accounts of superannuation funds means that the profits are entirely secret, thus aggravating the problem. This is not to recommend a narrow focus on the direct costs of dealing, as this could be counterproductive. Every market dealer knows that a large buyer or seller can move the price of the less liquid stocks, and competent dealers can easily justify their charges. These charges should, however, be disclosed.

Another conflict arises when investment managers are required to pay shelf fees for the right to be included on the investment menu of a master trust. If not disclosed, these would constitute a secret profit. But they represent a conflict even if disclosed, as fund administrators may be biased towards those managers that offer to make higher payments.

Business opportunities

A more difficult element of the conflict-of-interest prohibition is that which arises from business opportunities. Investment managers who find unusual investments that they regard as good value may face a conflict between investing in them on their own behalf and including them in their clients' portfolios. Buying on one's own account before buying for one's clients is clearly prohibited. But failing to buy the asset for clients at all is not as clear-cut, and may be justified on the grounds that it is inappropriate (for example, too speculative a use of trust money).

This argument has dubious provenance, as modern investment theory would suggest that risk is related more to general exposure to the market than to exposure to individual assets. It is perhaps even more dubious when the assets are held in a superannuation fund for internal staff—as might happen in a financial institution—which then appears to outperform the funds open to clients. The best way for investment managers to manage this particular agency risk is to hold all their personal assets, especially superannuation, in pooled funds that are available to their clients. This is required by some institutions, although the idea has not found its way into the ethical codes.

On another front, the right to participate in potentially lucrative initial public offerings involves a conflict of interest if the investment manager is allocated shares or underwriting commissions that are kept or passed on selectively to clients.

Self-investment and adviser-linked investments

The exemptions in the SIS Act for in-house assets include significant accommodation for corporate superannuation funds to make investments in the employer—if these investments were made before the relevant part of the legislation was passed. Public sector funds may also face pressure to invest in the debt of the sponsor. In both cases, investment returns may suffer.

Also worth mentioning, because it has led to a number of actions by APRA, is the practice of financial advisers recommending investment choices in which they have a personal interest. This is more prevalent among fringe operators, but major groups with private equity or other more exotic investment options are also compromised if the profits they make are not entirely disclosed.

Trustee Discretion over Fees

Trustees are entitled to remuneration for their services. However, the level of this remuneration should be disclosed and it should be predetermined. A contract that permits trustees to increase the fees paid to themselves places them in an impossible position of conflict. Any increase clearly benefits them and harms the members; thus, this type of contract should not be permitted.

The problem seldom arises in corporate funds, where trustees normally fulfil their duties as part of their general work obligations. The same is true of industry funds, although they are more likely to pay attendance fees or, in some cases, fees determined by an external body such as the Remuneration Commission. To the extent that these allowances can be determined objectively to compensate trustees for expenses or losses incurred as a result of their duties, they do not create a conflict. If the fees are significant, then mechanisms should be found to ensure that they are not determined by the trustees themselves.

It is common for retail funds to charge a fee that may be increased at the discretion of the trustee, normally with some period of notice. If members are entitled to move their accounts to another fund without penalty, then this may be an acceptable practice. But if their accounts are locked in—by the decision of the employer, for instance—then this discretion should not be exercised by the trustee without giving members a chance to change funds.

Conflicts Faced by Corporate and Life Insurance Directors

It would seem that the fiduciary duties of the directors of a corporate trustee are indirect, through their responsibility to the corporate trustee and its shareholders. In terms of the SIS Act,[37] they have a duty to exercise 'a reasonable degree of care and diligence' in ensuring that the trustee fulfils its duties.

It would not be surprising if the remuneration of directors were linked to the profitability of the trustee, or if their performance objectives included increasing revenue or reducing costs. Although the cost of their activities might have to be borne by members, as long as the activities themselves were legal, this would be unremarkable. It can be argued that a remuneration package that rewards directors for increasing business is in the interest of members. Directors do obviously face conflicts of duty when making decisions that might involve the corporate trustee in a conflict of interest. An inflexible application of the law would prevent them from making such decisions.

The same comments apply to life insurance directors, in the general law and in the Life Insurance Act 1995, because 85 per cent of their business is related to superannuation. Under the Life Insurance Act, they are required to put the interests of policy holders first where these might conflict with those of shareholders. This would seem to prohibit them from exercising discretion to increase policy charges unless, perhaps, policy holders had the right to surrender their contracts without loss.

5. COSTS AND RETURNS

This section looks in greater detail at the differences in costs between the various types of fund, and discusses whether they might be a consequence of some market or regulatory failure.

Costs

The typical costs of the different types of fund are reported in Clare (2001) and Rice and McEwin (2002) in their survey of charges in the superannuation industry. This section confirms most of their findings.

The costs of funds are reported to APRA, but not in a form that allows for easy comparison. The main reason is that expenses are not reported unless the assets are directly invested (see Table 4.2 above for the different types of indirect investment). Thus, with some minor exceptions, the charges of the investment managers of indirect investments, and the tax on investment income earned by pooled superannuation trusts and life insurers, are not reported. Funds invested entirely or almost entirely in life insurance policies may report no expenses at all to APRA; the life insurer pays them all.

The accounts of pooled superannuation trusts and life companies, but not of wholesale trusts, are reported to APRA. It is therefore possible to estimate the costs incurred in the underlying vehicles by examining their APRA returns.[38] The costs of life insurance companies appear to average some 1.9 per cent of assets per annum; those of pooled superannuation trusts average around 0.7 per cent of directly managed assets.

Using this information and the asset allocations shown in Table 4.3,[39] it is possible to estimate the total costs incurred by the different types of fund— before any deduction for tax, and without any allowance for the profit margins of life companies and pooled superannuation trusts (see Table 4.4). As funds pay tax at 15 per cent, members would probably be charged 15 per cent less than the figures shown in the final column. However, the profit margins of retail funds may more than make up for this.[40]

These costs do not include stock brokerage but probably include most other commissions. There may also be other costs that are netted off income. The totals are more or less consistent with the published charges of the larger industry and retail funds, although the incompleteness of the data means that the results should be treated as mere approximations.

The total costs of the entire industry can now be estimated (Table 4.5). It is assumed here that life company profit margins are about 25 per cent of costs,[41] and that banks account for some 60 per cent of the retail funds. While these assumptions are approximate, it does appear that fund management charges make up perhaps as much as 50 per cent of the non-interest fee, commission and other income reported by Australian banks and perhaps 25 per cent of their total revenue.[42] This would explain, in large measure, the importance attached to funds management by the banking industry. It would be interesting, although difficult, to investigate whether this plays a role in the high returns on equity enjoyed by the big Australian banks, and whether this could be ascribed to a lack of competition.

Table 4.3 Australia: Asset Allocation of Funds by Type of Fund

Fund Type	Total (A$ million)	Direct & Specialist Mandates (%)	Life Insurance Companies (%)	Pooled: Wholesale (%)	Pooled: Retail (%)	Assets of Funds Covered by Survey as % of Assets of All Funds
Corporate funds	55,104	45	7	44	5	83
Industry funds	62,579	44	3	41	12	98
Public sector funds	115,767	87	0	10	3	100
Retail funds	192,316	10	57	26	7	99
Small funds	127,504	66	12	22	0	0
Post-retirement streams	12,679	0	100	0	0	
Total	**565,949**					

Source: APRA (2003); APRA's unpublished quarterly survey.

Returns

Appendix A4.2 calculates the relative investment performance of the different types of fund after taking hidden expense differentials into account. Once this is done, it would appear that there is very little difference between the gross investment performance of corporate, industry, public sector and retail funds. This is to be expected and so tends to confirm the overall level of charges as determined here. While these results are inconsistent with the findings of Coleman, Esho and Wong (2003), the differences can be explained by the incorporation of hidden expenses and taxes.

Discussion

Australians are paying some 3 per cent of their total personal incomes in charges to the fund management industry, broadly defined. These can be broken down into three types of charges: distribution charges, administration charges and investment management charges.

Table 4.4   Australia: Funds' Costs as a Share of Their Assets by Type of Fund (%)[a]

Fund Type	Direct Charges	Specialist Mandates	Indirect charges by Life Offices	Indirect charges by Wholesale Managers	Indirect charges by Retail Managers	Total Charges
Corporate funds	0.48	0.24	0.07	0.32	0.07	1.17
Industry funds	0.65	0.19	0.03	0.30	0.18	1.35
Public sector funds	0.40	0.39	0.00	0.07	0.05	0.91
Retail funds	0.84	0.03	1.09	0.19	0.11	2.26
Small funds	1.22	0.00	0.24	0.16	0.00	1.62
Post-retirement streams			1.91			1.91

a   It is assumed that specialist mandate fees are 60 basis points per annum; that the wholesale holders of life insurance policies (corporate, industry and public sector funds) are charged only 100 basis points; and that retail unit trusts charge 150 basis points. These are no more than informed guesses based on discussions with industry participants and a sample of product disclosure statements.

Source: Author's calculations based on APRA (2001, 2003).

Distribution charges (retail funds)
The cost of distributing retail products amounts to some 10 per cent of new contributions, or as much as 1.5 per cent of the income of the 30 per cent of Australians who have superannuation in retail funds. This figure of 10 per cent is higher than the charges actually disclosed by the funds, but includes charges on rollovers from one fund to another in the numerator while excluding the rollovers themselves from the denominator. The justification for this is that rollovers are not new money, making marketing payments difficult to justify from a national or policy perspective. Including gross rollovers would halve the distribution costs of retail funds to 5 per cent, bringing them in line with disclosed costs.

Distribution costs appear to account for over 40 per cent of the total charges of retail funds. In return, investors receive some assistance in complying with the superannuation guarantee legislation, advice on financial planning and budgeting, help in negotiating Australia's complex tax and social security regulations, and advice on the choice of investment manager and asset class. Some of this is necessary but much of it is not. In particular, the investment

Table 4.5   Australia: Wealth Management and Insurance Industry Charges (A$ million)

	Direct Charges	Total Charges
Type of fund		
Superannuation funds		
Corporate funds	260	700
Industry funds	410	900
Public sector funds	460	1,200
Retail funds	1,600	5,000
Small funds	1,600	2,200
Post-retirement streams	0	300
Subtotal	4,330	10,300
Life companies		2,200
Public unit trusts		2,400
Total		**14,900**
Type of charge		
Distribution (retail funds)		2,100
Administration		7,200
Investment management		5,600
Total		**14,900**
Type of institution		
Life insurers		5,700
Banks		8,700
Other		500
Total		**14,900**

Source: Author's calculations based on APRA (2001, 2003) and other tables in the text.

advice provided by retail funds is of doubtful value (especially where advisers receive commissions related to their advice).

Mandatory disclosure of distribution costs does not appear to have reduced expenses elsewhere in the world and seems unlikely to do so in Australia. A more rigorous interpretation of the common law conflict-of-interest prohibitions may be necessary to reduce distribution costs significantly. Prohibiting the payment of commissions entirely would be draconian. An alternative might be to restrict the payment of commissions to circumstances in which the intermediary does not purport to give advice. This might be easier to manage if salespeople were to sell a limited range of products with specified terms and conditions. This is already the case in the United Kingdom, where stakeholder pensions are 'CAT marked'.[43]

Administration charges

Administration costs account for about half of funds' total charges. However, the costs of administering self-managed funds—averaging A$7,300 per fund per annum, or A$3,100 per member—are disproportionately high, amounting to about one-quarter of total charges. It is difficult to explain the higher costs of self-managed funds as being driven by their greater flexibility, given the enormous range of investment choice available in public offer funds. Indeed, direct property is the only type of investment *not* available in public offer funds and, as Roberts (2002) shows, self-managed funds make relatively little investment in this area.

Other possible explanations for the higher costs of self-managed funds are their outlays on expensive retail funds, or the opportunities self-management provides for reducing tax and circumventing the means test. Given that self-managed funds provide almost entirely for relatively well-informed, wealthy individuals who could use public offer industry funds if they chose to, and who might in any case be expected to be able to look after themselves in negotiations with administrators, the latter seems the most likely driver of the higher costs. This is wasteful; reducing tax is a negative sum game as the tax must be collected elsewhere and the costs are not recoverable.

Allocating administration charges (before tax) to the larger funds produces a cost of A$56 per member per annum for industry funds, A$136 for retail funds, A$168 for public sector funds and A$328 for corporate funds. These figures appear to be in line with the published charges of public offer funds. The costs of public sector and corporate funds may be understated to the extent that their administration is subsidized by the employer.

The differences in cost appear to be related to economies of scale, the difficulties of administering residual defined benefit schemes and the profit margins of the commercial enterprises (guessed as 25 per cent of costs). There may also be a difference in the level of service provided. A large part of the administrative costs of retail funds may be related to their more active quest for members; the high charges of corporate and public sector funds may be related to the higher average account balances of members, who are likely to take a more active interest in their accounts.

Given that the retail funds appear to make an adequate profit at an average annual charge of A$136 per account, we can make the heroic assumption that this provides the benchmark for a quality service. This would mean that unnecessary administrative charges in the superannuation system amount to over A$1.5 billion—or about half the total cost of superannuation. (This makes no

judgment about the administrative cost of insurance and other non-superannu-
ation investment contracts.) Of this, around 40 per cent can be ascribed to the
small self-managed funds and appears to be related to tax planning opportunities. The balance would appear to come from residual defined benefit expenses.
It would be well worth investigating ways of simplifying these, for example by
switching members to accumulation funds while providing investment guarantees.

Investment management charges

Investment costs seem to average 60–80 basis points annually. This is shy of
the charges displayed on the websites of some of the large retail funds, and
of the charges claimed for unit trusts, and about equal to the investment costs
claimed by industry funds. Members of superannuation funds would therefore
seem to be getting a relatively good deal, even if the profit margin in these
charges appears to be at least 50 per cent.

While the investment management industry is clearly a competitive one,
the high profit margins for this function do merit further investigation, perhaps
along the lines suggested by institutional economics (see section 3 above).
Investors should be educated to understand the random nature of investment
markets and the significance of costs for long-term returns. It should be emphasized that past performance is likely to predict future performance only in the
case of underperforming funds.

Although there ought to be scope for a reduction in superannuation investment charges, it is difficult to see how any significant savings could arise.

6. CONCLUSIONS

The higher costs of retail funds are largely explained by the costs of their distribution system. While a purported benefit of the system is that it includes
advice to members, much of this advice may be biased (because advisers are
paid by commission) or is unnecessary. The system also contains a number of
other conflicts of interest that may lead to instances of excessive charging. Part
of the distribution costs of retail funds, and what looks like the higher administration costs of self-managed funds, arise from the complexity of the tax and
social security codes and—in the case of the self-managed funds—the many
opportunities for tax planning.

The investment management charges of all funds appear to be high relative to the underlying costs. This is difficult to explain, as the costs are clearly
disclosed and there is significant choice and competition in this area. However, one factor appears to be investors' lack of knowledge about investment

markets, and in particular their failure to understand the impact of charges on long-term returns.

The main policy conclusions would seem to be as follows. First, where conflicts of interest exist, further action should be taken to eliminate them or mitigate their consequences. Second, the government should simplify the country's tax and social security regulations. Third, there is a need for investment education that emphasizes the significance of costs for long-term returns, the random nature of investment markets and the meaninglessness of differences in past performance—except in the case of underperforming funds. Finally, trustees should expressly be permitted to pay for financial advice for members without incurring any liability for wrongful advice.

APPENDIX A4.1: HOW SHOULD COMMISSIONS BE FUNDED?

There is clearly a need for a distribution network for life insurance and superannuation products, and for advice on income tax and means test management. If advice is desirable, how should it be funded?

The Previous System

When most advisers lived off front-end-loaded commissions on insurance policies, the business model would have been structured along the following lines.

- The agent would be paid, on average, 50 per cent of the first year's premium on each new policy in commission and very little if anything thereafter.
- If the average policy premium was equal to 2.5 per cent of the client's salary, then an agent's income per client would average:

    Client's salary $\times$ 2.5% $\times$ 50% = 1.25% of the client's salary.

- The agent would need to sell about 80 policies a year to earn as much as an average client. Usually it did not take long for agents to attain this level of income. In the meantime, the life insurance company employing the agent would provide some bridging finance to cover the first few months of training and establishment.
- If the agent was able to persuade each client to take out a new policy every four years, the agent would need to build up a portfolio of about 300 clients to maintain the same level of income.

In practice very few agents were able to find this number of clients, resulting in a high turnover of agents and many lapsed policies. While the policy holders lost money on lapsed policies (because they were unlikely to receive a refund) and the life companies bore heavy costs in building up agency forces, the agents themselves took significant financial risks—up to 80 per cent dropped out in the first two years, with many earning only minimal income during this period.

The Present System

The new rules of the game make front-end-loaded contracts unacceptable. Under the new commission structure for superannuation, agents are paid up to 4.5 per cent of the client's contributions (including rollovers) and up to 0.4

per cent per annum of the client's assets. The consequences of this system for agents and clients are as follows:

- If clients pay, on average, 12 per cent of their salaries into superannuation, on which the agent collects 3 per cent, and if they have accumulated one year's income in assets, on which the agent collects 0.3 per cent per annum, then the agent will take:

$$\text{Client's salary} \times 12\% \times 3\% + \text{client's salary} \times 0.3\%$$
$$= 0.66\% \text{ of the client's salary.}$$

- This means that the agent needs only (100/0.66), or about 150 clients, to earn as much as a client does on average, but that the agent is not viable until she has accumulated all 150. In the interim the agent will need to make up the shortfall in income elsewhere. This is very difficult for most agents, suggesting that there will be a decline in the number of new agents (as in fact appears to have been the case over the last few years). It should be noted, however, that one way for new agents to address the problem is to persuade clients to transfer their benefits from one fund to another, and earn a commission on the transfer.
- At the same time, the costs to clients have risen. Total charges under the new system are more than twice those of the old front-end-loaded system, reducing the benefit of a lifetime's investment by 20 per cent or more.

This system is obviously very much in the interests of existing financial advisers. As they reach retirement, they are apparently able to sell their renewal commissions to the life companies and banks at multiples of 2.5–4 times their annual value.

Towards a New, Fee-based System?

The most desirable system would be one in which payment for advice was separated from the decision on how much to invest, and where. At the moment, product providers do not want to offend financial advisers—their main source of business—by recommending fee-for-service brokers (although interestingly, fee-for-service advisers who give tax advice are exempt from registration under the Corporations Act).[44]

It is also difficult even for trustees with the best intentions to change the system. Members would rather pay for advice indirectly through their superannuation fund than pay for it directly, because of the tax advantages of doing so and because they do not have to take the cash out of their current household budget. On the other hand, it would be a brave trustee who paid for advice for members out of the fund. Such a trustee would rightly be concerned about falling foul of the sole purpose test contained in section 62 of the SIS Act, which does not permit superannuation monies to be used for any purpose other than those listed in the act: retirement savings, life insurance and the payment of commissions. Also, members might sue the trustee if the advice provided should prove to be inadequate. This is an area in which some clarification from the regulator would be helpful.

APPENDIX A4.2: INVESTMENT RETURNS OF FUNDS, 1997–2003

The investment returns of funds for 1997–2003 are shown in Table A4.1. They are included here to show that the apparent difference in investment performance between retail and industry funds is largely explained by the difference in hidden expenses. The returns provided to APRA are not intended to measure investment performance, and are not sufficiently detailed or accurate to be reliable for this purpose.

Table A4.1   Australia: Aggregate Gross Returns of Funds by Type of Fund (%)

	Corporate Funds	Industry Funds	Public Sector Funds	Retail Funds
Returns to end June[a]				
1997	20.07	15.85	17.93	12.02
1998	10.13	9.70	9.72	7.47
1999	8.45	9.35	9.17	8.83
2000	13.21	12.35	14.63	9.76
2001	5.87	5.43	4.57	4.94
2002	3.35	−0.85	−4.86	−3.48
2003	−0.53	0.90	−0.89	−0.53
Adjustments for indirect charges				
Expenses[b]	0.48	0.53	0.13	1.48
Income tax[c]	0.12	0.04	0.00	0.41
Capital gains tax[d]				
1997	0.32	0.08	0.01	0.60
1998	0.09	0.04	0.00	0.21

Table A4.1 (continued)

	Corporate Funds	Industry Funds	Public Sector Funds	Retail Funds
1999	0.05	0.03	0.00	0.33
2000	0.16	0.06	0.01	0.40
2001	−0.01	0.00	0.00	−0.01
2002	−0.10	−0.02	0.00	−0.36
2003	−0.09	−0.02	0.00	−0.23
Foundation units[e]				
1997				0.70
1998				0.53
1999				0.39
2000				0.30
2001				0.22
2002				0.17
2003				0.12
Estimated gross performance				
1997	20.99	16.50	18.07	15.20
1998	10.79	10.31	9.86	10.09
1999	9.07	9.96	9.31	11.44
2000	13.96	12.97	14.77	12.34
2001	6.43	6.00	4.70	7.04
2002	−2.92	−0.30	−4.74	−1.79
2003	−0.07	1.46	−0.76	1.24
Arithmetic average	**8.32**	**8.13**	**7.32**	**7.94**

a   The investment performance of all except corporate funds is based on quarterly averages as reported in APRA's *Superannuation Trends*; estimates of the performance of corporate funds are extrapolated from the performance of the larger funds participating in APRA's unpublished quarterly surveys.
b   The indirect charges of life companies and pooled superannuation trusts are estimated from the expenses reported for their underlying investments; the indirect charges of unit trusts are rough estimates based on a sample of product disclosure documents.
c   Assumes an income tax rate of 15 per cent on 4 per cent of the underlying assets.
d   Assumes a capital gains tax rate of 12.5 per cent on gross returns less 500 basis points, and that 50 per cent of future benefits are counted.
e   Foundation units arise from front-end-loaded contracts sold in the past, the costs of which are still being deducted from members' returns. The amounts shown here are informal estimates after discussion with industry participants.

Source: Author's calculations.

NOTES

* Particular thanks are due to Merrie Hennessy and Neil Esho for their considerable contribution to the process of writing this chapter. The author was employed by APRA when the paper was first written, but the views expressed here are his alone and cannot be ascribed to APRA.
1. These can be found on the superannuation section of APRA's website (http://www.apra.gov. au). They currently include APRA's *Quarterly Superannuation Performance* and *Annual Superannuation Bulletin*, which replaced *Superannuation Trends* in 2005. The latter has been used in this chapter.
2. Defined in part 5, division 2 of the SIS Act.
3. Defined in section 29B of the SIS Act and regulation 3A.03 of the SIS Regulations.
4. Defined in section 16 of the SIS Act.
5. This definition is not to be confused with that given in section 10 of the SIS Act, which refers to funds set up by some law or under the control of a state body.
6. See part 3A of the Superannuation Guarantee (Administration) Act 1992.
7. Defined in section 10 of the SIS Act.
8. Defined in section 10 of the SIS Act.
9. Defined in section 10 of the SIS Act and regulation 1.04 of the SIS Regulations.
10. Defined in, and administered in accordance with, the Retirement Savings Accounts Act 1997.
11. Defined in section 17A of the SIS Act.
12. These are defined as 'certain small funds' in section 121A of the SIS Act.
13. See part 5 of the SIS Regulations.
14. Defined in part 24 of the SIS Act.
15. Under section 83A of the SIS Act, a defined benefit fund is a public sector fund that has at least one defined benefit member (that is, a member who is entitled at some point to be paid a benefit related to salary); or a private sector fund that has at least one defined benefit member and arrangements whereby contributions are not hypothecated to individual members. Section 228 dispenses with the latter limitation but widens the definition of a defined benefit member to include members receiving a fixed pension. Regulation 1.03 of the SIS Regulations uses the section 228 definition, while the Superannuation Guarantee (Administration) Act 1992, which sets out the compulsory minimum contributions to superannuation funds, uses the definition given in section 83A.
16. Defined in regulation 1.03 of the SIS Regulations.
17. Here, Glover is quoting from *Bray v Ford* [1896] House of Lords Appeal Case 44, 51; see also *Phipps v Boardman* [1967] 2 House of Lords Appeal Case 46, 123.
18. In particular, part 6 of the SIS Act sets out provisions that require trustees to be prudent and free from inappropriate influences (direction).
19. Part 9 of the SIS Act.
20. Parts 15, 16 and 17 of the SIS Act.
21. Section 52(b) of the SIS Act.
22. Regulation 4.14(4) of the SIS Regulations.
23. Section 109 of the SIS Act.
24. Superannuation Circular No. II.D.5.
25. Part 8 of the SIS Act.
26. These are set out in section 52(8) of the SIS Act.
27. Defined in part 5 of the SIS Regulations in terms of the general power to make regulations set out in section 31 of the SIS Act.
28. The notion that people should begin to save early for retirement is demonstrably wrong—certainly if they want to own their own homes. This is because the net yield on superannuation assets is likely to be much lower than the interest on a mortgage, let alone other consumer debt.
29. Of the takeover by the National Australia Bank group of Lend Lease in 1998, it says:

The merger does not breach the concentration thresholds in any possible market. A number of possible markets were examined: broad 'funds management' market; 'wholesale' and 'retail' funds management markets; separate markets for life insurance, superannuation, retail investment products; and narrow markets based on particular products (the latter are the least likely market definitions due to considerable demand- and supply-side sub-stitutability). E.g., wholesale funds management—merged entity 7.4%, post-merger CR4 [concentration ratio of the top four firms] 35.2%; life insurance 22% and 60%; super 13.8% and 46.8%; retail investment products 20.3% and 50.3% (http://www.accc.gov. au/content/index.phtml/itemId/538590, accessed 23 March 2007).

30. Some of the issues related to disclosure are discussed at greater length in Bateman (2001).
31. The Financial Sector Reform Act (2001) and subsequent changes to the Corporations Act (2001).
32. Teele (1992) provides an example and gives instances of legal judgments and sections of the Corporations Act (2001) that have diluted the effects of the law.
33. Debatable perhaps, but see the definition of agency costs in *The Economist*'s useful econom-ics dictionary at <http://www.economist.com/research/Economics>.
34. Investment expenses, as reported by life insurance companies, amount to some 0.2 per cent of assets. Even allowing for some outsourcing not included in this figure, this is considerably lower than the 0.5–1.5 per cent charged under typical circumstances.
35. Retail funds held 57 per cent of their assets in life insurance companies in 2003, as can be seen in Table 4.3.
36. Maclean (2000) discusses how this problem can be managed and how it has been dealt with by the courts.
37. Section 52(8).
38. Life company expenses are estimated from APRA (2001), which remains the latest reported. The information on pooled superannuation trusts was obtained from a specially requested APRA statistical report.
39. APRA's quarterly *Superannuation Trends* reports the allocation of assets across the various investment channels but does not break it down by type of fund. Its quarterly survey of over 350 funds with assets of over A$60 million does not cover the small funds but accounts for some 94 per cent of the assets of the remainder. It therefore seems likely that its figures on asset allocation can be used as a reasonable approximation for the whole. The allocation of small funds' assets to the various investment channels is then estimated as a residual.
40. It would not be possible to determine objectively the profit margins of the different types of fund, even if all the data were available. This is because the determination and allocation of overhead expenses is necessarily subjective.
41. This figure can be justified by reference to the planned profit margins reported to APRA (see APRA 2001).
42. There is currently (March 2007) a gap between 2001 and 2005 in the statistics available on the APRA website. Table 6 of 'Australian Banking Statistics' gives a breakdown of the banks' fees and net interest income, as can be seen at <http://www.apra.gov.au/Statistics/Australian-Banking-Statistics-June-2001.cfm>. These statistics were derived from the June 2003 report.
43. 'CAT' refers to (limits on) charges, (wide) access and (standard) terms.
44. Corporations Regulations (2001), 7.1.29(4).

PART II

GLOBAL GOVERNANCE:
PRACTICE AND EXPERIENCE

5. Pension Supervision: Understanding International Practice and Country Context

Richard P. Hinz and Anca Mataoanu

1. INTRODUCTION

Over the past two decades, privately managed pensions have expanded from the exclusive purview of the wealthiest nations and a handful of colonial legacies to play a central role in retirement income worldwide. An explosion of private systems emanated from Latin America and Central and Eastern Europe in the 1990s as middle-income countries in transition struggled to find alternatives to financially unsustainable public systems and to establish pensions with labour market dynamics and incentive structures compatible with current demographic realities. Developing countries are increasingly attracted to private pensions because of their ability to provide a viable means to create high rates of income replacement for formal sector and higher-earning workers, and their potential to mobilize capital to facilitate financial market development and stimulate growth.

The design and operation of private pension systems are as varied as the settings and motivations behind them. All share extensive regulatory and supervisory systems that seek to establish and enforce a framework that enables them to function fairly and efficiently and provide a high level of security. Although there is a growing body of work on the theory and economics of private pension systems, it tends to focus on the financial implications and consequences of these arrangements rather than on understanding their operation and oversight. Very little consideration has been given to the way private systems are supervised or to the factors that determine the relationships between the design of a private pension system, the environment in which it operates and the manner in which supervision is most effectively undertaken.

Private pension funds have now been implemented successfully in a wide range of settings and circumstances. The extent of variation observed in the structure and operation of supervisory programmes throughout the world inevitably raises questions about optimal design and best practice. The commonality of their objectives suggests a greater similarity in approaches than is evident in experience. Despite this variation in organization and practice, there is at present no compelling evidence of the inherent superiority of any one type or style of pension supervision. This suggests that differences in the organization and operation of pension supervision programmes are substantially a function of the extent to which they are aligned with the environment in which they operate. An analytical framework that identifies the primary elements of private pension supervision and evaluates these in relation to factors that potentially explain differences in how they are implemented in various settings is therefore useful in understanding the nature of the supervisory process and differences in the design and initial implementation of private pension systems.

2. A THEORETICAL FRAMEWORK

The existing literature on supervision of banking and insurance provides a starting point to evaluate pension supervision and define a set of hypotheses to guide the analysis. This literature makes a clear distinction between regulation and supervision. Regulation is defined as the establishment of specific rules and standards, and supervision as the process of implementing the system and enforcing compliance with the rules. The reasons for and benefits of using such distinctions are discussed extensively in the literature (see Llewellyn 1999).

A first hypothesis guiding the analysis is that discernible patterns define and characterize several distinctive approaches or 'styles' of supervision. These patterns are generally differentiated by the degree to which the regulation and supervision are proactive and by the overall depth and intensity of supervision. Previous evaluations of pension regulation and supervision distinguish two primary 'styles': a typically Latin American proactive approach, and an older Anglo-American reactive model (Demarco, Rofman and Whitehouse 1998; Vittas 1998; Rocha, Hinz and Gutierrez 1999). A key issue in the analysis is whether these represent distinctive modes of supervision or simply define the ends of a continuum of possible approaches.

Work on the development of financial systems by Allen and Gale (2000, 2002a) points to a relationship between the stage of a country's economic development and its ability to rely on market mechanisms for financial sector supervision. An underlying motivation for all financial supervision is to address the inability of market mechanisms to address moral hazard and agency problems. A second hypothesis, therefore, is that supervisory activities are a function of a country's stage of economic development, with more developed economies more readily able to rely on market mechanisms and institutions to enforce the integrity of financial intermediaries such as pension funds. It is anticipated that the degree of openness and a more reactive approach to supervision will be strongly linked to levels of development. The same logic applies to countries where markets are open and many participants enter to provide advice or products to the consumers of pension services. In these markets, the intensity of the supervisors' efforts typically faces a capacity constraint and supervisors must rely on other methods to facilitate voluntary compliance with regulation.

The debate on the link between the stage of economic development and the structure of financial systems is frequently connected in the literature with discussions about legal traditions and the typology of legal systems. Levine, Loayza and Beck (1999) trace the linkages between legal origin and financial development and economic growth. Specifically, they find that legal origin accounts for cross-country differences in the financial development of bank and stock markets and explains international differences in long-run rates of economic growth, potentially relating legal systems and traditions to the organization and intensity of pension supervision.

The importance of a strong rule of law and governance for financial system stability has been recognized and explored by various authors. A technique for measuring the strength of the rule of law was developed by Kaufmann, Kraay and Mastruzzi (2003). A hypothesis derived from their work is that governance and the strength of the rule of law are important determinants of the degree to which countries can rely on the market or external parties to carry out supervisory activities.

Another factor that is relevant to the approach to supervision is the degree to which participation in pension systems is mandated or voluntary. Mandated pension systems require a large number of typically unsophisticated members to engage in enforced saving through pension funds, usually with the underlying economic risk to be borne by the participants. These types of arrangements can be expected to require higher levels of security and, consequently, more proactive and intensive supervision.

The working hypotheses may therefore be summarized as follows.

1. There are consistent patterns and relationships that characterize areas of emphasis and the overall intensity of pension supervision.
2. There is a relationship between the stage of a country's economic development and the intensity of its pension supervisory activities.
3. Countries with a large number of supervised entities cannot supervise comprehensively and must rely on other methods to facilitate voluntary compliance.
4. The underlying type of legal system and tradition is associated with the intensity of pension supervision.
5. Governance and the strength of the rule of law are important determinants of the degree to which countries can rely on the market to carry out pension supervisory activities.

6. Mandatory pension systems require more proactive and intensive supervision.

3. PRIMARY ELEMENTS OF SUPERVISION

Consideration of the factors that influence the design and operation of pension fund supervision requires the formulation of a framework to organize and classify the elements of these programmes. A framework for differentiating and evaluating programmes on the basis of variations in the way their elements are implemented enables a comparative analysis to discern potential explanatory factors.

The first step in this process is to identify and describe a set of primary functional elements (a typology) common to supervision programmes. Values based on an assessment of the depth and intensity of activities within each category are then assigned to each category across a representative sample of countries to provide the basis for comparative evaluation. The activities of pension supervisors can be considered to fall into six primary categories: licensing, monitoring, communication, analysis, intervention and correction. Each of these is described briefly below.

Licensing

Licensing activities restrict and control entry to the pension market through procedural requirements and criteria. These are commonly applied to pension funds or the entities that are permitted to sponsor or operate them. They can also be extended to individuals who perform important functions in the pension system (such as trustees) or to individuals or firms that are qualified to provide services (such as actuaries who evaluate the status of defined benefit plans). The modalities through which this function is exercised differ widely across systems, but in essence they all make use of a set of predetermined criteria to establish an entry barrier or to select a limited number of entrants.

Licensing is generally directed towards managing the risk of incompetent or unqualified firms or individuals entering the market or towards insuring against the results of negligent or risky behaviour by imposing capital or bond requirements. It may also, however, have the purpose of limiting competition or ensuring economies of scale in pension markets. Licensing can be seen as a mechanism to ensure public confidence in the private pension system by applying transparent standards and establishing security to warrant the integrity of funds.

Licensing regimes are differentiated by their restrictiveness, depth and periodicity. Some systems have virtually no entry barriers while others have very complex and strict standards applied by the supervisor. Licensing may be a requirement for all participants before they enter the market, for some participants only depending on their size or the structure of their assets, or for none of the participants. In cases where licences are issued, they may be issued just once (for the life of the supervised entity) or they may be subject to renewal each year (or potentially more often).

Monitoring

Monitoring activities involve the collection of information to enable the supervisor to track the status and actions of the pension funds within its jurisdiction. Monitoring commonly takes the form of mandatory submission of information on a regular basis or periodic reports to the supervisor. It may also include a range of other reporting requirements or more active forms of information collection. The common attribute is the provision of information that will either provide the basis for the supervisor's judgments and actions or make the activities of the pension funds more transparent. The potential recipients and users of this information include authorities undertaking supervision as well as the members of funds.

Monitoring activities can be defined in terms of both the scope and content of the information that is collected as well as the mode of collection. Common types of information collected include financial statements, schedules of transactions, information on individuals responsible for important aspects of fund operations (trustees, administrators, directors), actuarial analyses and information on the sponsors of pension funds.

Monitoring is often a passive activity in which the relevant institutions or individuals are required to submit information to the supervisor. It may also be a proactive function in which the supervisor periodically goes on-site to collect specific or supplementary information. Supervisors may also monitor the media for information, regularly exchange information or consult with other supervisors, and organize regular programmes of meetings with pension funds to collect information. An important form of monitoring is to establish venues where individuals or fund members can communicate with the supervisor and request scrutiny of a particular fund or activity. A distinctive approach of this type is the so-called 'whistleblower' requirements of some systems, which assign responsibility to certain individuals or parties to report knowledge of improprieties to the supervisor. Some monitoring systems also use independent third parties such as auditors or credit-rating agencies to produce or verify information.

Monitoring varies in terms of the type, scope and depth of the information that supervisors seek to utilize, as well as the parties who provide the information and the periodicity of the collection of information.

Communication

Supervisors engage in a full range of activities to communicate with pension funds. These are essentially the complement of monitoring activities in which the flow of information is from the supervisor to the funds. This can make it difficult in many instances to separate the two cleanly. Supervisors may communicate with the funds through the provision of regular reports on the industry, by announcing their priorities and compliance strategy, or by publicizing compliance actions. They may also engage in interactive communication by placing inspectors on-site where they can engage in daily communication with the funds, by meeting regularly with the funds to discuss issues of mutual interest, or through more formal processes in which changes in the activities of the funds are suggested and issues resolved through negotiation. Supervisors may also undertake outreach, education and training programmes to enhance funds' knowledge of the legal requirements or operation of pension systems. Supervisors often seek to communicate with a range of parties, including fund managers, service providers, members and the public.

The communication activities of supervisors have a wide range of goals and objectives. Some communication programmes are intended to inform pension funds about the intent and nature of the supervisor's activities, to maximize the capacity for cooperation and make interactions with the fund more efficient. Others are intended to advance understanding of the regulatory structure as well as the rights and responsibilities of funds and their members, in order to facilitate compliance with the rules or to advance the exercise of individual rights of action by members. Communication may also be intended to leverage resources and establish a climate of deterrence among funds, by publicizing the enforcement actions of the supervisor.

The three basic types of communication by supervisors are disclosure, outreach and education, and training. *Disclosure* is a means of communication with the public. Supervisors make public a portion of the information they receive, process or issue, in publications and in individual disclosure notes. Disclosure programmes are typically designed to provide the basis for individuals to scrutinize the activities of pension funds, in order to support private rights of action, ensure that funds are exposed to scrutiny, provide a deterrent to prohibited actions or enhance competition among funds. The utilization of and reliance on disclosure and the nature of these programmes are key indicators of the degree to which supervisory systems are reliant on indirect forms of compliance enforcement and market forces rather than directive interventions.

Outreach and education activities are undertaken to raise the awareness of the operation and requirements of pension systems. They may be directed towards the public and members of pension funds to educate them about their rights and responsibilities under the law, or towards the industry to raise awareness of compliance issues or understanding of supervisory standards or operations. They may take the form of publications, websites or regular programmes of consultation with the industry, on an individual or collective basis. Like disclosure, the nature and extent of outreach and education programmes are indicative of the underlying style and approach of supervision. Systems in which little effort is made to interact in this manner will typically be more directive in nature, relying nearly exclusively on action by the supervisor, while programmes with extensive outreach and education activities will place greater weight on the role and action of third parties in the supervisory process. Programmes of this type are also a form of preventive rather than remedial supervision, because their ultimate goal is to educate practitioners about how to remain in compliance and prevent problems by enhancing the capacity of third parties to provide oversight.

In some countries, the supervisor also provides more formal *training* to ensure that the managers of pension funds are adequately prepared, or as a specific requirement prior to some form of licensing or entry control. This may be general training in the law, training in response to significant changes to the law, or training in specific areas of fund operation such as risk management and investment practices, the criteria for evaluating third-party service providers and compliance with technical regulatory requirements.

The communication activities of pension systems are differentiated by their scope and purpose. Supervisory systems that impose strong controls and place little reliance on external or market processes are very directive in their communication with funds regarding compliance issues, and are likely to engage in few activities designed to facilitate compliance or enhance deterrence. Systems with more procedurally oriented standards or a greater reliance on external processes will engage in a more interactive communication process. They will typically have far more extensive outreach and education programmes that support negotiated settlement of compliance issues, and rely on deterrence and third-party actions to support direct compliance activities.

Analysis

The manner and extent to which supervisors analyse and evaluate the information they receive from pension funds is usually closely linked to the system's legal and regulatory approach. Legal frameworks that are based on quantitative standards lead supervisors to develop extensive systems for measuring the financial status and activities of funds against normative standards. This often involves complex calculations for individual funds that may be undertaken as frequently as daily. Pension systems founded in the Anglo-Saxon tradition of trust law tend to be oriented towards comparative analysis, and hence follow a less frequent process of evaluating funds against benchmarks or the behaviour of the entire industry. The analysis in these systems may also be less focused on the outcome of financial decisions than on the process of decision making, and on determining the relationships among the various parties involved in managing the assets and affairs of the funds.

The measurement and analysis element of supervision can therefore be evaluated on the basis of the purpose, frequency and intensity of the activity. Systems that are very intensive and proactive undertake analysis very frequently, with the intention of discerning as quickly as possible, if not in advance, when a fund may be drifting outside an established standard of behaviour or violating a requirement. These attributes may also be associated with risk-based approaches to supervision, in which complex algorithms or 'scoring' systems based on extensive calculations may be the basis for decisions about supervisory interventions.

At the other end of the spectrum are systems that are oriented towards keeping funds within a loosely defined and often situational or relative set of standards. Here, analysis is far less frequent and intensive. This represents an approach that relies more on external or market forces, or, in some circumstances, the presence of extensive regulation and oversight of other aspects of financial market operation.

Intervention

All supervisory programmes are continually faced with decisions about whether and how to intervene in the operation of pension funds. It is often difficult to separate intervention from some of the key aspects of communication with funds. Interventions may take the form of explicit and immediate requirements carrying the force of law for funds to either undertake, or desist from engaging in, certain activities. In other systems, interventions may be in the form of findings that are presented to the funds for a response. The process of intervening in the latter circumstances is likely to be in the form of negotiation through which issues are resolved, or a process of litigation through the civil courts, where the ultimate resolution is reached through a judicial process.

A key issue that defines the nature of interventions is the force of authority given to the supervisor and the nature of the process through which interventions occur. In some countries the supervisor has the authority to intervene when a finding is made that a fund is, or may be, approaching non-compliance. Fund managers may in some cases be provided with very little if any recourse to negotiation or appeal procedures. In other countries the supervisor has little capacity to impose sanctions unilaterally and must instead intervene through a far less directive process of consultation, notification and perhaps negotiation. The most basic and important feature of the notification of compliance action is the manner in which individual funds are notified by the supervisor when they are deemed to be out of compliance with legal requirements. This may range from regularly scheduled interaction that occurs as often as daily in some countries, to formal notices. In some cases the supervisor simply issues directives to the fund to make changes. The manner of this sort of intervention and the nature of the process that follows, whether completely directive or a form of negotiated settlement, are perhaps the aspects of the supervisor's activities that most define the nature and style of supervision. Another key variation is the involvement of third parties in interventions. Some systems require all action to be taken through the courts. Others establish a formal process of appeal to a specially constituted group.

Interventions by supervisors are therefore differentiated partly by the degree to which they are proactive or occur only after conclusive evidence of non-compliance is established. They are also distinguished by the extent to which they are directive and represent a unilateral exercise of authority against which there is little or no appeal, or conversely are a process of negotiation and adjudication.

Correction

As is the case with any form of compliance enforcement, the ultimate, and perhaps most important, element of pension supervision is the capacity to take corrective action. Although it may seem conceptually difficult to separate correction from intervention, the types and purposes of corrective action may vary across supervisory systems that are otherwise quite similar. This variation makes corrective action an important element to evaluate on its own.

There are essentially three types of corrective action: punitive, remedial and compensatory. Supervisory programmes may engage in all three types or their authority may be limited to just one. *Punitive actions* are designed to impose penalties on funds for actions deemed adverse to the interests of members. Penalties are usually in the form of fines paid to the supervisor; these may be retained by the authority or become part of public revenue. The intent of punitive actions is to establish deterrence and punish behaviour that falls outside the standards.

Remedial actions are those taken by a supervisory authority to remedy the consequences of a failure to comply with the law. They are essentially a way of reversing the outcome of non-compliance. Remedial actions may simply require the fund to return to a prior status or to cease certain actions. In some cases, they may involve financial sanctions that are limited to rectifying any direct result of negligence or malfeasance by the responsible parties. They may also be applied to correct abuses of the favourable tax status afforded to pension funds or to repair harm suffered by parties involved in transactions with the funds. The primary intent of these corrective actions is to rectify any direct negative outcomes and prevent a recurrence. Of course, they may also have a deterrent effect, but it is more indirect.

Compensatory actions go beyond remedial outcomes to seek to compensate aggrieved parties for both the direct and indirect effects of violations. Rather than simply reversing the outcomes, they are intended to compensate affected parties for the consequences of actions determined to be inappropriate. Compensatory damages will typically be applied in conjunction with remedial actions. Actions of this type have a strong deterrent intent, but they also have the purpose of ensuring that harm is minimized.

The corrective activities of supervisory systems are distinguished by the degree to which they are solely focused on remedial outcomes, correcting problems as they arise, or extend into the arena of compensation and punitive provisions that attempt to establish a more self-enforcing regime of deterrence.

4. METHODOLOGY

Comparative analysis of the attributes of the supervisory programmes of different countries requires the development of a method to assign descriptive values to each of the primary elements of supervision. To achieve this, an approach that assigns a summary value of 1 to 5 for the intensity of activities within each of the elements has been developed. These values are compared with some of the characteristics of the pension system and basic information about the macroeconomic and developmental environment in which it operates, to assess whether there is any relationship between design, context and supervisory practices.

The summary score for each element is derived from a set of five attribute scales that measure the degree of intensity and intervention. This approach is taken because supervisory systems represent an array of attributes deemed to represent a set of choices made along a spectrum of possible alternatives. Although each function of a supervisor could conceivably be assigned a unique descriptive scale, there is sufficient commonality in the purpose and nature of the elements to allow them to be condensed into a common set of scales, one or more of which is applied to each element. The score for each element is assigned by considering such factors as the frequency of reporting, the amount and type of information reported to the supervisor, the amount of analysis that underlies supervisory decisions and interventions, the degree to which the supervisor has authority to unilaterally direct funds to take certain actions, the intensity and direction of communication activities, and the overall regime for the application of sanctions. The five scales that describe the attributes of supervision are shown schematically in Figure 5.1.

Figure 5.1   Intensity Scales for Pension Supervision Activities

Restrictive ←——————————————————————→ Open

Proactive ←——————————————————————→ Reactive

Comprehensive ←——————————————————————→ Exception based

Directive ←——————————————————————→ Negotiated

Corrective ←——————————————————————→ Deterrent

This approach is selected not only because it describes the full range of attributes observed among supervisory systems, but also because it does this in a manner that evaluates the elements in relation to the degree to which they represent interventions to address market imperfections or to directly secure the interests of pension fund members. A score of 1 represents elements with the characteristics shown on the left side of the scales and a score of 5 represents elements deemed to be consistent with the characteristics on the right side.

These scales are consistent with the analysis of supervisory styles and methods outlined in the limited literature on the subject. The values on the left represent supervisory methods that have previously been described as 'draconian' (Vittas 1998) 'proactive' or 'highly prescriptive' (Rocha, Hinz and Gutierrez 1999), with those on the right described as flexible or reactive. The scales effectively differentiate between methods on the basis of the depth, intensity, periodicity and intent of the supervisor's activities. The following provides a practical illustration of how such a scoring mechanism works.

Restrictive systems impose high entry barriers in which the supervisor requires the submission and validation of extensive information prior to the licensing or approval of operations of pension funds, trustees, pension fund managers, custodians and so on. Market entry is generally restricted to a small number of entities that meet rigorous standards. In our scoring scheme, such a system would receive a score close to 5 for the licensing and analysis functions. A score of 1, in contrast, would be assigned in instances where there is no (or minimal) involvement of the supervisor in assessing the qualification for market entry of funds and other relevant participants. Such systems are sometimes characterized as open and the approach of the supervisor is deemed to be reactive.

Supervisory environments are reactive or exception based when the supervisor has little or infrequent interaction with the supervised entities and intervenes, in a remedial fashion, only to restore compliance with the legal standards. In such regimes, intervention is often triggered by external actors such as whistleblowers or auditors rather than arising as a result of the regular monitoring conducted by the supervisor.

At the other end of the spectrum, supervisors are perceived to be proactive when they intervene on a regular basis to address violations of standards pre-emptively or to prevent what is perceived to be undesirable behaviour. This sort of approach typically involves intensive interaction between the supervisor and the pension funds through frequent collection of information and regular consultations on issues such as investment management decisions.

The exercise of supervisory authority may range anywhere between a directive, unilateral intervention to restore compliance and a negotiated, participative process. The actual position between these two extremes depends on the nature and scope of authority provided to the supervisor, the supervisor's degree of independence and the availability of legal venues to enforce compliance and impose sanctions.

5. CROSS-COUNTRY EVALUATION

This section describes pension supervision in eight countries within the analytical framework just outlined. Each country description is accompanied by a chart that displays the intensity of supervision activity on a scale of 1 to 5 for every functional element, based on the methodology described above.

Australia

The retirement system in Australia consists of three pillars: a means-tested, taxpayer-financed old age pension; a mandatory, tax-supported occupational superannuation[1] plan; and a voluntary pillar (Figure 5.2). Superannuation schemes are structured as trusts, in the tradition of English trust law. The Australian Prudential Regulation Authority (APRA) is an integrated supervisor for the entire financial system.[2] It oversees the activities of a superannuation system with about 7,000 funds holding assets of more than $A800 billion.

The Australian supervisory system is viewed as very open. Many superannuation funds can enter the market without going through any kind of licensing procedure,[3] while others must seek approval only for their trustees. Like most systems founded in the English common law tradition, the underlying legal framework utilizes the flexible and process-oriented prudent person standard to control the investment of pension funds.

APRA monitors information obtained from trustees and informal sources such as the media and whistleblowers. The intensity of its monitoring activity is relatively low, since the amount of information that is reported and disclosed to APRA is fairly limited. It is mandatory for superannuation funds to submit

Figure 5.2   Australia: Intensity of Supervisory Activities

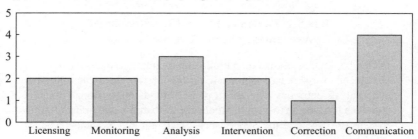

financial statements, known as statutory returns, on a yearly basis. Those funds that use derivatives to hedge risk must also submit risk management statements that disclose their policy for managing portfolio risk.

Pension trusts themselves handle most of the responsibilities related to disclosure of information to members, complaints by members, decisions about portfolio management and measurement of results. In this respect APRA's role is very limited, suggesting a reactive, exception-based approach. Moreover, the trustees widely outsource these responsibilities to specialized financial service providers, adding another layer of intermediaries to the process. APRA is not involved in checking the performance of these intermediaries.

Although the monitoring, analysis and much of the communication that APRA carries out are reactive, the outreach component of the communication function is highly intensive. APRA publishes a large amount of material on superannuation policy as well as the performance measurement of funds and makes this easily accessible on its website. It has also initiated an international outreach effort to share experience with other integrated supervisors around the world. APRA reaches out to trustees by providing training and guidelines on compliance with regulation, principles for safe administration, and reporting and disclosure requirements.

In October 2003, APRA began to implement a risk-based approach aimed at tailoring the frequency and intensity of its interactions with pension funds to the risk profiles of the supervised entities (see Box 5.1). APRA estimates risk profiles based on several indicators, including the probability of fund failure, the impact of an eventual failure and the quality of fund management. Although implementation is still in the early stages, it is likely that this approach will reduce the number of interventions in funds and increase activity in the more preventive-oriented supervision functions such as monitoring, communication and analysis.

In the context of our conceptual framework, therefore, the Australian supervisory system can be classified as open, with moderately reactive monitoring, communication and analysis functions and a moderately corrective intervention

Box 5.1: PAIRS and SOARS: A Risk-based Assessment Approach to Supervision

In October 2003, the Australian Prudential Regulation Authority (APRA) introduced a risk-based approach to the performance measurement and analysis activities inherent in pension fund supervision. This new approach is based on two central tools: the Probability and Impact Rating System (PAIRS) and the Supervisory, Oversight and Response System (SOARS).

PAIRS is APRA's main risk measurement tool. Currently applied to roughly 3,000 regulated entities, it generates two estimates: the probability of fund failure over a five-year horizon; and the impact of entity failure should it occur. The probability of fund failure is obtained by looking at the ability of the fund to manage risk and its capital position. A precise measure of a fund's ability to manage risk is difficult to ascertain, but an estimate can be obtained by analysing the fund's internal systems for corporate governance, its degree of internal compliance, the composition and performance of its board and executive management, and so on. The impact of entity failure is calculated as a measure of the entity's size and of the amount of assets it administers.

SOARS is the tool used by APRA to determine the level of intervention that best fits the risk profile of the supervised entities, obtained by using PAIRS. For each of the four supervisory stances prescribed by PAIRS, SOARS prescribes corresponding mandatory interventions. For 'normal entities', a regular schedule of on-site inspections every two years is applied. For 'oversight entities', APRA imposes stricter capital requirement provisions, engages more in communication and performs more frequent visits. 'Mandated improvement entities' are subject to vigorous intervention. The business of 'restructure entities' is transferred to other entities.

This system is still too new for any relevant performance measures to apply. It will be interesting to monitor its activity in the future and obtain information on the accuracy of its predictions—especially with regard to the probability of failure—based on actual data from the entities. It will also be important to observe the performance of the entities after the APRA interventions dictated by SOARS, to assess whether the system actually improves the efficiency of the organization and allows a better allocation of supervisory resources. If positive effects do emerge, consideration should be given to implementing similar instruments in other countries, where the environment permits.

mechanism. The introduction of risk assessment tools should gradually cause APRA to become more proactive in communication, monitoring and analysis, with the stated goal of preventing rather than correcting behaviour.

The United States

The United States has a universal public social security system that targets a modest salary replacement rate of 40 per cent on average (Figure 5.3). It is supplemented by an extensive voluntary occupational pension system that includes more than 700,000 privately managed funds. These funds are regulated and supervised by two bodies: the tax authority, the Internal Revenue Service, which administers the provisions relating to minimum funding and distributions, and the terms required for benefits to qualify for preferential tax treatment; and the Employee Benefits Security Administration (EBSA) of the US Department of Labor, which administers the provisions relating to standards for the investment and management of assets and the reporting and disclosure of information.

The system is fully open, with no requirement for private pension funds to obtain a licence or advance approval to operate. The supervision of the system is highly reactive, with interventions occurring almost exclusively on an exception basis. The supervisory authorities primarily intervene on the basis of specific requests or information indicating problems with a particular employer or pension plan. The supervisory system is moderately oriented towards monitoring and disclosure, with requirements for the provision of extensive financial and operating information. However, this is only provided annually, or less frequently in the case of the smaller plans. The supervisors have limited analytical and evaluation programmes, which are largely used to identify possible problems for further investigation rather than as the basis for corrective actions.

The supervisory system in the United States is strongly oriented towards information disclosure and private rights of action rather than extensive intervention by the supervisory authorities. It relies on private auditors rather than

Figure 5.3   United States: Intensity of Supervisory Activities

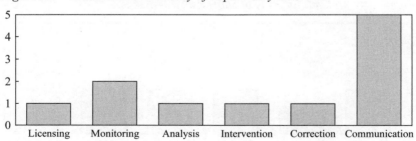

direct oversight for verification of the completeness and accuracy of financial disclosure. It provides very limited capacity for pre-emptive interventions and corrective actions, generally requiring supervisors to notify pension funds of findings of violations of the law and often achieving corrections through negotiated settlements. The supervisors have relatively weak authority to take corrective actions and must bring civil actions in the courts when unable to resolve issues through negotiation. The law does not allow supervisors to impose punitive or compensatory sanctions, beyond modest penalties and excise taxes for certain types of violations of the law.

In recent years, the supervisors have become more oriented towards providing education, technical assistance and voluntary compliance programmes through which they attempt to prevent problems by educating practitioners about the law and raising the awareness of individual participants about their rights and responsibilities to monitor the activities of their employer's plans. Supervision in this system is therefore characterized by a strong emphasis on communication.

Ireland

In Ireland, pension provision is managed primarily through occupational and personal voluntary plans organized as trusts (Figure 5.4). Several institutions have supervisory responsibility for the pension system but the primary supervisors are the Pension Board for occupational pension plans and the Department of Enterprise, Trade and Employment for personal pension plans. The Pension Board is a specialized institution that supervises close to 100,000 pension funds holding assets of € 44 billion.

Like the Australian system, Ireland's pension system relies heavily on the institution of the trustee and on the prudent person rule (see Box 5.2). As a result the Irish system is open, with very few barriers for pension funds to enter the market. The Pension Board does not issue any licences *per se*; rather, pension trusts are approved by revenue commissioners and register with the Pension Board before entering the market.

Figure 5.4   Ireland: Intensity of Supervisory Activities

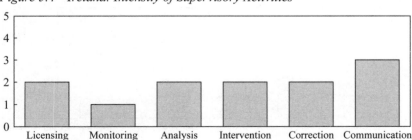

Box 5.2: The Prudent Person Rule

The prudent person rule is increasingly used as a behaviour-oriented standard for participants in financial markets and as a building block for governance systems. A typical formulation of the prudent person rule is contained in section 404(a,1B) of the Employee Retirement Income Security Act (ERISA) of the United States, which states that a fiduciary must discharge his or her duties with 'the care, skill, prudence and diligence under the circumstances then prevailing that a prudent man acting in a like capacity and familiar with such matters would use in the conduct of an enterprise of a like character and with like aims'.

The prudent person rule originates in trust law, where the institution of 'trust'—usually a mass of assets—is managed by the 'trustee' for the benefit of another person. Rather than focusing on the administrative process itself, the prudent person rule focuses on the general conduct of those responsible for administering trust assets. It generates legal duties and responsibilities that establish fiduciary obligations. In this way it seeks to minimize potential divergences of interest in relationships where one party is particularly vulnerable to another (the principal–agent problem). Effective enforcement of legal liability is essential for successful implementation of the rule.

The prudent person rule is a good model of governance because it combines obligation and duty with accountability, without necessarily invoking the state or its regulatory agencies. It is a simple rule that is general enough to avoid the conflicts and inefficiencies generated by jurisdictional overlaps. It gives formal status to the entities to which it is applied, allowing independence from competing interests and a minimum of intervention in the administrative process itself.

In the context of pension provision, the prudent person rule is applied in various ways. In countries that share a trust-based law system, it applies to fiduciaries, with very few additional quantitative or qualitative restrictions set forth in laws and regulations. In other countries, it is accompanied by quantitative rules limiting self-investment or investment in risky assets, rules limiting the use of custodians and so on.

Since, by definition, the prudent person rule assigns very general standards of conduct, interpretation is required to ensure ongoing compliance and to sanction misbehaviour. The role of the regulatory agencies in interpreting and implementing the rule becomes crucial for successful implementation, especially in countries that have little experience with this concept (code-based law systems).

The Pension Board monitors the activity and conduct of plan trustees and other participants in a passive, reactive manner. Whistleblower rules play a key role in the monitoring activity of supervision. In Ireland, auditors, actuaries, trustees and other parties involved in the pension provision process are required to report perceived violations to the authority. One can argue that heavy reliance on whistleblowers means that detailed monitoring activities are delegated to them, thereby reducing the monitoring responsibilities of the supervisor. This characteristic underscores the highly reactive character of Irish pension supervision. Indeed, the system design places nearly all of the burden of measurement and analysis on the shoulders of the trustees and auditors.

The Pension Board is not very active in its communication activities. There is a strong emphasis on information disclosure from pension funds and trustees to members, employers and other participants, but no requirement for them to report regularly to the supervisory authorities regarding future investment policies and performance indicators. Trustees must have their accounts audited yearly and have all documents available to present to the supervisor upon request, but there is no interaction during the review process. The Pension Board issues guidelines or guidance notes on the duties and responsibilities of plan trustees as well as codes of practice on specific aspects of their responsibilities. It is also involved in the provision of appropriate training for trustees. Much of the communication is outsourced to a separately constituted pension ombudsman who investigates and decides complaints and disputes involving occupational pension plans.

Despite its strong powers to carry out proactive investigations in auditing pension funds for compliance, in practice the Pension Board rarely uses this power. In 2002, it audited only 165 schemes out of a total of 100,000 and initiated just 74 investigations. For this reason, we consider intervention to be highly reactive and exception based in Ireland.

An interesting feature of the Irish pension supervision system is that the Pension Board is granted wide discretion to intervene in the event of non-compliance and very strong corrective power. It has the power to prosecute offences in court, with penalties ranging from fines to the imprisonment of trustees. Although there is a high punitive discretion available to the supervisor for instances of non-compliance, these correction and intervention powers are primarily used remedially, to restore lost rights to members or to ensure compliance with regulations.

Hungary

Hungary has a relatively new system comprising three pillars: a mandatory public first pillar; a mandatory, fully funded, privately managed second pillar; and a voluntary, privately managed third pillar (Figure 5.5). The Hungarian Financial

Figure 5.5   Hungary: Intensity of Supervisory Activities

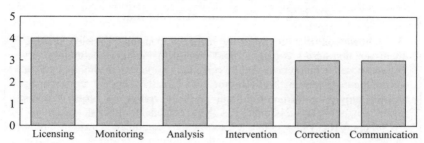

Supervisory Authority (HFSA), established in 2000, is an integrated supervisor for the entire financial sector, including pensions. The number of privately managed pension funds in Hungary is very small. Correspondingly, the market concentration is very high: six funds hold 87 per cent of the total membership and 83 per cent of the total value of assets, which amounted to ∉ 1.7 billion in 2003. The supervisory act implemented by HFSA has a proactive structure directed towards ascertaining compliance with regulations by investigating the supervised entities' fulfilment of internal control mechanisms.

Since the funded component of the Hungarian pension system is fairly new, HFSA coordinates a licensing process focused on ensuring compliance with the fairly restrictive legal standards for market entry. Funds have to obtain licences to establish a fund, initiate fund operation, implement benefit regulations and start the provision of fund services. They must produce extensive and detailed documentation to obtain these licences and register with the tax authorities and other institutions before applying for a licence. Licences are now permanent, replacing a more intensive temporary licensing arrangement.

HFSA's monitoring activity is very focused. Pension funds report information on transactions daily to the supervisor so that it can check compliance with the country's strict investment regulations in real time. In practice HFSA checks this information only randomly, but it does carry out detailed examinations of the funds' accounting and internal control systems. It also receives quarterly and annual reports from the funds to support the monitoring of fund performance.

In terms of the measurement and analysis of fund performance, the Hungarian supervisor uses benchmarks of market performance to assess the risk level and investment performance of fund portfolios. These ratios are calculated and reported by the supervised entities themselves. In the future, HFSA is planning to move to a value-at-risk (VAR) approach to assessing potential risk and allocating oversight resources (see Box 5.3). This should allow it to fine-tune its risk assessments, thus reducing the extent of its measurement and intervention activities. HFSA communicates with the supervised entities in an interac-

Box 5.3: The Value-at-Risk Model

As defined contribution, privately managed pension provision arrangements expand across countries, final retirement incomes become increasingly exposed to market risk. While considering investment choices that will secure the long-term goals of retirement welfare, the administrators, managers and supervisors of pension funds must also mitigate a variety of risks: credit risk, market risk, liquidity risk, legal and operational risk and so on.

Value-at-risk (VAR) models are accepted by banking and insurance regulators as a standard tool to quantify risk and control exposure to market risk. Value at risk is defined as the maximum potential change in the value of a portfolio of financial instruments, with a given probability over a certain time horizon. This estimation starts by marking to market all the assets in a portfolio. Then, based on the probability distribution of market returns over a defined period of time, potential losses are estimated. The motivation for this approach is that improper estimation of risk at the underlying asset level leads to suboptimal capital allocation, with severe consequences for the profitability or financial stability of institutions.

Risk management techniques based on the VAR approach are widespread in the banking and insurance sector. They are also starting to become popular in the pension arena, in countries that have solid defined contribution, privately managed pillars for retirement income provision. The approach has many applications and is used both for risk management and for regulatory purposes. The Basel Committee on Banking Supervision and the Bank for International Settlements require financial institutions such as banks and investment funds to meet capital requirements based on VAR estimates.

The main purpose of introducing a VAR approach to risk management and capital regulation is to tie capital requirements more closely to the underlying risk of the assets in a portfolio. This exercise is especially important for pension funds and insurance companies, since they operate on a mandate that stipulates that their capital shall be sufficient to cover future liabilities and claims, usually over a long-term time horizon.

Among the countries that have introduced risk management tools based on VAR principles, Mexico is a prominent example. In Mexico, portfolio composition and asset value are reported daily at market value, allowing for close estimation of the probability distributions for returns. Risk exposure is also managed through investment rules that restrict asset categories, counterparty exposure limits and benchmarking of liquidity indicators. This approach replaced an older system that measured risk using average weighted maturity calculations. As VAR tools are introduced, the weight of these quantitative restrictions in the risk management tools portfolio is decreasing, allowing for a more market-linked and modern regulatory regime. Another country that is currently considering implementing a VAR approach is Hungary.

tive, negotiated way. It initiates consultations with fund managers on a regular basis, holds information sessions and issues guidelines.[4] It also reaches out to the entire sector by publishing regular findings on good practices for sustainable fund administration.

On-site inspections and investigations of pension funds are quite frequent and comprehensive, covering a large number of official documents.[5] Currently there are three types of on-site inspection: comprehensive, targeted and follow-up. These inspections may target just one fund or a group of funds. This situation makes HFSA's intervention activity intensive, if less so than in Chile, for example. The fact that most of the interventions are aimed at restoring compliance together with the low incidence of compliance actions indicates that, while intensive, the activity of HFSA is mainly directed towards deterrence. HFSA anticipates that the need for comprehensive on-site inspections will fall with the introduction of a VAR monitoring mechanism.

The primary means of imposing sanctions is through the issuance of what are known as resolutions. These are formal pronouncements by HFSA stating specific findings of non-compliance with the law and standards. These statements are intended to inform supervised entities about their state of non-compliance and suggest corrective actions. Other possible interventions are suspension of member recruitment, withdrawal of operating licences and penalties. The corrective actions that HFSA applies are mainly aimed at restoring compliance with the applicable requirements and preventing the occurrence of adverse events that could affect the financial sustainability of the fund. Very few of these actions have any punitive character.

Mexico

Mexico has several vehicles for defined contribution, privately managed retirement savings (Figure 5.6). The main one is a mandatory occupational pension system for salaried employees. There is also a form of voluntary occupational pension scheme through which employers can offer an additional option to save for retirement. A voluntary personal pension system is also in place, mainly for the self-employed.

One of the most important features of the Mexican system is that the management of funds is separated from investment activity, and entrusted to two separate institutions: the 13 Administradoras de Fondos para el Retiro (AFORES), which are the fund administrators and managers, and the Sociedad de Inversión Especializada en Fondos para el Retiro (SIEFORES), which are specialized retirement saving investment funds. These institutions are legally separate and they have to go through separate approval processes before being allowed to function. The main supervisor is the Comisión Nacional del Sistema de Ahorro para el Retiro (CONSAR), a specialized pension supervisor. It

Figure 5.6　Mexico: Intensity of Supervisory Activities

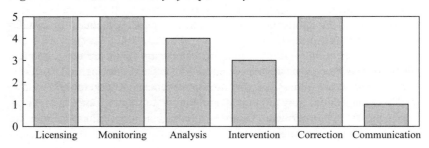

takes a proactive approach to supervision, establishing mechanisms to prevent operating risk in the activity of fund managers and fund investors rather than acting after a violation has occurred.

The supervisor controls access to the market by enforcing very strict capital and reserve requirements. The AFORES and SIEFORES have to be licensed separately. To obtain a licence, they must prepare and submit a large number of documents attesting to their compliance with regulation, including a self-regulation programme. This process is very similar to the one in place in Hungary.

CONSAR monitors the detailed, transaction-based information provided daily by the supervised entities through a computerized information system that allows for integrated surveillance. In addition, since 2002 CONSAR has used the VAR method to monitor the risk of pension funds and tailor interventions. This method captures the volatility of the different risk factors that affect the investments of the SIEFORES. Value at risk is calculated and reported daily to CONSAR by an independent consultant.

CONSAR's intervention activity is intensive and directive. It makes at least one on-site visit per year to each entity and may request additional on-site visits at any time. The triggers for additional inspections include risk analysis, sanctions, and information from comptrollers and external auditors.[6]

The main corrections applied by CONSAR are fines, which cannot exceed the equivalent of 5 per cent of the paid-in capital and reserves of a company. These fines have a punitive role and are quite numerous. In 2002, CONSAR applied 19,910 corrections, most of them fines. The supervisor may also take administrative action to correct bad behaviour.

It is important to emphasize a few key elements of the Mexican approach to pension supervision. Since its creation, CONSAR has worked to develop mechanisms to prevent risk in the operation of the AFORES and SIEFORES, rather than acting after a violation has occurred. It has therefore moved from the reactive to the proactive side of the spectrum. CONSAR has updated its supervision models from surveillance of accounting registries to integrated surveillance of a broader range of processes through the introduction of advanced information technology.

While CONSAR collects a great deal of information, it does not focus on disclosure. That is primarily the responsibility of the fund administrators, the AFORES. They are required to make comprehensive information on each of the SIEFORES available on their websites, including general risk management policies; market, liquidity and credit risk indicators; graphs showing historic and risk-adjusted rates of return; and the administration fees charged to members. They must also publish a breakdown of the portfolio of each SIEFORES each month in a newspaper with nationwide distribution.

Chile

Saving for retirement in Chile is done primarily through a system of mandatory, private defined contribution pension schemes where assets accumulate in individual accounts (Figure 5.7). Workers can also save for retirement through voluntary savings accounts, and the self-employed can contribute voluntarily to the private pension schemes offered by banks and insurance companies.

There is patrimonial and legal separation between pension fund administrators—the Administradoras de Fondos de Pensiones (AFPs)—and the funds themselves. With some restrictions, contributors may choose among the different pension fund administrators. The supervisor, Superintendencia de Administrados de Fondos de Pensiones (SAFP), is a specialized institution regulating the establishment, structure, functions and power of the AFPs. It is an autonomous public body under the Ministry of Labor and Social Provision.

As in Mexico and Argentina, SAFP carries out a very detailed and intensive screening process before allowing a pension fund administrator to enter the market. Eligibility for a licence is also contingent on the AFP fulfilling conditions related to capitalization, insurance and management personnel.

Because pension fund administrators are so heavily regulated, SAFP's actions are focused primarily on ensuring compliance with those regulations.

Figure 5.7   Chile: Intensity of Supervisory Activities

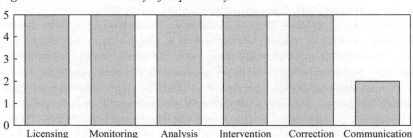

Both its monitoring and its measurement and analysis functions are very intensive. Most of the analysis is done by SAFP's Risk Classification Commission, which is responsible for approving securities, assigning a risk classification to each of those securities and assessing investments in foreign assets.

Intervention is also very intensive. SAFP not only analyses the portfolio choices of its constituent pension fund administrators, but takes part of the responsibility for investment by issuing approval for certain securities. SAFP can therefore be considered to play a proactive role in *managing*—not just assessing—the risks associated with the funds' investments.

Communication with the supervised entities has a relatively low intensity and is directive. The pension fund administrators are required to report regularly to SAFP on the real yield of investments and on portfolio composition. SAFP has the power to approve, or withhold approval for, investment in certain assets based on the results of the monitoring and analysis process. Because there are no legal rules for whistleblowers, the main source of information on non-compliance is the supervisor itself. That is why we consider the communication process to be directive. Communication with members is the responsibility of the pension fund administrators.

SAFP corrects instances of non-compliance by levying fines or by initiating and supervising winding-up procedures. Corrections of this kind have a punitive character and serve as a deterrent against non-compliance.

Argentina

Argentina has a multi-pillar pension system with a mixed public–private second pillar (Figure 5.8). The second, public pillar has two components: a fully funded defined contribution plan and a pay-as-you-go component. Employees can choose between the two components, but all workers must be enrolled in one of these mandatory plans. Pension funds are administered by the Administradoras de Fondos de Jubilaciones y Pensiones (AFJPs); pension fund assets are independent and separated from the AFJPs. The supervisory institution for the pension fund administrators is the Superintendencia de Administradoras de Fondos de Jubilaciones y Pensiones (SAFJP).

As in Mexico and Chile, the pension market is very concentrated, with just 12 AFJPs (in December 2003) administering P46 billion in pension assets.[7] Regulation of the Argentine pension system has been very conservative, with strict licensing procedures, restrictions on investments, and requirements for funds to maintain special reserves and achieve minimum investment returns.

The monitoring activity conducted by SAFJP is very intensive and proactive. The agency routinely examines information on pension fund operations reported by, or requested from, the funds. The information it monitors is transaction based. The supervisor reviews the financial statements prepared by fund

Figure 5.8   Argentina: Intensity of Supervisory Activities

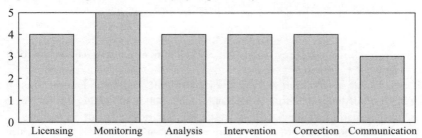

administrators and matches them with information provided by custodians, financial institutions and the capital market. Transactions are valued at prices set by SAFJP, based on information provided by the market and valuation criteria established by the regulations. The supervisor has the right to request additional information and to make both regular and *ad hoc* inspections to enforce compliance.

The Argentine supervisor also checks whether funds are complying with the mechanisms for disclosure to members and beneficiaries, and reviews their advertising plans. All these activities require very intensive communication between the supervisor and the fund administrators, and between the supervisor and the public. Every trimester, SAFJP makes public a comprehensive document containing information on the performance of funds, licences that have been approved or suspended, levels of commission, the number of members and beneficiaries in each scheme, the current value of the funds and the distribution of investments.

SAFJP corrects non-compliance by levying fines and enforcing compensatory mechanisms. The supervisor may enforce corrective procedures when systemic weaknesses are observed in one or more of the critical processes carried out by pension fund administrators. The corrective elements of the pension supervisor in Argentina are primarily punitive, although they also have a remedial component. In this important respect Argentina differs from Chile and Mexico, where the corrective function is predominantly punitive.

Hong Kong

Hong Kong has a three-pillar pension system: a publicly managed, tax-financed social safety net; a mandatory, privately managed, fully funded provident scheme; and a voluntary personal savings and insurance pillar (Figure 5.9). Within the mandatory provident scheme, a plan can be set up as a master trust governing multiple companies, as an industry scheme for an entire sector or as an employer-sponsored scheme. The supervisory authority in Hong Kong

Figure 5.9   Hong Kong: Intensity of Supervisory Activities

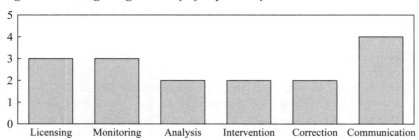

is the Mandatory Provident Fund Authority (MPFA), established in 1998. All schemes are managed as individual accounts and must be set up under a trust structure, with the trustees to be approved by MPFA.

The number of privately managed schemes in Hong Kong is much smaller than in other countries where pension regulation is based on trust law. The number of mandatory reporting requirements and adequacy criteria is correspondingly much higher, but the market can still be described as an open one.

Although there are no formal licensing procedures for funds apart from the need for trustees to be approved, MPFA monitors and validates funds' compliance with capital adequacy requirements. The monitoring function of MPFA is moderately intensive. Although the volume of information reported to the supervisor is fairly large, trustees and auditors serve as an intermediary layer for monitoring this information. The trustees of master trusts, industry schemes and employer-sponsored schemes must submit an annual return containing mainly financial information, a statement of investment policy, and a report on internal controls that includes an assessment from an independent auditor on general performance and compliance with capital requirements. Trustees must also publish annually a consolidated report that is submitted to MPFA, and make it available to members upon request. Communication to members is generally the responsibility of the trustees. The supervisor ensures transparency by making up-to-date information about trustees and corrective activities available on its website.

Apart from these traditional sources of information, MPFA relies on whistle-blowers (usually auditors), who must report instances of non-compliance to it. The supervisor undertakes very little measurement and analysis; this is the responsibility of the trustees and auditors.

Investigations and other types of intervention occur when the supervisor believes there has been non-compliance. MPFA may suspend or withdraw approval for trustees when the level of non-compliance exceeds a certain limit. It may also initiate and supervise a winding-up procedure if a pension scheme is unable to fulfil its responsibilities to members.

This approach to supervision, particularly with regard to interventions and interactions, suggests a reactive approach that is typical of systems in which pension funds are established under trust law. Among the countries included in our analysis, the activities of MPFA in Hong Kong appear most closely to resemble those carried out by the Australian regulatory authority, with the exception of monitoring activity. MPFA monitors a large volume of information in a more proactive way than its Australian counterpart.

6. COMPARATIVE ANALYSIS

Presence of Supervisory Styles

The most basic question to be asked about the classification of supervisory systems is whether there are any consistent patterns that would support an overall summary characterization of each type of system—whether there are discernible 'styles' of supervision. The scales used to assign values to each element of a system are broadly based on the intensity (that is, depth and frequency) of the activities carried out by the supervisor. The most general hypothesis to be evaluated is whether supervisory systems may be deemed to be of consistently higher or lower intensity based on the various primary elements examined. If the components of a supervisory system fall consistently along such a scale, it becomes easier to compare the system with a variety of factors related to the environment in which it operates, and formulate some explanatory relationships. High levels of variation among the attributes would make such relationships far less meaningful.

Two groupings of the elements indicate that the countries examined do exhibit consistent supervisory styles. Figure 5.10 shows the distribution of four of the elements most closely associated with direct interventions in the activities of funds: licensing, analysis, intervention and correction. The clear pattern supports the proposition that there is consistency in the degree of intensity within various systems, allowing them to be characterized as generally proactive or reactive. This, of course, simply confirms that these supervisory systems are, at least by these measures, relatively consistent in their approach, which is to be expected if they are to be able to function as a cohesive programme. It is important to note that the countries appear to fall across a continuum of styles rather than clustering at the two extremes. The United States and Australia can be characterized as essentially reactive systems, while Mexico and Chile are strongly interventionist and proactive in character, with Hungary and Hong Kong occupying the middle ground.

The element that is rather strongly negatively correlated with others is communication. The prevalence of communication activities apparently increases

Figure 5.10   Correlation among Primary Elements of Pension Supervision: Licensing, Analysis, Intervention and Correction

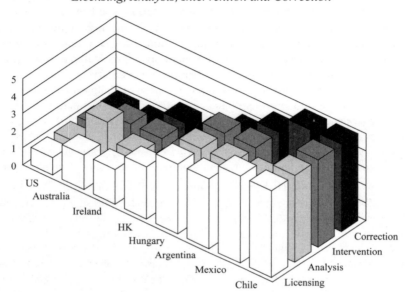

in proportion to the degree to which other activities are reactive or exception based. This is intuitively logical, because education and technical assistance are a likely adjunct to programmes that rely on external actors and market forces to induce compliance with regulations. They are perhaps best perceived as a type of agency cost to the regulator. Figure 5.11 shows the relationship between monitoring activities and communication, where the connection is perhaps most direct; however, it applies to nearly all of the other elements as well. This leads to the conclusion that supervisory systems have a broad distribution of characteristics, patterns or styles, ranging from a largely reactive approach with a strong emphasis on communication to a strongly interventionist approach where considerably less effort is devoted to providing information to the regulated entities

The presence of relatively consistent patterns allows us to compare the components of a supervisory system with the factors that define the environment or context in which the supervisor operates. This permits an assessment of whether supervisory style is related to a country's legal and economic environment. The environmental factors that might potentially determine a country's approach to supervision include the overall level of economic development, the degree to which capital markets are developed, the capacity for reliance on legal procedures and private actions, and the country's legal tradition. The pathways of causality among these factors are potentially complex. These fac-

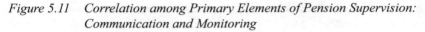

Figure 5.11   Correlation among Primary Elements of Pension Supervision: Communication and Monitoring

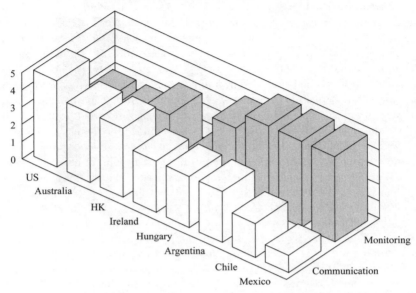

tors may simply constrain the feasible design of the pension system or they may more narrowly determine how any system would be supervised within such an environment. Whether the relationships are more general or specific to pension supervision, an initial evaluation of these relationships provides useful insights on the alignment of approaches to supervision and the environment in which they operate.

Level of Development

The simplest of these comparisons is the relationship between overall level of economic development and supervision. This is considered by comparing per capita GDP to the characteristics of the pension supervision. Figure 5.12 shows the scores for the main operating characteristics of the sample of countries arrayed from left to right in relation to the per capita GDP of the country.

The analysis indicates a strong relationship between overall level of economic development and the approach to private pension supervision. Countries with the highest income levels are associated with supervisory approaches that impose fewer entry barriers and qualifications for pension funds and are less intensive and intervention oriented. Those with a lower per capita GDP are associated with more proactive methods of supervision and are less likely to rely on market discipline to control their pension systems. As indicated in

*Figure 5.12   Primary Elements of Supervision and GDP per Capita
(PPP US$)*

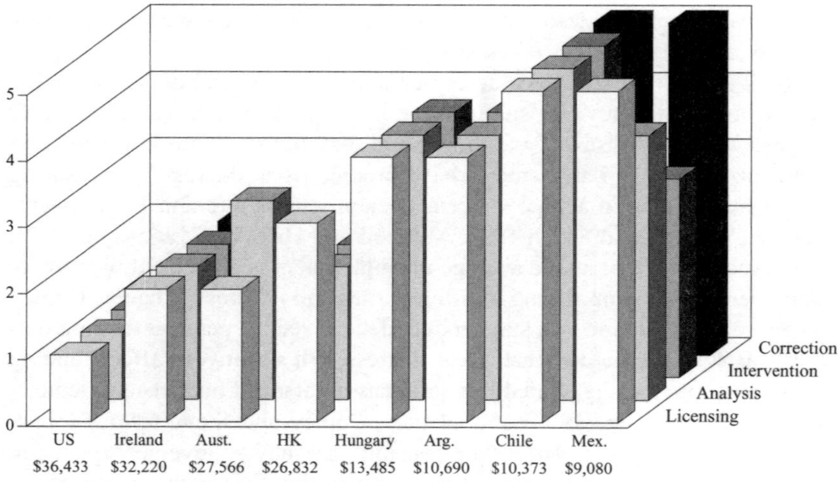

Source: EIU Country Data, 2002 series.

Figure 5.11, the supervisory systems of countries with higher levels of development are more oriented towards reliance on communication.

There are several possible explanations for this relationship. The wealthier countries tend to provide more widely available social safety nets and universal social security systems, so they are likely to be able to sustain greater levels of risk in their private pension systems. Private pensions are consequently likely to be a less significant proportion of overall household wealth in these countries. This makes them better able to take risk in search of higher returns, leading to less restrictive supervisory regimes. Lower-income countries—especially those that, for fiscal reasons, have established private pension schemes to replace or supplement public programmes—have a much lower capacity to sustain risk. They are also likely to have large fiscal exposures through the various kinds of public guarantees that are usually required to enact such reforms.

To a significant degree, the relationship is likely to be a result of the underlying nature of the pension system and the markets in which it operates. The countries with the higher per capita income levels tend to have voluntary occupational systems that operate as second-tier forms of financial intermediation. The pension funds in these countries are investing their assets in highly regulated financial markets, or in pooled investment products managed by other regulated institutions. The business of fund management is more developed, and the supervisor is able to utilize this primary regulation to diminish the

Figure 5.13 *Primary Elements of Supervision and Financial Market Development (ratio of market capitalization of traded companies to GDP)*

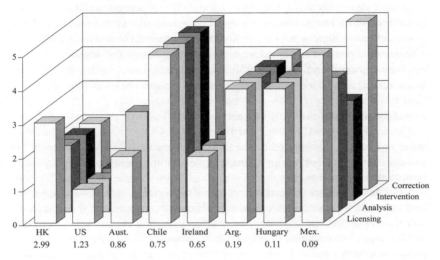

Source: Beck et al. (2000).

degree to which interventions are required. In contrast, the lower-income countries may not have the same institutional foundation to rely on, and must therefore manage these risks through a more proactive approach. The following sections examine some of the possible relationships in more detail.

Capital Market Development

The ratio of stock market capitalization to GDP provides a measure of the depth of financial markets and financial market development (Levine, Loayza and Beck 1999). Figure 5.13 shows countries ordered according to this measure. The expectation would be that in well-developed markets there are a large number of participants and a high level of primary or direct regulation of financial products. Competition among these actors fuels institutional development and creates venues for third-party oversight; these may take the form of comprehensive accounting rules or established auditing practices. In such systems, all these layers of financial intermediation and professional affiliation are governed by primary market regulations that support less intensive supervisory oversight. Also, the high level of integration between the different branches of the financial industry allows for the development of fungible financial professionals, limiting the need for specialized pension supervision.

Although in general there is a relationship between the depth of capital markets and the approach to supervision, this does not fully explain the patterns shown in Figure 5.13. Some of the countries with relatively high levels of market depth, such as Chile, have approaches to supervision that are more proactive, while other countries with thinner markets, such as Ireland, have a less intensive approach. This indicates that other factors are also likely to influence the patterns of supervision. Some less quantitative descriptors of the environment are therefore potentially useful in understanding the impact of the environment in which pension funds operate on supervisory techniques.

Legal Systems and the Rule of Law

As mentioned in the introduction, Levine, Loayza and Beck (1999) trace the linkages between legal systems, financial development and economic growth, finding that legal origin accounts for cross-country differences in the development of bank and stock markets. Pension supervision systems are similarly grounded in the legal framework within which they operate, and it seems likely that the importance of this factor may be similar (and closely related) to that of a country's overall level of economic development. The sample of countries considered here can be divided into those whose legal system is based on a civil code system (Argentina, Chile, Mexico and Hungary) and those whose legal system is derived primarily from English common law (Australia, Hong Kong, Ireland and the United States.

A comparison of the characteristics of supervisory practices and the type of legal system indicates that countries that share legal traditions based on English common law rely heavily on trustees and whistleblowers in the exercise of pension supervisory activities. These are entities that are external to the supervisory authority and subject to a regulatory framework that relies heavily on the application of a prudent person standard. This process-oriented standard, which imposes responsibilities (and liability) on parties assigned specific duties in the management of pension funds, is another potential factor explaining the low levels of intervention and the negotiated and corrective nature of sanctions observed in English common law systems. Reliance on these parties for signals of non-compliance shifts much of the monitoring and analysis activity from the supervisor to private third parties. This is a possible explanation for the low levels of monitoring and analysis done in-house in countries where the legal system is based on English common law.

The opposite is true for countries that base their legal systems on rule-based civil codes, which are slower to adapt to changes in the economic and social environment (Beck and Levine 2004). Pension systems based on civil codes typically have a more intensive and directive character and a punitive rather than compensatory approach to corrective actions and sanctions.

*Figure 5.14   Rule of Law Index and Average Score of Intensity of
Supervisory Activities*

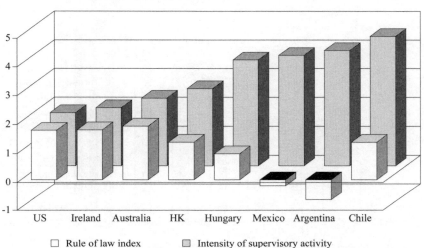

☐ Rule of law index   ▨ Intensity of supervisory activity

Source: Kaufmann, Kraay and Mastruzzi (2003).

Rule of law—the extent to which formal legal systems are consistent and reliable—may also determine the extent to which supervisors are able to function in a more reactive manner and rely on markets and third parties to undertake some of the basic monitoring and analysis functions. To test this hypothesis, the sample of countries is compared to the relevant measure from a rule-of-law indicator developed by Kaufmann, Kraay and Mastruzzi (2003) (Figure 5.14). This indicator is derived from statistical compilation of various measures of the quality of a country's legal system and governance. Even though the countries' relative positions on the rule-of-law indicator are not precise enough to sustain an exact country ranking, Figure 5.14 does provide some insights into the connections between the style and intensity of supervision.

It appears that higher levels of governance and rule of law are associated with supervisory systems that are less intensive, less directive and more reliant on third-party oversight and market mechanisms. The capacity to pursue compliance issues through the courts in a reliable manner enables supervisors to function in a more reactive and less intensive manner, because it gives them a greater capacity to achieve correction of problems after the fact and to make financial recoveries on behalf of fund members. This approach is buttressed by the ability to rely extensively on private rights of action to enforce compliance. High levels of governance and rule of law create opportunities for members of pension funds to pursue their individual rights of action through a negotiated

*Figure 5.15   Primary Elements of Supervision and the Number of Privately
Managed Pension Funds*

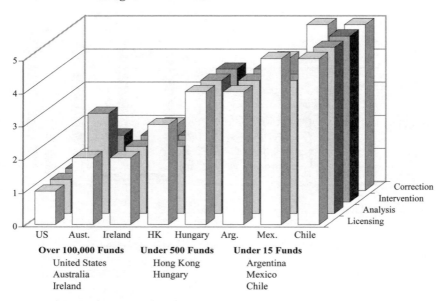

Over 100,000 Funds   **Under 500 Funds**   **Under 15 Funds**
   United States   Hong Kong   Argentina
   Australia   Hungary   Mexico
   Ireland   Chile

Source: Websites of respective supervisory authorities.

process of litigation. This can reduce the need to enforce detailed protective
mechanisms proactively through intensive supervisory activities.

Number of Pension Funds

A key determinant of the capacity of supervisors to engage in proactive methods of supervision is the number of entities they supervise. Figure 5.15 shows
supervisory systems in relation to three groupings by number of pension funds.
The largest systems, those supervising over 100,000 funds, have responsibility
for a number of entities that is many times the number of staff employed by the
supervisor; some have more than 1,000 pension funds within their jurisdiction
for each member of staff. The middle grouping, those supervising less than
500 funds, represents ratios of funds to staffing that are below 10. Those with
a relatively small number of funds, less than 15, have more staff than funds for
which they are responsible.

The analysis indicates that there is an association between the number of
funds and the approach to supervision. Only the countries with a small number
of funds engage in the more intensive methods, while those with a large number
of funds have a pattern of less intensive interventions and greater reliance on

communication activities. This seems to provide an explanation that reconciles some of the variations found in the comparison between supervisory style and the depth of financial markets. Hong Kong and Chile, for example, have more developed financial markets but a relatively small number of funds. This seems to be associated with a greater level of intensity of supervision than might be anticipated solely on the basis of the depth of their financial markets.

Adding measures of financial market depth and the potential scope of responsibility of a pension supervisor provides further insights into the factors associated with the variations in supervisory methods. These lend credence to the perception that countries with market-based, financially developed economies are able to rely on these markets to protect the rights of pension plan members. They can therefore afford to have a supervisory style that is reactive, with low-intensity intervention, exception-based analysis and remedial correction.

Mandatory and Voluntary Systems

The unifying concept for virtually all measures of supervision is the need to manage and limit risk. One of the primary determinants of the capacity to bear risk is whether a pension system is imposed on the population and represents the primary source of retirement income (resulting in a very low risk tolerance) or is a voluntary addition to the retirement savings of individuals (who may therefore be willing to trade off risk for higher potential returns and flexibility). A key design issue for voluntary pension systems is the level of direct and opportunity costs associated with very intensive and proactive supervisory methods. Imposing a high supervisory burden may limit the willingness of employers and others to sponsor or manage pension funds. Funds managed on a collective basis in which assets and management are pooled may also be able to manage risk more effectively without the need for intensive supervision.

Figure 5.16 arrays the supervisory methods in three groups: voluntary occupational systems, mandatory occupational systems and mandatory individual pension systems. It indicates that there is a relationship between the intensity measure of the elements of supervision and the underlying nature of the pension system. Occupational systems in the United States, Australia and Ireland are generally less intensive in their approach, while the mandatory systems of Latin America exhibit the opposite pattern.

7. CONCLUSIONS

A variety of observations and conclusions may be drawn from the description and analysis of these patterns of private pension supervision. At the most

*Figure 5.16   Type of Retirement Income Provision System:
Mandatory versus Voluntary*

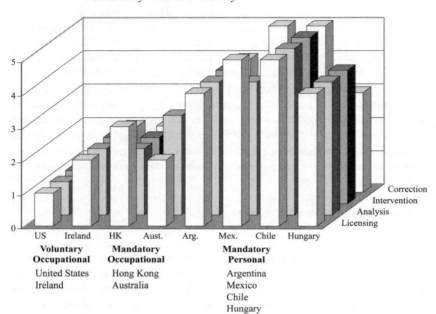

general level, there is considerable variation in the way that each of the primary elements of pension supervision is implemented. The individual systems, however, exhibit relatively consistent styles when their component elements are placed on a scale of relative intensity. This supports the perception that there is a range of supervisory approaches, varying from the very intensive, proactive and directive approach of Chile to the reactive, exception-based style of the United States. More significantly, it illustrates that there is a continuum of styles along this spectrum. This suggests that there are not just one or two normative models for supervision; rather, a variety of factors influences and determines an appropriate method of supervision.

Evaluating the relationships between possible explanatory factors and the patterns of the intensity of supervision is, however, more problematic. The limited sample of countries examined and the subjective nature of any scoring method limit observations to the consideration of potential relationships rather than the development of determinative formulas. Difficulties in assessing the pathways of possible causality also accentuate the limitations of explanatory models. It is very hard to differentiate the factors that may determine the organization and structure of a funded pension system from those that influence the nature of the supervision applied to it. It is likely that various economic and legal environments simultaneously lend themselves to certain types of pension funds and strongly influence the type of supervision that is feasible or effective. For these reasons, while the observations about the relationships between conditions and supervision provide useful insights into the process of matching form to function and aligning methods to the realities of prevailing conditions, their application to the design of supervisory techniques and institutions cannot be approached in a predictive or mechanistic fashion.

Keeping in mind these important caveats, a number of useful observations about context and supervision may be derived from the analysis. Increasing levels of per capita GDP and greater depth of capital markets are negatively correlated with the intensity of supervisory practices. The first of these, a broad proxy for overall economic development, provides more of a reference point than explanatory power because of its linkage to all of the other potential influences examined. More developed countries nearly always have commensurate development of financial markets and legal institutions and are much more likely to be able to support voluntary pensions or rely on employers to manage occupational programmes. The relationship to capital market development, however, provides some insights into the conditions required for supervisory systems to leverage various other forms of primary market oversight and formulate their activities as a form of tertiary supervision. This results in the focus on monitoring and exception-based interventions observed in these settings. It also enables supervisors to rely on private third-party monitoring mechanisms such as auditors and actuaries.

The legal environment exerts a similar influence on supervisory methods. Conditions in which there is a strong reliance on rule of law and the integrity of governance in public and private institutions create the capacity to relax licensing and other entry barriers and rely on indirect and less frequent forms of monitoring and intervention. Conversely, environments characterized by lower respect for the rule of law require more intervention by public authorities. An important factor in this process is likely to be the ability to rely on disclosure of information and private rights of action as a significant adjunct to compliance enforcement by public authorities. The capacity to utilize third parties and rely on private actions through a process of civil justice—perhaps even simply the presence of and confidence in a commercial code of conduct and private adjudication—is likely to be a common attribute of the economic and legal factors at play in this process.

Environmental factors also influence the structure of pension systems and dictate the form and intensity of supervision. Countries with mandatory individual systems are associated with very restrictive and intensive approaches to supervision. Not coincidently, these same countries have systems with a very small number of funds. Countries with strong rule of law and governance have occupational arrangements with a large number of funds. The ability to

Figure 5.17   Intensity of Supervision

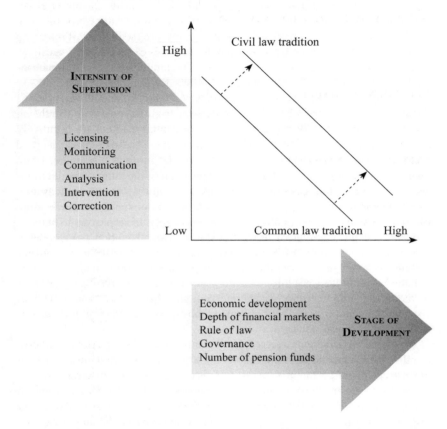

overcome the agency and moral hazard challenges associated with sustaining employer-managed systems is directly linked to the ability to supervise these systems in a less proactive manner. No doubt the imperative to limit the regulatory burden and compliance costs in a voluntary system is a key factor in strengthening this relationship.

Taken together, these factors suggest the relationship between context and supervision illustrated schematically in Figure 5.17. The conditions shown on the horizontal axis interact to influence the nature of the supervisory style observed in the different countries. Countries with higher levels of per capita income and financial market development are associated with stronger rule of law, stronger governance institutions, voluntary pension systems and occupational sponsorship. These factors combine in a variety of ways to lead to supervisory systems that are more open, less proactive and less directive; they both influence and reflect the underlying nature of the pension system.

The degree to which these factors enable supervisory systems to function in a less intensive manner is broadly influenced by the underlying legal and cultural environment, as depicted by the parallel lines for the two basic types of legal system. An equivalent set of conditions in a civil law environment is likely to lead to a more intensive style of supervision than might be present in a common law environment. This is because common law systems are associated with countries that have more developed capital markets and voluntary occupational systems, but also because they are more conducive to flexible regulatory regimes, negotiated processes and, perhaps most importantly, the capacity to utilize third parties and private rights of action as compliance enforcement tools.

This framework allows some useful observations about the general nature of the relationships between environmental factors and supervisory systems, potentially enabling policy makers to assess where their supervisory systems reside in relation to the environment in which they operate. There are, however, limits to the applicability of these relationships that may shift significantly the position that a given country might otherwise be expected to occupy.

One of the most important of these is a country's legal culture and tradition. Countries that have adopted an Anglo-Saxon common law may be far more conducive to more open and less directive systems than might otherwise be anticipated by their economic conditions. Conversely, very highly developed countries with a civil code tradition may be constrained in their ability to adopt the more negotiated systems and reliance on private rights of action that such a model would predict.

In addition, such a model is relatively static and may provide more insights into the relevance of initial conditions for a pension system than into the dynamics of its evolution. At this point, the experience with the way in which supervisory systems evolve with the conditions around them is far too limited to allow any assessment of whether countries will maintain these relationships as their economies and pension systems develop.

Evaluation of these relationships does provide a useful framework, some relevant points of reference and some valuable insights into the importance of prevailing conditions for the design and implementation of private pension supervision. It illuminates the extent to which the intensity and form of supervisory activities are a function of the matching of methods to environment, directing attention to this matching process rather than the formulation of normative models in the development of guidelines for best practice. By doing so, it provides a useful starting point for the introduction of new systems in the continuing reform process and some guideposts by which existing supervisors can consider their future course.

NOTES

1. In Australia the term 'superannuation' is preferred to 'pension' for historical reasons; retirement benefits used to be paid as lump sums at retirement.
2. APRA supervises banks, securities, insurance companies and pension funds. The Australian Securities and Investment Commission and the Australian Taxation Office share some superannuation supervisory responsibilities with APRA.
3. There are approximately 3,000 such funds at present.
4. HFSA reports more success in obtaining compliance from such communication activities than from administering punitive corrections like fines.
5. The frequency of inspection is every two years for mandatory pension plans and every two to three years for voluntary plans. There were 160 on-site investigations in 2001.
6. In 2002 CONSAR made 74 on-site inspections, 56 per cent of them to the AFORES.
7. There has been a process of concentration in the sector, with the number of administrators halving from 24 when the system began to 12 in 2003. At the end of 2003, nearly 70 per cent of contributors were affiliated with just four AFJPs, with the largest (Memoria Trimestral de la SAFJP) covering almost one-quarter of the market.

6. Governance of Public Pension Plans: The Importance of Residual Claimants

Gregorio Impavido

In most developing countries, public pension funds are used for developmental and social objectives that are often not consistent with the provision of adequate, affordable and sustainable retirement income for plan members. The problem of public pension fund management appears to be related to a weak control structure for the plans. This is often inadequate to resolve the conflict of interest between management and stakeholders stemming from the separation between management and control and the coordination failure caused by a dispersed set of stakeholders. In particular, although representative boards should allow for appropriate monitoring by active members, it is often the case that politics rather than sound portfolio theory guides asset allocation.

This chapter has three main sections. In the first, I provide a summary exposition of the corporate governance mechanisms that, in the economic literature, are identified as useful in limiting the conflict-of-interest problem stemming from the separation of ownership and control, and from the dispersed nature of ownership. This section does not claim originality and draws considerably on Becht, Bolton and Röell (2003) and Shleifer and Vishny (1997). In the second section of the chapter, I summarize the results of a survey of the governance practices of a large sample of public pension plans in less developed countries and discuss the relationship between poor governance and the performance of public pension funds. In the third section, I attempt to draw lessons from the economic literature on corporate governance that can be used to improve the governance of public pension fund management. These sections draw considerably on Impavido (2002) and Hess and Impavido (2004) but they complement these works in two important ways: (1) by focusing on corporate governance from the point of view of the economic literature, rather than the management literature as in Hess and Impavido (2004); and (2) by explicitly recognizing the multi-constituency problem of public plans. My conclusions follow in section 4, where suggestions for reforming the control structure of public plans are made.

1. THE COLLECTIVE ACTION PROBLEM OF SHAREHOLDERS

The economic literature on corporate governance essentially focuses on two related issues. The first relates to the resolution of the conflict of interest that derives from the separation of control from ownership in a firm. This separation allows for the possibility that the objectives of shareholders are not aligned with the objectives of the company's managers. In the economic literature, this is referred to as a market failure due to asymmetric information over the actions of management; a principal–agent problem arises and monitoring becomes essential to ensure that the managers' actions are aligned with shareholders' objectives. The second issue concerns the resolution of the collective action problem of shareholders caused by a dispersed ownership. Dispersion discourages monitoring by any single shareholder and, with fixed costs of monitoring, a collective action problem arises. Addressing the collective action problem amounts to addressing the conflict-of-interest problem mentioned above; the two are obviously related.

Becht, Bolton and Röell (2003) identify five main governance mechanisms that may mitigate the collective action problem of shareholders. These are: (1) ownership concentration and financial intermediation; (2) the threat of takeover as a means to temporarily encourage managers to behave; (3) the board of directors; (4) executive compensation; and (5) fiduciary duties. The objective of these governance mechanisms is to limit the agency problems associated with varying degrees of ownership dispersion and varying degrees of separation between ownership and control. Their effectiveness is generally measured in the literature by their impact on shareholder value. However, a less developed literature on common agency and multiple constituencies, relevant for the analysis of public pension fund governance, has used other efficiency criteria, including measures of the welfare of other stakeholders.[1]

In the next four subsections, I briefly summarize the main lessons that can be drawn from the literature regarding the effectiveness of each governance mechanism listed above. I then look at the problems associated with departing from shareholder value as the criterion used to measure efficiency before discussing the main lessons that can be drawn from this summary of the corporate governance literature.

Ownership Concentration and Financial Intermediation

The rationale for having a somewhat concentrated ownership in the hands of large shareholders is to overcome the free-riding problem of dispersed owners in monitoring managers' behaviour. A shareholder with a large interest in the firm should have an incentive to produce the necessary effort to monitor management. Alternatively, the literature has looked at the role of financial inter-mediaries such as banks in monitoring the performance of borrowers (firms) on behalf of lenders (depositors).[2] As monitoring devices, both ownership concentration and debt are ways of protecting and avoiding the duplication of monitoring by small investors (Becht, Bolton and Röell 2003).

The interest in large shareholders as a form of governance mechanism prob-ably stems from the observation that, with the exception of the United States, some form of ownership concentration is the norm in OECD and developing countries. When considering large shareholders, the economics literature often looks at large investors like pension funds. However, pension fund manag-ers are thought not to have sufficient incentives to monitor firms on behalf of their beneficiaries, as they do not benefit directly from producing the effort required. It is likely that the interest in pension funds as active shareholders in the United States is related more to the Employee Retirement Income Secu-rity Act (ERISA), which requires fund managers to vote at shareholder meet-ings, than to the effectiveness of pension funds as active monitors. Despite the suggestion that concentrated ownership or the presence of large investors improves efficiency, the empirical literature has found ambiguous results on the impact of ownership dispersion or concentration on firms' performance.

Financial intermediaries such as banks may, however, be efficient corpo-rate governance mechanisms, since monitoring borrowers' actions is a way for banks to improve the return on their lending (Shleifer and Vishny 1997). In particular, banks could be used to improve the screening of projects (Broecker 1990), to audit and punish borrowers (Diamond 1984; Gale and Hellwig 1985; Krasa and Villamil 1992) and to prevent opportunistic strategies on the part of the borrower (Holström and Tirole 1997). The scope for bank monitoring depends on the capacity (or incapacity) of investors to carry out their own monitoring. The effectiveness of bank monitoring depends largely on the size of the bank, allowing it to achieve economies of scale in monitoring. Above all, it depends on the existence of a solid core of profitable and reputable banks whose cost of monitoring is less than the surplus gained from exploiting these economies of scale. In other words, banks need to be well managed.[3]

The Threat of Takeover

The rationale for including hostile takeovers among corporate governance mechanisms is related to the fact that if managers underperform, this is nor-mally reflected in lower shareholder value. A corporate raider may be able to target enough shareholders to take over the firm at this low value, fire the underperforming managers, improve performance and earn the rent from this higher shareholder value. By identifying the non-performing managers, cor-porate raiders may also perform the function of reducing the asymmetry of information between managers and owners.

Most of the theoretical research has focused on the *ex post* efficiency of hostile takeovers, that is, the impact of takeovers on shareholder value, the usefulness of takeover defences (Burkart 1999), the takeover process itself, and its optimal regulation (Hirshleifer 1995). It has focused less on *ex ante* efficiency, that is, on the effectiveness of hostile takeovers in changing management behaviour. The empirical literature reflects the focus of the theoretical literature. It confirms the existence of large premiums for target shareholders and tends to support the idea that takeover defences may not be efficiency enhancing. This is because takeover defence mechanisms increase the bargaining power of target shareholders, allowing them to extract a higher rent in the takeover process. Higher rents are extracted at the expense of other shareholders in the firm so that the overall *ex post* efficiency of takeovers is not necessarily maximized. In any case, whatever the interest of the literature in hostile takeovers, these are rarely used even in the United States, where the more dispersed ownership would suggest a higher incidence of such takeovers (Becht, Bolton and Röell 2003).

The Board of Directors

Boards of directors are a form of delegated monitoring internal to the firm. Delegation introduces another layer between shareholders and managers, and directors must have the right incentives to fulfil their role.[4] Therefore, when analysing the effectiveness of the board of directors as a monitoring device, two aspects need to be considered: (1) the alignment of objectives between managers and directors; and (2) the alignment of objectives between directors and shareholders.

Essentially, the issue is whether directors would side with management, shareholders or neither. Ideally boards would side with shareholders, but in practice they are often 'captured' either by management or by the dominant shareholder. Hence, the presence of outside or independent directors is considered essential to strengthening the effectiveness of boards (Bhagat and Black 1999). Inside, or executive, directors are managers of the firm. They bring to the board extensive knowledge of the firm, but they are expected to have a conflict of interest with shareholders and to support the CEO's interests over those of the shareholders. Outside, or non-executive, directors have no employment, business or family relationship with the firm or its shareholders. They are generally considered to be sufficiently independent of the CEO to be capable of protecting the rights of shareholders. In summary, executive directors are expected to manage and non-executive directors are expected to monitor.[5]

In practice, however, the degree of independence of outside directors is often limited. CEOs have a strong influence over their appointment, and minority directors who oppose management risk being dismissed. Finally, the rationale for independence from the CEO (more effective monitoring) does not apply to situations of concentrated ownership. In such situations, independence is required from both management and controlling shareholders in order to protect the interests of minority shareholders (Becht, Bolton and Röell 2003).

The theoretical literature is essentially limited to the two issues of appointment and the optimal distribution of inside and outside directors. One of the main findings of this literature is that the ability of the board to monitor management is a function of its independence. However, this ability decreases with time the longer the good performance of the manager with the firm continues (Hermalin and Weisbach 1998, 2001). The reduced ability of the board to monitor management and the possibility of minority directors being dismissed suggest that fixed-term appointments to the board are to be preferred to open-end appointments. Finally, the decreasing ability to monitor could lead to cycles in firm performance. Hence, hostile takeovers become an important complement to the monitoring mechanism of both managers and boards when boards are the least effective (Hirshleifer and Thakor 1994, 1998).

The empirical literature on the role of boards is large.[6] It has focused on the impact of the board on firm performance, mainly controlling for board composition, board independence and board *modus operandi*. The results so far have been ambiguous, however.

Executive Compensation

Appropriate compensation packages are also among the governance mechanisms used to align managers' and owners' objectives. The economic literature has studied the relationship between executive compensation and capital structure, investment decisions, mergers, dividend policies and the relative effectiveness of accounting versus stock-market-based performance measures (Murphy 1999).

The theoretical literature essentially provides a rationale for associating different elements of the executive compensation package with well-defined performance measures that shareholders can observe. As far as salaries and bonuses are concerned, compensation packages tend to be composed of a 'basic' salary; *ad hoc* bonuses aimed at motivating short-term performance; and multi-year bonuses and stock participation products aimed at motivating long-term performance. Since the salary component is often not based on any specific performance measure, but rather on the average salary of the executive's peers, it is not considered adequate to inform owners about a manager's actions. Stock participation products such as stock options are considered effective at aligning the short-term objectives of the manager with the long-term objectives of the firm and its owners. Other important elements of executive compensation packages are pension benefits and severance pay.

The empirical literature does not support the idea that compensation packages are designed following the prescription of the theoretical literature; rather, in the United States at least, managers have considerable influence in determining their own pay at the expense of shareholders (Becht, Bolton and Röell 2003). Factual evidence shows that stock options and stock ownership are the major pay–performance elements of compensation packages. However, there is little empirical evidence that the observed increase in stock-based incentives over the last two decades is linked to improved managerial performance (Murphy 1999).

Shareholder Value and Collective Principals

The previous subsections provided an overview of the impact of five main corporate governance mechanisms on, essentially, shareholder value: the principal efficiency criterion that governance rules and mechanisms need to maximize.[7] In this subsection, I discuss how the inclusion of other efficiency criteria affects the usefulness of the corporate governance mechanisms described above. Before opening this discussion, I briefly discuss the traditional rationale in the economic literature for regarding shareholder value as the principal criterion for measuring good corporate governance.

This traditional view stems from Fisher's intertemporal investment theory of a firm developed under two critical assumptions: (1) what matters are the preferences of the principals (the owners of the firm); and (2) owners all face the same marginal rate of transformation of wealth in different states of the world. Two central results, known as the Fisher separation theorem,[8] state that: (1) firms' investment decisions are independent of the consumption preferences of their owners; and (2) firms' investment decisions are independent of the financing decisions or capital structure of the firm. In other words, firms' investment decisions can be 'separated' from their financing decisions. Alternatively, firms' investment decisions can be separated from owners' attitudes towards investment. More generally, separation between ownership and control is feasible and does not affect the value of the firm.[9]

It is easy to identify two main problems with this reasoning. The first is related to the observation that not all shareholders face the same marginal rate of transformation of wealth in different states of the world. The second is related to the observation that there are other constituencies beyond owners who also have an interest in the management of the firm.[10] In both circumstances, a collective action problem among shareholders arises and shareholder value may no longer be the optimal efficiency criterion.[11]

Under these circumstances, it is not clear what the optimal control structure of the firm should be and whose interests should prevail. One idea is to include directors representing the interests of all constituencies. However, boards that include directors representing all stakeholder groups are uncommon under normal conditions.[12] Also, by including directors who represent all constituencies, there is a risk that board size may become so large that effective monitoring becomes impractical. Moreover, the ability of these representatives to protect the rights of their constituents or to influence corporate policy is not clear. Shareholder directors have, for example, been known to exclude employee directors from meetings at which sensitive information is discussed (Becht, Bolton and Röell 2003).

The inclusion of other stakeholders' interests in the objective function of the firm is essentially the underlying difference between the 'Anglo-Saxon capitalism' of the United States and the United Kingdom and the 'stakeholder capitalism' of countries like Germany and Japan. In the first entrepreneurial model, the firm is viewed as an instrument to create wealth for shareholders. In the second, it is viewed as a means to allow different groups of people to cooperate to achieve their own objectives. In their comparative analysis of the two forms of governance, Allen and Gale (2002b) conclude that stakeholder capitalism is a superior form of governance when markets are imperfect and incomplete, as in the presence of labour market rigidities. This result depends strongly on the authors' interpretation of labour market rigidities. More precisely, the impossibility of firing non-performing individuals implies that managers and employees are encouraged to cooperate and preserve the long-run viability of the firm as the only means to preserve their source of income. In this way, the time horizon of managers and employees is extended to coincide with the time horizon of the firm. In other words, shareholders' and managers' objectives are aligned.[13] Despite the intellectual simplicity of the argument and the challenge of the conclusions, the major shortcoming of the model is that it looks only at a partial equilibrium. It is not clear that in a general equilibrium framework, labour market flexibility is still not Pareto improving.

Irrespective of which form of capitalism is superior, the inclusion of specific stakeholders' interests may be optimal under specific circumstances. For example, by including creditors in the governance framework of ailing companies, the perverse incentive of shareholders to 'gamble' with the future of the firm can be limited.[14] This is because debt holders receive substantial protection in the liquidation process of a firm and may have an incentive to bring forward liquidation to protect their rights. Shareholders have the least protection during the liquidation process, and therefore may wish to delay liquidation in the hope of achieving a higher value through continuation.

More generally, however, the inclusion of other stakeholders among principals has the tendency to weaken further the effectiveness of the corporate governance mechanisms summarized in this section. The common agency literature underlines the difficulty of aligning the objectives of management and stakeholders when the latter have multiple and possibly inconsistent objectives.[15]

Key Lessons from the Corporate Governance Literature

The literature on corporate governance finds that boards are *per se* weak monitoring mechanisms. They become a more effective means to control managers' actions when complemented by the other monitoring mechanisms summarized in this section.

The literature provides ambiguous results on the individual effectiveness of these other mechanisms. For instance, there is little evidence that hostile takeovers maximize *ex ante* efficiency, that is, that they discipline managers. Takeovers also tend to benefit only the targeted shareholders, with a probable negative impact on *ex post* efficiency. Given their limitations, institutional and regulatory mechanisms are often in place to limit the occurrence of hostile takeovers. In practice they are rare. Ownership concentration is regarded as a means to promote shareholder activism, but it is not clear that shareholder activism by pension funds is incentive compatible. Ownership concentration also raises concerns about the protection of the rights of minority shareholders. Debt as a monitoring mechanism may be efficient, but it is essential that the lender itself be well managed. In the case of ailing companies, debt may be an efficient way to compensate for the 'gambling' tendency of owners. Well-designed executive compensation packages may increase *ex ante* efficiency but factual evidence seems to suggest that the practice does not follow the theory. Also, managers have excessive influence in determining their own compensation packages.

Finally, there is the issue of which is the right efficiency criterion to maximize. Most governance mechanisms are designed to maximize shareholder value. However, with uncertainty and incomplete markets, it is not clear that this is necessarily the optimal criterion under all states of the world. The inclusion of other stakeholders' interests in the maximization problem of the firm is likely to reduce further the effectiveness of the governance mechanisms discussed above. In such cases, the prescriptive power of the corporate governance literature is even weaker.

2. GOVERNANCE OF PUBLIC PENSION PLANS

In this section I summarize the limited but growing literature highlighting the importance of governance for the performance of public pension funds.[16]

The empirical literature on the relationship between governance and public pension fund performance is largely based on US data. It indicates that governance determines key investment strategies, which in turn affect performance. Independent performance evaluations are associated with better investment policies, while frequent performance evaluations are not significantly associated with performance. The size and composition of the board are not significantly associated with performance. Nevertheless, there is a general consensus that directors should be fit and proper to undertake their role, not too numerous, and appointed through a transparent process which clearly shows their competence and suitability for the job (Impavido 2002). This could involve rigorous minimum qualification hurdles, a transparent review process by a special selection committee, or public hearings.

There is a larger body of factual evidence linking the poor performance of some public pension funds to undue political intervention. Political involvement in the investment choices of public pension funds, and of financial intermediaries in general, takes various forms. For instance, in many countries governments impose explicit social and developmental objectives on financial intermediaries that are often inconsistent with their financial viability. Even when explicit mandates are absent, governments may rely on their powers of coercion to ensure either sufficient demand for their debt to finance public expenditure or sufficient demand for other securities to finance connected entrepreneurs and public enterprises. Sometimes regulations require commercial banks to meet reserve and liquidity requirements by holding government paper. Finally, in both developing and developed countries, commercial banks, insurance companies, pension funds as well as public pension plans may be required to invest in specially issued and non-marketable government instruments offering below-market yields. The impact of politics, rather than sound portfolio theory, on investment performance can be so detrimental that in many countries the returns of public pension funds are lower than the interest rates paid by banks on individual savings accounts (Iglesias and Palacios 2000).

Hess and Impavido (2004) surveyed the public pension fund governance practices of 26 plans in developing countries. They found substantial variance in (1) general mandates and (2) investment policies and investment regulations.

General mandates
Plans tend to have mandates that vary from explicit exclusion to explicit inclusion of social and developmental goals in investment policies.

Some countries have only commercial mandates. For instance, the Canadian Pension Plan Investment Board (CPPIB), a professional investment management corporation, has the sole objective of investing funds received from the Canada Pension Plan (CPP) in a way that maximizes returns without incurring undue risk. This purely commercial investment mandate is to be pursued by taking into account the factors that may affect the funding of the CPP and its ability to meet its financial obligations. The legislation establishing the CPPIB does not foresee any other objectives for the corporation. Similarly, the Namibian Government Institution Pension Fund has no social mandate to invest in targeted industries, with investment regulation aiming to achieve liquidity and the diversification of risk. The New Zealand Superannuation Fund has an explicit commercial investment objective, and funds are managed by an independent governing body with clear accountability (Frances and McCulloch 2003).

In other countries, plans may not have formal social mandates but these are included *de facto* in the plan investment policy. For instance, the Social Security and National Insurance Trust (SSNIT) of Ghana has the legal objective of investing in assets with adequate yield and liquidity at an acceptable risk level, but the investment policy produced by the board includes social and developmental objectives not explicitly defined in the law. In addition to housing finance and industrial real estate, the SSNIT provides student loans indexed to inflation at a subsidized rate. The Indian Employee Provident Fund also has no formal social mandate, but the objectives of the fund appear contradictory. One objective is to ensure the complete safety of employees' funds. Others include: (1) withdrawals for specific purposes such as housing, major medical expenses, children's education and marriage; (2) channelling funds to the government sector; and (3) paying a reasonable return to employees. Other countries have explicit social mandates. For instance, until recently Singapore's Central Provident Fund was required to have all its assets invested in non-tradable government securities, allowing pension assets to be used to finance government consumption or investment without any form of transparency.[17] The Social Security Fund of Cyprus has around CYP3.3 billion (37 per cent of estimated 2007 GDP) invested in non-tradable Treasury bills. Because these are essentially an interagency transfer, EU accounting standards do not consider them as part of gross domestic debt. The objectives of the Korean National Provident Fund are: (1) ensuring long-term financial stability; (2) contributing to economic and social development; and (3) increasing beneficiaries' welfare. Until recently this policy was implemented by lending to the government at non-market rates, through the requirement to purchase non-tradable government bonds and through minimum deposit requirements.

All the plans surveyed by Hess and Impavido (2004) have some type of explicit or implicit mandate beyond, or in place of, maximizing return without incurring undue risk. These mandates include a requirement to invest in government bonds (national, state, provincial or municipal) (48 per cent), investment in social projects such as housing (24 per cent) and investment to achieve general economic development objectives (32 per cent) (Table 6.1).

Investment policies and investment regulations
Typically, the investments of public pension funds are subject to quantitative investment rules. Commonly, restrictions apply to foreign investments,

Table 6.1   Investment Mandates (% of plans surveyed)

Type of Mandate	%
Any explicit mandate beyond maximizing return without incurring undue risk	100
Requirement to invest in government bonds	48
Mandate includes developmental projects such as real estate development	24
Mandate includes general economic development objectives	32

Source: Hess and Impavido (2004).

equities and loans. For instance, 57 per cent of the plans surveyed by Hess and Impavido (2004) cannot invest abroad, 14 per cent have restrictions on equities and 19 per cent have restrictions on loans (Table 6.2).

The problems associated with these types of restrictions are often compounded by the limited investment opportunities available in the countries concerned (Iglesias and Palacios 2000). A limited investment universe implies that actual investment portfolios are not adequately diversified. For instance, the average plan in Hess and Impavido (2004) has 35 per cent of its assets allocated to government bonds, 25 per cent to bank deposits and 15 per cent to equities (Table 6.3).[18] A limited investment universe also implies that actual investment portfolios are *de facto* skewed towards investments associated with developmental or social goals. For instance, public pension plans in Honduras have only a general mandate to protect the benefits of their members and are prohibited from investing abroad. As a result, portfolios are heavily skewed towards housing-related member loans, often at subsidized rates.

Table 6.2   Investment Policy Restrictions (% of plans surveyed)

Type of Investment Restriction	%
Quantitative limits on investment	57
Restrictions on loans	19
Restrictions on equities	14
Restrictions on foreign investments	57

Source: Hess and Impavido (2004).

Table 6.3   Portfolio Allocation (% of total assets)

Type of Investment	Average	Median	Minimum	Maximum
Government bonds	35	20	0	98
Bank deposits	25	23	0	93
Equities	15	7	0	63
Loans	6	2	0	39
Corporate bonds	4	2	0	22
Real estate	8	2	0	52
Other	4	1	0	23

Source: Hess and Impavido (2004).

3. IMPROVING THE GOVERNANCE OF PUBLIC PENSION PLANS

The corporate governance literature surveyed in section 1 is essentially concerned with the misalignment of objectives between owners and managers. It appears, however, that the essential problem for public pension fund management is fundamentally different, and precedes, in terms of priority, the problem of aligning managerial and stakeholder objectives. The factual evidence reported above suggests that multiple (and unclear) plan mandates induce a strong bias in the control structure of the plans themselves. This, in turn, has a negative impact on fund performance. Therefore, the identification of key stakeholder groups in public plans is an important step necessary for defining clearer objectives for plans and improving their control structure. Once the control structure is improved, it becomes possible to address the collective action problem of key stakeholders. These two issues are discussed below.

Identifying the Key Stakeholders of Public Plans

The rationale used here to identify key stakeholder groups in public pension plans is the same as that followed by Besley and Prat (2003). Key stakeholders should be identified on the basis of the residual claim structure of the fund.

Residual claimants are supposed to have the strongest incentive to monitor managers' actions, as they directly bear the consequences of the actions taken by the manager. In other words, those groups that bear the consequences of the policy decisions implemented by the fund manager should be making the decisions in the first place. Besley and Prat (2003) argue that for private sector defined contribution plans (with no guarantees), the residual claimant is the active contributor; for defined benefit plans, the residual claimant is the sponsor. This would imply that decisions taken on asset allocation should be taken by contributors in the case of defined contribution plans and by the sponsor in the case of defined benefit plans.

For public pension plans, things are not so straightforward. Four stakeholder groups are usually identified as having an interest in the management of public pension plans: (1) active members; (2) the government; (3) employers; and (4) taxpayers. Active members (contributors, retirees, survivors and dependants) have a direct interest in the amount of benefits paid by, and the amount of contributions paid to, the plan. The government has an interest in both the administrative costs of running the plan and its performance, as these will affect the effectiveness with which a pension policy is implemented (the provision of adequate benefits, for instance). Employers are interested in the level of contributions paid to the plan. Finally, taxpayers are the natural stakeholders of public defined benefit plans and any defined contribution plans with minimum return guarantees,[19] as they bear the ultimate obligation to maintain the targeted funding levels.[20]

Among these four groups, some have a more direct interest in pension plan performance than others. It is fair to say that active members and taxpayers have the most direct interest in pension plan performance, while the government has only an indirect interest. This is also true for employers, whose share of pension contributions could easily be considered as a minimum gross wage requirement that needs to be contributed by employees.[21]

Taxpayers and active members are the residual claimants in public pension plans, and therefore should have stronger representation on the board of directors than other groups. However, experience shows that employers are often represented on the boards of public pension plans; taxpayers are never explicitly represented;[22] and the government, as plan sponsor, often has higher representation (on average) than employers and employees. Hess and Impavido (2004) also confirm that the control structure of public plans is not based on the notion of residual claimant. In their survey, on average, 31 per cent of board directors represent the government, 27 per cent represent employees[23] and 13 per cent represent employers (Table 6.4).

The lower than average representation of active members on many boards helps explain why the investment policies of public sector funds are often exposed to undue political influence. Another part of the explanation is that 68 per cent of employee representatives are trade union members, and thus more likely to be politicized. Finally, the manner in which directors are nominated may also contribute to the explanation. Hess and Impavido (2004) find that although the average proportion of *ex officio* directors is relatively small, 70 per cent of directors are appointed by the government. Moreover, in 10 of the 26 plans surveyed, the entire board consists of government-appointed

Table 6.4   Board Composition (% of board)

Type of Director	Minimum	Maximum	Mean	Median
How director is selected				
Ex officio	0	85	19	0
Appointed	9	100	70	82
Elected	0	91	14	0
Group director represents				
Trade union	0	62	18	20
Employer association	0	38	13	0
Other employee association	0	38	9	0
Government as plan sponsor	0	100	31	25

Source: Hess and Impavido (2004).

directors. Hence, while government-appointed directors should represent non-government interests, it is likely that the influence that governments have on the nomination process will seriously limit the ability of the appointed directors to independently execute their functions.

The natural mandate of pension fund managers and the optimal control structure of public pension plans should be evident once it is recognized that residual claimants in public pension plans are active members and, more generally, taxpayers. If the interests of residual claimants are to be favoured, the likely consequences would be that: (1) public pension fund mandates would be based on efficiency indicators linked to financial performance and risk;[24] (2) active members would be granted more (if not exclusive) control over decision making than is the case at present; and (3) if practical reasons preclude taxpayer representation on the board, clear disclosure procedures (such as periodic reporting to parliament) would be put in place to inform taxpayer representatives about the performance of plans.

Addressing the Collective Action Problem of Key Stakeholders

Even if active members are granted more decision-making responsibility on the boards of public pension plans, this does not ensure that effective monitoring of management will take place. Active members are a dispersed group of stakeholders, so a governance structure that reduces the collective action problem of public plan stakeholders is still necessary. Here, we look at the governance mechanisms discussed in section 1 and discuss how they can be applied to public pension plans.

Unlike corporations, public pension plans cannot benefit from all of the mechanisms discussed above. For instance, market mechanisms such as takeovers do not apply to public pension plans, which are usually mandatory: pension fund members cannot simply 'vote with their feet' and leave the plan. Again, pension plans do not borrow, so debt cannot be used as a monitoring device. Finally, the use of large investors as delegated monitors is impossible for the same reason: there is no shareholding capital in public pension plans. The only mechanisms that can be used are the board of directors, executive compensation and fiduciary duties.

This is clearly not enough to exploit the complementary nature of the governance mechanisms used for corporations. Hence, in order to improve plan performance, strict governance standards should apply to the board of directors. These would cover: (1) the composition of the board; (2) the functioning and organization of the board; (3) the transparency and accountability of the activity of the board; and (4) statements of investment policies. These aspects are discussed in turn below.

The composition of the board of directors should be such that, in general, only individuals with adequate investment and business expertise in areas such as economics, accounting, actuarial science, finance, investing, banking and business are selected. A transparent and credible mechanism is needed for the appointment of directors. This should be an open and transparent process in which an independent body, such as parliament or an expert committee, is consulted. An appropriate balance should be sought with respect to the number of directors, noting that, in general, a limited number of governors maximizes the effectiveness of the board. Also, since it is likely that qualified individuals will not be found among active members of public plans, the number of independent directors with appropriate qualifications should be maximized. This would also improve transparency and help reduce the collective action problem of dispersed stakeholders (such as active members) or more distant stakeholders (such as taxpayers) (Impavido 2002; Hess and Impavido 2004).

Owing to the problem of bias in the control structure of public plans, the functioning of the board should be governed by clear and publicly disclosed behavioural control mechanisms. This would entail introducing and adhering to internal governance structures and processes, to minimize mismanagement and fraud. For instance, a code of conduct for directors, guidelines on conflicts of interest and clearly defined fiduciary duties would need to be developed either as separate plan documents or as part of a comprehensive governance manual. A governance committee would also be needed, to recommend policies, guidelines and procedures; to make recommendations on the board's effectiveness; to monitor the application of the code-of-conduct and conflict-of-interest guidelines; and to conduct periodical governance assessments (Impavido 2002; Carmichael and Palacios 2004).

Internal and external performance and governance audits are essential to increase transparency in fund operations, thereby improving accountability (Impavido 2002). The likelihood of mismanagement or undue influence would be drastically reduced if the public were informed regularly about such issues as the structure and performance of the governance framework as well as the financial performance of the fund. An internal audit committee should be formed with responsibility for overseeing financial reporting, external and internal audits, information systems, and internal control policies and practices.

Finally, public pension funds should produce sound statements of investment policies. At the same time, there should be a transparent process for disclosing to the public how the investment policy is to be implemented and adhered to. There is a vigorous debate about whether public pension funds should invest in equities and whether they should be allowed to lend to members. On this last issue, Carmichael and Palacios (2004) clearly highlight the difficult issues linked to lending to members. When member loans are allowed, there is a need to solve the difficult exercise of separating admissible loans to members from non-admissible loans to related parties. Funds must establish transparent and rigid rules for eligibility and policies for dealing with defaults.

The investment policy document should clearly express the desired asset mix needed to match assets and liabilities. It could also describe the role and composition of the investment committee; how investments are recorded; short-term as well as long-term performance measures; the universe of vehicles that can be used to meet these measures; risk tolerance guidelines, in terms of either quantitative limits or the outcomes of asset–liability models; and reporting, compliance and performance review requirements. The investment policy should also establish due diligence criteria for investment transactions, the valuation of underlying assets,[25] the accounting treatment of assets[26] and the procedures to be used for approving investments.[27] Above all, the targeted long-term performance measures should be consistent with the targeted long-term funding ratio for the plan.

4. CONCLUSIONS

This chapter has reviewed the economic literature on corporate governance, surveyed the governance practices of a large number of public pension funds in developing countries and discussed the applicability to public pension funds of the corporate governance mechanisms traditionally used by firms. The general conclusion that can be drawn from this exposition is that the traditional governance mechanisms used by corporations to address the collective action problem of shareholders appear to have limited applicability to the governance of public pension plans.

Two specific governance problems are likely to have a detrimental effect on fund performance in developing countries. The first relates to the control structure of public pension plans. Multiple (and unclear) plan mandates induce a strong bias in the control structure of plans. This is generally designed to give equal representation to a large number of stakeholders on the board of directors. However, in practice the government often has higher representation (on average) than employers and employees. Together with non-transparent appointment procedures, the lack of fit and proper tests for directors and the presence of *ex officio* directors, this suggests that governments have more influence over board decisions than other stakeholders. The control structure of public plans should instead be aligned with the residual claimant structure of the plan. As residual claimants of public pension plans, active members and, more generally, taxpayers should be granted more control over board decision making. This can only be achieved if clear commercial mandates are provided for in the law or in plan documents.

The second governance problem relates to the collective action of plan stakeholders. Agency theory should be useful in improving the governance of public pension plans. However, traditional delegated monitoring mechanisms such as takeovers, debt or financial intermediaries clearly do not apply to the governance of public plans. This implies that public pension boards lack the complementary support of other governance mechanisms commonly used in corporations. For public pension plans, it is likely that an increased use of independent directors and the introduction of explicit behavioural controls will strengthen the monitoring function of boards. Both of these should diminish conflicts of interests between directors and management and increase overall transparency and accountability to plan members.

NOTES

1. Shareholder value (here simply the stock market share valuation) may not be the right efficiency measure to maximize to promote the alignment of managers' and owners' incentives. There is a debate between the 'Anglo-Saxon model', which looks at shareholder value as the ultimate efficiency measure to maximize in a firm, and the 'stakeholder capitalism model', more prevalent in Europe but well established in Japan as well, which includes other stakeholders' interests in the efficiency maximization problem.
2. See Diamond (1984) for the first treatment of financial intermediation as delegated monitoring.
3. Further discussion of debt as a monitoring device is conducted later in this section, where issues related to multiple stakeholders are considered.
4. Concentrated shareholders, financial intermediation and boards of directors are all forms of delegated monitoring. With delegated monitoring, the classic problem of 'who monitors the monitors' arises.
5. In some jurisdictions, such as France, Germany, Austria and Hungary, the distinction between executive and non-executive directors is formalized by the adoption of a two-tier governance structure where a management board is monitored by a supervisory board.

6. See Bhagat and Black (1999) and Hermalin and Weisbach (2001) for surveys on the role of boards.
7. In this chapter, shareholder value is used to indicate: (1) profit maximization, (2) discounted cash flow streams or (3) the discounted stream of dividends in case of certainty; or (4) the expected value of the discounted stream of dividends in case of uncertainty. For the sake of simplicity, we do not consider cases where these measures differ.
8. The Fisher separation theorem holds in the case of complete markets and certainty and, under specific circumstances, in the case of: (1) complete markets, uncertainty but shareholder unanimity about value maximization; and (2) incomplete markets and shareholder unanimity about value maximization.
9. When everybody faces the same marginal rate of transformation of wealth, it is not important who makes the decisions about investment allocation. In this case, optimal investment decisions imply that the discounted dividend stream is maximized, and this in turn allows owners to maximize consumption. Even if owner-consumers have heterogeneous consumption preferences, they can move to higher utility indifference curves through the use of side transfers.
10. These may include creditors, employees, local community representatives, environmental representatives, pensioners or any other group with some material tie to the firm.
11. Obviously, if side transfers were allowed, this statement would not hold true. However, in reality the transfers among shareholders or other constituencies that would be needed to compensate for the different marginal rates of wealth transformation are either not allowed or impractical.
12. Some corporations in Germany are required by law to have employee representatives on the board. However, the degree of representation varies by sector and can be as low as zero in the media industry, for instance. In the Netherlands, the boards of directors of some corporations are required to act in the interests of the company and are not appointed by shareholders. In France, companies have the option to have one-tier or two-tier boards. Austria, Hungary and Germany have two-tier boards.
13. Notice that this result is obtained by Allen and Gale (2002b) with less than completely rigid labour markets. The impossibility of firing managers is considered here only to facilitate the exposition.
14. See, for instance, Aghion and Bolton (1992), Berglöf and von Thadden (1994) and Dewatripont and Tirole (1994).
15. See, for instance, Bernheim and Whinston (1985, 1986), Dixit (1996) and Dixit, Grossman and Helpman (1997).
16. See, for instance, Mitchell and Hsin (1997), Iglesias and Palacios (2000), Useem and Mitchell (2000), Impavido (2002), Carmichael and Palacios (2003) and Hess and Impavido (2004).
17. The requirement to invest pension assets in (non-tradable) government securities is equivalent to an explicit social mandate to the extent that it is accepted that government consumption and investment have a strong developmental component. Such a requirement raises the obvious concern about the effective level of funding of the plan.
18. Although this cannot be inferred from Table 6.3, more than 20 per cent of plans have at least 80 per cent of their assets allocated to government bonds or bank deposits.
19. Such as provident funds with explicit or implicit guarantees or notional defined contribution plans.
20. Taxpayers are called upon when plans become actuarially unbalanced. This is especially evident when the plan is pay-as-you-go and taxpayers need to maintain a given or increasing level of benefits in the face of insufficient contributions.
21. Many countries have minimum wage regulations that ensure a socially acceptable minimum consumption level. Mandatory participation in a public pension plan with, say, contributions fully paid by the employer is equivalent to a minimum wage rule. The only difference is that the portion of the gross wage that comes under this rule cannot be consumed and must be saved for retirement.
22. Ensuring taxpayer representation on the board of directors encounters practical difficulties. Many jurisdictions have resorted to transparency regulations requiring periodic reporting to parliament on the management of the fund as a way of ensuring *de facto* representation.
23. Through trade unions and other employee associations.

24. Legitimate efficiency indicators indirectly linked to performance could include achieving a given funding level, achieving a set investment return target or reducing administrative costs. In any case, plan mandates should be clearly stated to facilitate the adoption of measurable goals against which the performance of the plan and of its governors and administrators can be measured (Impavido 2002).

25. Some general criteria might be that the plan cannot purchase securities that are not interest bearing or interest accruing, do not offer dividends and do not pay income; that securities cannot be purchased above their market value; or that an approved appraiser is required for the purchase of all properties, with fresh valuations to be undertaken by an independent qualified appraiser at least annually.

26. For instance, equities are normally carried on the balance sheet at market value, with the market value for quoted ordinary shares and preferred shares being the 'last price' quoted by the stock exchange. Unquoted shares whose fair value cannot be measured reliably may be valued at the lower of the cost and net realizable value. Long-term securities such as government bonds, corporate bonds, mortgages and preference shares with fixed redemption dates could be carried on the balance sheet at the amortized value, with any premium or discount arising on the purchase of these investments amortized to income over the period to maturity.

27. For instance, the investment committee should require that each investment be recorded, and signed by both a plan officer and the chair of the committee authorizing the investment.

7. Benchmarking the Performance of Superannuation Funds

Hazel Bateman and Robert J. Hill

In this chapter we survey some of the main index benchmarks used by Australian superannuation (pension) funds to evaluate the performance of fund managers. In recent years there has been a proliferation of specialist investment funds; this in turn has caused a proliferation of index benchmarks. Nevertheless, the benchmark of choice in Australia for equity funds is still the S&P/ASX 200 index. We consider some alternative ways in which benchmarks could be constructed, particularly with respect to the choice of weights, the frequency of rebalancing, the choice of index number formula and the treatment of dividends. We argue that such alternative benchmarks warrant further investigation. The chapter concludes by exploring some of the implications of a mismatch between investment style and the underlying benchmark.

1. PERFORMANCE BENCHMARKS FOR SUPERANNUATION

Superannuation funds are a major element of the Australian financial industry, with total assets in excess of A$1.25 trillion, equivalent to over 100 per cent of GDP, invested across a wide range of Australian and international assets. In mid-2007, 32 per cent of assets in the default strategies of superannuation entities were held in Australian equities, 24 per cent in overseas equities, 16 per cent in securities, 8 per cent in cash and 8 per cent in property (APRA 2007).

Superannuation is the main source of retirement saving for many Australian retirees, so fund performance is crucial. Under standard assumptions,[1] a 1 percentage point reduction in the annual rate of return over a 40-year period translates to a reduction in the retirement accumulation of over 20 per cent. It is therefore essential that superannuation fund trustees work to maximize returns on member accounts over the long term.

Performance benchmarks are important for superannuation funds. They help to measure the investment performance of fund managers, they provide superannuation fund members and trustees with a reference point for monitoring the performance of investment options and the superannuation fund in aggregate and, importantly, they may affect the behaviour of fund managers (Blake and Timmermann 2002).

In recent years there has been rapid growth in the number and sophistication of the investment choices offered by superannuation funds. A decade ago the typical industry fund offered no investment choice, with contributions generally placed in a single multi-manager diversified fund. This has evolved into a menu of choices comprising:

- multi-manager diversified options associated with names such as 'conservative', 'balanced' or 'growth', with varying proportions of bonds/fixed interest and shares/property;
- single manager diversified options, where fund members can choose both the type of diversified fund and the fund manager (that is, they can choose from a menu of diversified investment managers);
- multi-manager asset class options, where fund members can choose their own asset allocation across multi-manager asset classes (cash, fixed interest, shares, property and so on); and/or
- single manager asset class options, where a choice is given of both asset class and fund manager (that is, members can choose from a menu of single-asset investment managers, or even individual equities).

Current practice varies between superannuation funds of differing types and sizes, with the retail funds and public offer industry funds offering the most investment options. The Retail Employees Superannuation Trust (REST) typifies the current offerings of industry funds, with six multi-manager diversified options (capital stable, cash plus, core strategy, balanced, diversified and high growth) and six multi-manager asset class options (cash, Australian and international shares, Australian shares, bonds, property and international shares). Another industry fund, Sunsuper, offers even more choice, with five multi-manager diversified options (conservative, moderate, balanced, growth and aggressive), nine single-manager diversified options and 19 single-manager, single-asset options. At the other end of the scale is public sector fund QSuper, whose menu comprises four multi-manager investment options.

Each of the investment options, whether it is single manager or multi-manager, single asset class or diversified, is associated with a performance benchmark. The benchmarks for the illustrative investment options offered by QSuper, REST and Sunsuper are set out in Appendix A7.1.[2] The greater investment choice now being offered by superannuation funds has given rise to a multitude of performance benchmarks across investment options.

The typical performance benchmarks for illustrative investment options are summarized in Table 7.1. For the multi-manager diversified options, typical performance benchmarks include peer group benchmarks (where performance is compared to the median or mean return of similar funds) or returns relative to the consumer price index (CPI), the cash rate, the 90-day bank bill rate or a similar product (such as cash management accounts or retirement savings accounts). In some cases absolute returns are specified. For the asset class options (both multi-manager and single manager), the typical performance benchmarks are more specific. We focus in this chapter on stock market indices. In this context the standard benchmark for both the single and multi-manager Australian equity investment options offered by superannuation funds is the S&P/ASX 200 or 300 accumulation indices.

2. AUSTRALIA'S INSTITUTIONAL BENCHMARK: THE S&P/ASX 200

The Australian share market has in excess of 1,500 companies. Standard and Poor's (S&P) in conjunction with the Australian Stock Exchange (ASX) maintains a number of indices to measure the movements in share values resulting from equity trading on the ASX.[3] These include both price and accumulation indices. Price indices measure the capital gains or losses that occur from investing in an index portfolio excluding dividend payments, while accumulation (or total return) indices include dividend payments.

S&P's Australian equities market indices include the S&P/ASX 200, 300, 20, 50 and 100, the S&P/ASX MidCap 50, the All Ordinaries, the S&P/ASX Small Ordinaries and the S&P/ASX Industrial and Resources Indices. The main features of each of these indices are summarized in Appendix A7.2. The S&P/ASX 200 accumulation index is the institutional benchmark index for the Australian market, so it is no accident that it is the benchmark generally used by superannuation funds for their equity investment options.

Broad Structure of the S&P/ASX 200 Price and Accumulation Indices

The S&P/ASX indices are of the chained Laspeyres variety. The index level reflects the total market value of all component stocks relative to a particular base period.

The S&P/ASX price indices (PI_t) are calculated as follows:

$$PI_t = PI_{t-1} \times \sum_{n=1} [P_{n,t} \times (S_{n,t-1} \times A_{n,t-1})] / \sum_{n=1} [P_{n,t-1} \times (S_{n,t-1} \times A_{n,t-1})]$$

Table 7.1   Benchmarks Used by Funds for Typical Investment Options

Investment Option	Typical Performance Benchmark
Multi-manager diversified	
Conservative, balanced, growth, high growth and so on	Outperform mean/median of similar funds CPI Cash rate 90-day bank bill rate Return from cash management trusts Return from bank retirement savings accounts Absolute growth of x per cent per annum No specific benchmark
Multi-manager by asset class	
Cash	UBSW Bank Bill Index Return from cash management trusts CPI
Australian shares	S&P/ASX 300, S&P/ASX 200
International shares	MSCI World ex Australia Index
Shares	Combination of S&P/ASX 300 and MSCI World ex Australia Index Outperform balanced funds CPI
Australian sustainable shares	S&P/ASX 200
International sustainable shares	MSCI World ex Australia Index
Sustainable shares	Outperform similar funds CPI
Property	S&P/ASX 200 Listed Property Index Mercer Unlisted Property Index CPI
Australian fixed interest	UBSA Composite Bond Index
International fixed interest	UBSWA Composite Bond Index
Fixed interest	UBSWA Composite Bond Index Combination of UBSW Composite Bond Index, UBSW Inflation Linked Bond Index and Salomon Government World Bond Index CPI
Single manager by asset class	
Cash	UBSW Bank Bill Index UBSWA Bank Bill Index
Australian shares	S&P/ASX 200, S&P/ASX 300
International shares	MSCI World ex Australia Index
Sustainable shares	S&P/ASX 200
Property	S&P/ASX 200 Listed Property Index
Australian fixed interest	UBSA Composite Bond Index
International fixed interest	Citigroup World Government Bond Index (ex Australia) UBSWA Composite Bond Index

Source: Derived from Appendix A7.1.

where $P_{n,t}$ is the price of stock n at time t; $S_{n,t}$ is the number of shares outstanding of stock n at time t; and $A_{n,t}$ is the investable weight factor of stock n at time t.

In the stock market index literature, it is more common to write the chained Laspeyres formula as follows:

$$PI_t = \sum_{n=1} [P_{n,t} \times (S_{n,t-1} \times A_{n,t-1})] / B_t$$

where B_t is referred to as the index divisor at time t. The divisor is calculated as follows:

$$B_t = \sum_{n=1} [P_{n,t-1} \times (S_{n,t-1} \times A_{n,t-1})] / PI_{t-1}.$$

The S&P/ASX total return (accumulation) indices (TR_t) are calculated as follows:

$$TR_t = TR_{t-1} \times \sum_{n=1} [(P_{n,t} + D_{n,t}) \times (S_{n,t-1} \times A_{n,t-1})] / \sum_{n=1} [P_{n=1n,t-1} \times (S_{n,t-1} \times A_{n,t-1})]$$

where $D_{n,t}$ is the daily dividend paid on one unit of stock n at time t.

The official daily index closing values for the S&P/ASX price and accumulation indices are calculated after the market closes and are based on the last traded price for each constituent.

Features of the Benchmark Equities Index for the Australian Market

To be eligible for inclusion in the S&P/ASX indices, stocks must be listed on the ASX and be institutionally investable. For a company to be institutionally investable, it must have sufficient liquidity, sufficient free float and sufficient market capitalization.

Liquidity refers to the dollar value traded. A company must be sufficiently liquid to enable institutional investors to buy in or sell out of the company without severely distorting the share price of that stock.

Free float is the portion of shares that is freely available for trading in the market, that is, not held by the government, government agencies, controlling and strategic shareholders or partners, or other entities that hold more than 5 per cent of the stock (excluding financial institutions). Stocks are deemed ineligible for inclusion in the S&P/ASX indices if their free float is less than 30 per cent.

Market capitalization is adjusted so that it reflects only the free float of the company. The adjustment is called the investable weight factor (IWF). A company's index market capitalization is calculated by multiplying the company's price by the number of ordinary shares by the IWF. Therefore, the IWF represents the proportion of the company that is included in the index.

One important additional feature of the S&P/ASX indices is that companies that have dual listings are only included in the index of the primary listing country. This issue rose to prominence in Australia when News Corporation relocated to the United States in 2004. As a result, even though it was still listed on the Australian stock exchange, it was no longer included in any S&P/ASX indices. We return to this issue in the next section.

The weights for the S&P/ASX price and accumulation indices are based on companies' IWFs (which themselves are based on free float capitalization). All S&P/ASX indices are market capitalization weighted. Therefore, the company with the largest free float market capitalization will have the largest weight and impact on the index. As of 31 December 2005, for the S&P/ASX 200 this was BHP Billiton, with a free float market capitalization of 9.2 per cent. The IWFs are reviewed annually as part of the April quarterly rebalance, except where any single event alters the free float of a security in excess of 5 per cent. In this case, changes to the IWF are implemented as soon as practicable.

The constituents of the S&P/ASX price and accumulation indices are also reviewed periodically, although the intention is to minimize turnover among index constituents. Constituent companies are rebalanced quarterly (or when significant corporate events occur), with market capitalization and liquidity assessed using the previous six months of data. This may result in index deletions and additions. Quarterly rebalance changes take effect on the third Friday of December, March, June and September (except for the S&P/ASX 300, which is rebalanced twice a year). The free float and IWF of all S&P/ASX index constituents are reviewed during the March rebalance.

Except in the case of significant corporate events, deletions from and additions to the index are made only at the time of the quarterly rebalance. Companies are added to the index only where there has been a deletion, which may happen in the event of acquisition, insufficient market capitalization, insufficient liquidity, liquidation or company restructuring.

3. BENCHMARK DESIGN: SOME INDEX NUMBER ISSUES

Weighting Schemes

One of the most important characteristics of a benchmark is its weighting scheme. All the S&P/ASX indices are market capitalization weighted. This is not the only option, however. Here we consider three alternative weighting schemes.

An *equally weighted benchmark* assumes that an equal amount of money is invested in each stock in the portfolio. S&P recently started computing an equally weighted version of the S&P 500 index. Block and French (2002) argue that this weighting scheme better matches the investment style followed by many fund managers in the United States, and hence provides a more appropriate benchmark. Certainly, following an equally weighted strategy leads to a more diversified portfolio than does allocating funds according to market capitalization. This is a particularly important issue in Australia, where in mid-2007 the 10 largest stocks accounted for nearly 40 per cent of the total market capitalization of Australian equities listed on the ASX. To use the ASX 200 as a benchmark, therefore, is to encourage fund managers to construct highly concentrated and hence potentially risky portfolios. A switch to an equally weighted benchmark might stimulate significant diversification. For large funds, however, such diversification may not be attractive, because it would require them to make significant investments in smaller and hence less liquid stocks. Such funds might experience non-trivial adverse price movements when buying and selling lower-liquidity stocks.

A *price-weighted benchmark* assumes that the portfolio consists of one unit of each stock. This is the weighting scheme used by the Dow Jones Industrial Average. Price weighting is hard to defend, since it is not clear why any investor would want to follow such a strategy. It implies investing more in stocks sold in high denominations. Moreover, stock splits are problematic for price-weighted indices (see Hill 2004).

Finally, a *market trade-weighted benchmark* could be constructed based on the number of shares traded. For example, if four million Telstra shares were traded on a particular day, then this would be the number of Telstra shares in the benchmark portfolio on the following day. The properties of such an index are not well understood. In particular, it is not clear exactly what can be deduced if an index weighted by shares traded rises more than the corresponding index weighted by market capitalization. Certainly the former index will tend to be more volatile. Whether it constitutes a useful benchmark for fund managers remains to be seen.

Rebalancing

Market capitalization indices must be rebalanced periodically to reflect changes in the number of shares outstanding and/or on free float. The free float adjustment introduces a subjective element. That is, it may be desirable to adjust the weight of stocks downward where a significant proportion of the shares is not on free float. For example, a large fraction of News Corporation shares is held by members of the Murdoch family, and hence is not available to investors. Since the company's relocation to the United States, this has been more of a problem for the construction of the global S&P 500 than for the Australian indices. The important point here, though, is that it is not always clear exactly where the line between liquid and illiquid shares should be drawn.

News Corporation's relocation raises another important issue. Although it still had a secondary listing on the ASX, News Corporation was removed from the S&P/ASX indices in 2005. This remained the case until it was reinstated in 2007. S&P removed News Corporation to avoid double counting of firms in its regional indices. It is not clear that this was in the best interests of Australian investors, however, because fund managers whose performance was benchmarked against S&P/ASX indices were reluctant to hold the stock for fear of departing too much from their target benchmarks. In other words, after News Corporation's deletion from the S&P/ASX indices, many fund managers were forced to sell their holdings. It was due to lobbying from these same fund managers that S&P later reversed this decision.

The timing of rebalancing is of greatest significance for equally weighted indices, where the portfolio must be adjusted periodically so that an equal amount of money is invested in each stock. That, after all, is the whole point of an equally weighted index, although it is not clear how often such rebalancing should occur. It could be done daily, weekly, monthly, quarterly or yearly. The frequency of rebalancing can significantly affect the index (Hill 2004).

The Index Number Formula

Whenever the reference portfolio changes due to rebalancing, this raises the question of how the index itself should be computed. The Laspeyres formula is not the only option. Below, we contrast Laspeyres with Paasche.

Laspeyres: $PI_t = PI_{t-1} \times \sum_{n=1} [P_{n,t} \times (S_{n,t-1} \times A_{n,t-1})] / \sum_{n=1} [P_{n,t-1} \times (S_{n,t-1} \times A_{n,t-1})]$

Paasche: $PI_t = PI_{t-1} \times \sum_{n=1} [P_{n,t} \times (S_{n,t} \times A_{n,t})] / \sum_{n=1} [P_{n,t-1} \times (S_{n,t} \times A_{n,t})]$

Paasche differs from Laspeyres in that it uses the current period's basket of shares as the reference point rather than the basket of the previous period. In general, the Paasche and Laspeyres price indices will give different answers. A number of other price index formulas have also been proposed in the index number literature. Perhaps the best known is the Fisher index, which is the geometric mean of Laspeyres and Paasche.

The choice of formula is not so important for market capitalization-weighted indices, since for such indices the difference between $(S_{n,t-1} \times A_{n,t-1})$ and $(S_{n,t} \times A_{n,t})$ will tend to be small, and hence Laspeyres and Paasche should approximate each other closely. The divergence between Laspeyres and Paasche becomes rather more significant for an equally weighted index whenever the portfolio is rebalanced. The divergence becomes bigger still for market trade-weighted indices, where the difference between the reference portfolios for consecutive periods could be huge.

For most purposes, the Laspeyres index is the correct formula to use, since it tracks the change in the value of a portfolio of assets over time. However, the other indices also provide useful information and warrant further investigation in the stock market context.

The Treatment of Dividends

From a benchmarking perspective, it seems clear that stock market indices should include dividend payments. Over a period of years, the compounding effect of dividend payments may cause the difference between an index inclusive of dividends (referred to as a total return or accumulation index) and one exclusive of dividends to become surprisingly large. The reinvestment of dividends also raises some interesting issues. Fisher (1966) distinguishes between indices that assume dividends are invested in the stock that pays the dividend versus indices that assume that the dividends are invested across all stocks according to market capitalization. Two further possibilities would be to assume that dividends are invested equally in all stocks or that they are invested in government bonds. The implications of these assumptions for accumulation indices warrant further investigation.

Pre-announcement of Index Replacements

Stocks entering a popular index often jump in price immediately following the announcement. This is because index-tracking funds (passive or active) must buy the stock to rebalance their portfolios to match the target index. Conversely, stocks leaving the index fall in price as funds unload them. This raises the issue of whether or not changes in an index should be pre-announced. If they are, then the index will tend to rise more slowly, since the initial rise in the price of stocks entering the index will not be included while the fall in the price of stocks leaving the index is included. If changes are not pre-announced, the reverse holds. Some evidence on the size of this effect in Australia is provided by Chan and Howard (2002). It is not clear which approach is preferable from a benchmarking perspective.

4. MISMATCHES BETWEEN BENCHMARKS AND INVESTMENT STYLES

The performance of a fund manager should be judged against her stated investment style. It is important, therefore, that the reference benchmark is tailored to fit the style. This raises the question of how many investment styles should be recognized. When taken to the limit, there is an infinite number of styles and each fund manager performs exactly as expected given her style. Therefore, to obtain meaningful results, the number of styles that is recognized must be restricted in some way.

Investment styles differ along a number of dimensions. For example, a fund may invest equal amounts in each stock in the portfolio, invest amounts in proportion to each stock's market capitalization or use some other weighting scheme. It may focus on stocks in a particular sector, across a whole stock market or across different stock markets. It may concentrate on large, medium or small capitalization stocks, value or growth stocks, high or low-beta stocks, and so on.[4]

How many different investment styles should be distinguished? The Global Industry Classification Standard (GICS) identifies 11 market sectors. Alternatively, a fund could focus on large, medium or small capitalization stocks, or on growth or value stocks. This yields a total of 15 styles. Of course, we could also consider a style that focuses on small capitalization stocks in a particular market sector. Following this approach, we would immediately have 55 different strategies. That is, the large, medium, small, value or growth styles could be applied to each of the 11 GICS market sectors or to the whole market. Ultimately, the number of different styles that should be recognized depends on what strategies are actually being followed by fund managers. Each style implemented in the market needs its own benchmark.

There are at least two reasons why a fund might wish to set an investment style for its managers. First, there is the need to balance investments across sectors. For example, if the fund is currently underweight in one market sector, it may ask a manager to build a portfolio in that sector. Second, a particular investment style may yield gains from specialization. A manager who deals exclusively with small capitalization stocks, for example, is likely to develop a more detailed knowledge of this sector that may allow her to outperform non-specialists. This raises the question of whether there is an optimal level of specialization. The disadvantage of specialization is that it reduces the manager's freedom of action, and imposes constraints on the degree of diversification, thus implying greater risk.

Specialization also raises the possibility of a mismatch between a fund manager's performance benchmark and her investment style. For example, the S&P 500 index outperformed its equally weighted equivalent index in the United States during the 1990s because of the strong performance of some of the largest stocks. Therefore, if fund managers were following an equally weighted investment style, the S&P 500 would have been a misleading benchmark against which to evaluate their performance. A second example is provided by sustainable funds such as the AMP Capital Sustainable Future Australian Share

Fund. Its performance benchmark is currently the ASX 200 index, yet it is not clear that this provides an appropriate benchmark for such a fund. Rather, what is required is a benchmark comprised only of sustainable stocks. As far as we are aware, no such benchmark currently exists.

More generally, a number of possible mismatches may occur. The benchmark may be narrower in focus than the investment style. This in a sense corresponds to the example just given. The S&P 500 portfolio is a much more concentrated (that is, less diversified) portfolio than the equally weighted S&P 500. Alternatively, the benchmark may be broader than the investment style. Suppose, for example, that a fund manager is required to construct a portfolio of biotechnology stocks, but the benchmark is for the health care GICS. If the performance of biotechnology stocks differs on average over the period of interest compared with the performance of other stocks in the health care GICS, the benchmark will be biased. A third possibility is that the benchmark may simply be wrong, as would occur if a manager is investing in small capitalization stocks but is evaluated using a large capitalization benchmark.

When a mismatch exists between style and benchmark, this may have one of two consequences. First, the evaluation of a fund manager's performance may be incorrect. Alternatively, the fund manager may adapt her style to fit the benchmark. In this case the benchmark will provide an appropriate evaluation. The problem now is that the manager will not have followed the strategy desired by the fund.

5. CONCLUSION

Superannuation funds rely on benchmarks to evaluate the performance of investment managers as well as to provide fund members and trustees with a reference point for measurement of the performance of investment options and the fund in aggregate.

Index benchmarks at present are almost invariably market capitalization weighted and use the Laspeyres formula. In this chapter we have considered some alternatives to these assumptions. By changing the assumptions it is possible to generate a much wider array of benchmark indices. At present the properties of these alternative benchmarks are not well understood. However, it seems likely that at least some will provide information that would be of use to superannuation funds, and hence warrant further investigation. In particular, the implications of a mismatch between investment styles and benchmarks deserve greater scrutiny.

APPENDIX A7.1: FUNDS, INVESTMENT CHOICES AND THE ASSOCIATED BENCHMARKS

Investment Option	Performance Benchmark (Objective)
QSUPER (public sector fund) **Multi-manager diversified**	
Cash	Average return over one year of 0.5% below the cash rate after administration fees but before tax
Cash Plus	Average return over three years of cash rate + 0.75% per annum after administration fees but before tax
Balanced	Average return over five years of cash rate + 2% per annum after administration fees but before tax
High Growth	Average return over 10 years of cash rate + 3% per annum after administration fees but before tax
REST (industry fund) **Multi-manager diversified**	
REST Capital Stable (60% bonds, 16% Australian shares, 10% cash, 5% international shares, 9% other)	Average return above inflation over the medium term *and* outperform CPI + 1% per annum over a rolling three-year period
REST Cash Plus (90% cash, 10% bonds)	Outperform the UBSW Bank Bill Index over a rolling two-year period
REST Core Strategy (30% bonds, 25% Australian shares, 15% overseas shares, 15% property, 10% cash and unlisted equity)	Outperform CPI + 3% per annum over a rolling four-year period
REST Balanced (45% bonds, 25% Australian shares, 14% overseas shares, 7% property, 9% cash and unlisted equity)	Outperform CPI + 2% per annum over a rolling three-year period
REST Diversified (20% bonds, 40% Australian shares, 19% overseas shares, 12% property, 9% cash and unlisted equity)	Outperform CPI + 3% per annum over a rolling four-year period
REST High Growth (5% bonds, 45% Australian equity, 25% overseas shares, 16% property, 9% cash and unlisted equity)	Outperform CPI + 4% per annum over a rolling five-year period

Appendix A7.1 (continued)

Investment Option	Performance Benchmark (Objective)
Multi-manager by asset class	
100% cash	Perform in line with the UBSW Bank Bill Index (before tax and after fees) over a rolling one-year period
100% shares (70% Australian shares, 30% overseas shares)	Outperform benchmark return (before tax and after fees) over a rolling three-year period; benchmark calculated using S&P/ASX 300 accumulation index and MSCI World ex Australia Index in $A
100% Australian shares	Outperform S&P/ASX 300 accumulation index over a rolling three-year period (before tax and after fees)
100% bonds	Outperform benchmark return (before tax and after fees) over a rolling two-year period; benchmark calculated using UBSW Composite Bond Index, UBSW Inflation Linked Bond Index and Salomon Government World Bond Index in $A
100% property	Outperform the Mercer Unlisted Property Index over a rolling three-year period (before tax and after fees)
100% international shares	Outperform the MSCI World ex Australia Index in $A over a rolling three-year period (before tax and after fees)
SUNSUPER (industry fund) **Multi-manager diversified**	
Sunsuper Conservative (12–20% cash, 11–32% fixed interest, 0–6% property, 10–25% Australian shares, 6–22% international shares)	No specific benchmark; modest returns with limited longer-term capital growth
Sunsuper Moderate (2–11% cash, 7–29% fixed interest, 0–10% property, 20–35% Australian shares, 12–31% international shares)	No specific benchmark; moderate returns over the medium to long term
Sunsuper Balanced (0–30% cash/fixed interest, 0–11% property, 20–45% Australian shares, 12–35% international shares, 0–7% infrastructure, 0–7% private equity)	No specific benchmark; strong long-term growth (way ahead of inflation)

Appendix A7.1 (continued)

Investment Option	Performance Benchmark (Objective)
Sunsuper Growth (0–20% cash/fixed interest, 0–15% property, 30–50% Australian shares, 15–40% international shares, 0–7% infrastructure, 0–11% private equity)	No specific benchmark; returns significantly ahead of inflation over the long term
Sunsuper Aggressive (0% cash/fixed income, 0–20% property, 35–65% Australian shares, 25–55% international shares)	No specific benchmark; high returns substantially ahead of inflation over the long term
Single manager diversified	
AMP Capital Balanced Growth	Moderate capital growth and some income
AMP Capital Sustainable Future Balanced Growth	Moderate capital growth and some income
Credit Suisse Capital Growth	Capital growth and some income
QIC Growth	Long-term growth
SSgA Passive Balanced Trust	Closely track the monthly rates of return of a composite benchmark
AMP Capital High Growth	High returns over the medium to long term
Credit Suisse High Growth	High growth over the long term
SSgA Indexed Growth Trust	Closely track the monthly rates of return of a composite benchmark
QIC High Growth	Long-term high growth
Single/multi-manager by asset class *Capital guaranteed*	
Sunsuper Capital Guaranteed	Closely approximate USB Bank Bill Index (after tax and fees) over a rolling five-year period
SSgA Australian Cash Trust	Closely track monthly rates of return relative to UBSWA Bank Bill Index with net returns reinvested
Cash/Australian fixed interest	
Sunsuper Australian Fixed Interest	Outperform UBSWA Composite Bond Index by 0.5% (before fees and taxes) over a rolling five-year period
SSgA Australian Fixed Income	Closely approximate the UBSWA Composite Bond Index

Appendix A7.1 (continued)

Investment Option	Performance Benchmark (Objective)
International fixed interest	
Sunsuper International Fixed Interest	Outperform UBSWA Composite Bond Index by 0.5% (before fees and taxes) over a rolling five-year period
SSgA Global Fixed Income	Closely approximate Citigroup World Government Bond Index (ex Australia) hedged back to $A
Property	
SSgA Australian Listed Property	Closely track returns of S&P/ASX 200 Listed Property Accumulation Index
Australian shares	
Sunsuper Australian Shares	Outperform S&P/ASX 300 accumulation index by 1–2% (before fees and taxes) over a rolling five-year period
AMP Capital Australian Shares – Equity Fund	Outperform S&P/ASX 200 accumulation index over a rolling 12-month period
Macquarie Australian Shares	Outperform S&P/ASX 200 accumulation index over a rolling 12-month period
Maple-Brown Abbott Australian Shares	Outperform S&P/ASX 200 accumulation index over a rolling 12-month period
Merrill Lynch Investment Managers Australian Shares	Outperform S&P/ASX 200 accumulation index over a rolling five-year period
International shares	
Sunsuper International Shares	Outperform MSCI World Index (ex Australia) by 1–2% (before fees and taxes) over a rolling five-year period
SSgA Global Index Plus Trust – Unhedged	Outperform MSCI World Index ex Australia by 0.75–1% with net dividends re-invested (expressed in $A unhedged)
SSgA Global Index Plus Trust – Hedged	Closely track monthly rates of return of a composite benchmark with exposure to both equity and fixed income assets
Credit Suisse International Shares – Unhedged	Outperform MSCI World Index ex Australia before fees and taxes
Credit Suisse International Shares – Hedged	Outperform MSCI World Index ex Australia before fees and taxes
Lazard Sunsuper Opportunity (International Securities)	No benchmark
QIC International Shares	High capital growth in the long term

Source: Websites of the individual funds.

APPENDIX A7.2: AUSTRALIAN STOCK MARKET INDICES

S&P/ASX 200

This is the institutional benchmark index for the Australian market. It was introduced in April 2000 and replaced the All Ordinaries as the primary gauge for the Australian equity market. It serves the dual purpose of being a broad benchmark index while maintaining the liquidity characteristics of narrower indices. Constituents are rebalanced quarterly using the previous six months of market capitalization and liquidity data. The S&P/ASX 200 represented approximately 80 per cent of the total market capitalization of the Australian market in mid-2007 (equal to around $A1.25 trillion). At that time, the largest company had a weight of 9.4 per cent and the top 10 companies accounted for around 41 per cent of market capitalization.

S&P/ASX 300

The S&P/ASX 300 adds 100 small capitalization stocks to the S&P/ASX 200. Constituents are rebalanced half-yearly using the previous six months of market capitalization and liquidity data. The index represented 81 per cent of the Australian market in mid-2007.

S&P/ASX 20

The S&P/ASX 20 index consists of the 20 largest and most liquid stocks in the Australian market. Constituents are rebalanced quarterly using the previous six months of market capitalization and liquidity data. In mid-2007, this index accounted for 46 per cent of the market capitalization of Australian equities listed on the ASX.

S&P/ASX 50

The S&P/ASX 50 represents the Australian component of the S&P Global 1200 index. High liquidity and significant market capitalization are prerequisites for inclusion in this index. Constituents are rebalanced quarterly using the previous six months of market capitalization and liquidity data. In mid-2007, this index represented 63 per cent of the market capitalization of domestic equities listed on the ASX.

S&P/ASX 100

This index comprises large and mid-capitalization stocks. Constituents are rebalanced quarterly using the previous six months of market capitalization and liquidity data. The index represented approximately 74 per cent of the total market capitalization of the Australian market in mid-2007.

S&P/ASX MidCap 50

This index consists of stocks in the S&P/ASX 100, excluding those in the S&P/ASX 50. The index provides a benchmark for large, active managers where the emphasis is on having a portfolio with sufficient liquidity. Constituents are rebalanced quarterly using the previous six months of market capitalization data. In mid-2007 the index represented around 11 per cent of the total capitalization of the Australian market.

All Ordinaries Index

Since the introduction of the S&P/ASX 200 in April 2000, the purpose of the All Ordinaries has been to act as Australia's equity market indicator. The index represents the 500 largest stocks on the ASX. It is rebalanced annually in March on the basis of market capitalization. Liquidity is not considered. In mid-2007, the index comprised 95 per cent of the Australian market. The top 10 companies represented over 40 per cent of market capitalization.

S&P/ASX Small Ordinaries Index

This index consists of stocks included in the S&P/ASX 300 index, but not in the S&P/ASX 100 index. The index provides a benchmark for small capitalization investments. Constituents are rebalanced in March and September using the previous six months of market capitalization and liquidity data. The index represented around 7 per cent of the total market capitalization of the Australian market in mid-2007.

S&P/ASX Industrial and Resources Indices

These indices are calculated for the S&P/ASX 100, 200, 300, Small Ordinaries and MidCap 50 indices. The constituents of the industrials and resources indices are determined by the Global Industry Classification Standard (GICS) assigned to each stock. The GICS system consists of 11 sectors: financials (excluding property trusts), property trusts, materials, consumer discretionary, industrials, consumer staples, telecommunications, energy, health care, utilities and information technology.

There has been considerable change in these weightings over the past 25 years or so as Australia has evolved from a resources-dominated market to one dominated by financials. In 1980 resources represented 62 per cent of the market and financials 7 per cent. By mid-2007, resources represented less than 20 per cent of the market and total financials in excess of 40 per cent.

NOTES

1. These assumptions are: 9 per cent superannuation contributions over 40 years for a worker on average earnings; an inflation rate of 0 per cent per annum; productivity growth of 1 per cent per annum; a benchmark real rate of return of 5 per cent per annum; no taxes; and no administration or investment fees or charges.
2. These performance benchmarks refer to the performance objectives communicated to fund members in the menu of investment choices. They may or may not be exactly the same as the performance benchmarks included in the contracts with individual investment managers.
3. For details, see S&P (2004a, 2004b, 2007).
4. In the benchmarking literature, style is sometimes defined more narrowly to refer to the choice between a growth or value-oriented investment strategy.

PART III

COUNTRY STUDIES

8. Public Sector Pension Governance, Funding and Performance: A Longitudinal Appraisal

Tongxuan (Stella) Yang and Olivia S. Mitchell*

Public pension plans are the mainstay of retirement security for millions of public sector employees around the world. In the United States, these plans have traditionally been of the defined benefit variety, holding around US$3 trillion in assets (Ilkiw 2003) and covering a range of state and local civil servants, teachers and university professors, and uniformed workers (firefighters, police). Although these pensions play a key role in US labour and capital markets, they are experiencing serious funding problems due to their assets standing well below the levels needed to cover the promised benefits. According to Bonafede, Foresti and Dashtara (2007), 80 per cent of the 64 state retirement systems that reported actuarial data for 2006 were underfunded, with the average underfunded plan having an assets-to-liabilities ratio equal to 79 per cent. Of the 108 state retirement systems that reported actuarial data for 2005, 84 per cent were underfunded, with the average underfunded plan having an assets-to-liabilities ratio equal to 82 per cent.[1] A large number of stakeholders stand to lose if public pension funding ratios sink, including retirees, who may suffer benefit cuts, and taxpayers, who may have to pay for the underfinanced benefit claims.[2] Such pension liabilities may also reduce the ability of governments to attract and retain high-quality employees,[3] influence the credit ratings of pension plans and potentially increase the risk premiums for public debt.[4]

Traditionally, US public pension plans have differed from their corporate counterparts in that they are not subject to national regulation shaping funding targets, how they must be managed, what they can invest in and how they report their performance. Rather, each of the states and many localities structure their boards according to local rules, set investment and performance targets independently, and manage their pensions according to local practice. For this reason, there is a rich variety of experience with alternative governance and reporting structures in the public plan arena that can be used to assess the determinants of successful public plan funding.

In this chapter we employ a newly constructed longitudinal dataset on state and local pensions to evaluate how funding status responds to governance structures and investment strategies. We use longitudinal data to describe public pension funding patterns over the last decade and discuss the investment performance of the plans. Next, we construct an empirical model to explore the determinants of public pension investment performance and funding. Our results point out the governance and disclosure factors that are of key interest to policy makers and stakeholders seeking to make public plans more resilient in the international arena.

1. AN OVERVIEW OF PUBLIC SECTOR PENSION PLAN FUNDING AND INVESTMENT PERFORMANCE

Public pension plans in the United States have been surveyed approximately biennially over the last decade by the Public Pension Coordinating Council (PPCC). The resulting data files, known as the PENDAT surveys, capture a wide range of public retirement system practices related to plan administration, membership, benefits, contributions, funding and investments.[5] We summarize key information gleaned from these surveys in Table 8.1, which shows the number of state and local plans reporting over time as well as their asset holdings and liabilities.

The data show, for instance, that the state and local plans surveyed held a median US$1.7 billion in assets in 2000, with reported liabilities of around the same magnitude. The distribution is quite skewed, so mean plan assets and liabilities in the sample are about US$10 billion. Following convention, we define the stock funding ratio as the ratio of assets to the present value of vested funded liabilities; that measure stood at approximately 100 per cent in 2000. This factor is indicative of whether a pension plan's assets are sufficient to collateralize promised benefits in the long run (Mitchell and Smith 1994).[6] In contrast, the flow funding ratio captures the ratio of required to actual annual contributions in a given year; the evidence shows that the PENDAT plans met their annual contribution target in 2000 with a ratio of just over 100 per cent.

Panel A of Table 8.1 shows that reported public pension assets and liabilities grew over time, with assets rising more quickly than liabilities. This produced enhanced funding ratios throughout the 1990s. For instance, stock funding stood at only 86 per cent and flow funding at 90 per cent in 1990, but both measures had risen to around 100 per cent by 2000. These averages conceal substantial diversity; the stock funding ratios in our sample ranged from 0 to 500 per cent.[7] Panel A also indicates that contributions fell slightly during

Table 8.1   United States: Public Plan Assets, Liabilities, Funding and
Contribution Patterns, and Public Plan Investment Performance

	1990	1991	1992	1994	1996	1998	2000
A. Public plan assets, liabilities, funding and contribution patterns (in 2000 dollars)							
Assets (US$ million)							
Mean	1,847	1,759	2,559	3,336	3,836	5,938	10,300
Median	290	139	424	653	498	741	1,726
Liabilities (US$ million)							
Mean	2,420	2,186	3,202	3,946	4,398	6,176	10,000
Median	344	164	450	682	557	761	1,691
Stock funding ratio (%)							
Mean	86.45	89.85	89.58	87.42	89.02	94.00	98.63
Standard deviation	50.44	48.42	44.76	34.34	22.78	22.17	22.64
Flow funding ratio (%)							
Mean	89.50	99.97	95.02	97.88	97.59	99.63	101.42
Standard deviation	32.99	45.36	32.40	18.34	11.05	27.56	28.22
Contribution rate (%)							
Mean	12.88	13.49	13.63	13.93	12.78	11.96	11.84
Standard deviation	9.69	9.58	10.44	10.04	9.88	8.27	10.08
B. Investment performance: real returns							
1-year return (%)							
Mean	2.81	11.02	5.75	-0.59	10.79	13.53	2.44
Standard deviation	4.60	7.76	3.08	3.89	3.74	4.52	5.97
Average 5-year return (%)							
Mean	7.77	6.54	6.84	5.23	8.40	11.28	10.71
Standard deviation	2.53	1.76	1.64	1.17	1.85	2.31	2.42
Sample size (no.)	124	203	144	174	228	190	125

Source: Authors' computations using PENDAT 1990–2000.

the period, in response to good investment performance. Panel B of the table shows public plan investment performance over the decade. During the 1990s, managers obtained positive real single-year returns in all years but one. On the other hand, one-year returns were quite volatile, reaching a high of 13.5 per cent in 1998 and a low of –0.6 per cent in 1994; the cross-sectional standard deviation reached 7.8 per cent in 1991. Naturally, five-year average returns were smoother, ranging from 5.2 to 11.3 per cent, with correspondingly less volatility.

In the following section, we examine funding over time and across plans, and explore how these are linked to investment returns and governance factors.

2. PREVIOUS PUBLIC SECTOR PENSION RESEARCH

Most early studies on public pensions were of a descriptive and cross-sectional nature, so they did not evaluate specific explanations for the outperformance of some public plans.[8] A few analytical works did investigate the determinants of public plan funding outcomes using a single-equation, cross-sectional approach, and a smaller set developed a multi-equation approach to control for possible endogeneity. For our purposes, the outcomes of particular interest in that body of literature are pension funding measures and investment returns; the control variables included attributes such as governance (mainly board composition, management practices and reporting practices) and investment practices (for example, whether the plan had restrictions on specific investment categories). We summarize these studies in Table 8.2.[9]

Most previous studies have used single-equation models to relate outcomes of interest to control variables. For instance, Inman (1985) linked teacher pension funding patterns to environmental variables; he concluded that underfunding was more pronounced in older, more industrialized cities and in poorer rural states. Hsin and Mitchell (1994) also used cross-sectional data to evaluate the determinants of public pension plan funding, including fiscal stress and governance. They concluded that actuarial assumptions (specifically, assumptions about interest rates, wage growth rates and amortization periods) appeared to be set strategically to meet changing fiscal situations. A subsequent analysis by Mitchell and Hsin (1997) again employed cross-sectional data to link both funding and investment performance outcomes to governance variables such as board composition. The authors found that funding was enhanced by the presence of in-house actuaries and by the requirement for pension board members to carry liability insurance. Funding was lower when states were experiencing fiscal stress and when employees were represented on the board.

In another single-equation regression study, Mark (1997) employed panel data for 1972–91 to explore funding practices across states and over time. He concluded that underfunding was a mean-reverting process rather than a random walk. He also reported that stock market returns and fiscal budget surpluses had positive effects on funding, and that more frequent actuarial studies caused underfunding to revert more quickly to equilibrium. However, he did

Table 8.2   *United States: Summary of the Empirical Findings of Previous Research on Public Plan Funding*[a]

	StockFund	FlowFund	ROR
ENDOGENOUS VARIABLES			
StockFund		>0 Sig: Mitchell & Smith (1994)	
FlowFund			
ROR			
EXPLANATORY VARIABLES			
Governance structure			
Board composition			
% active members	<0 Sig: Mitchell & Hsin (1997)[b]	NS: Mitchell & Hsin (1997)	NS: Useem & Mitchell (2000); Mitchell & Hsin (1997); Coronado, Engen & Knight (2003)[b]
% retired members	<0 Sig: Mitchell & Hsin (1997)	NS: Mitchell & Hsin (1997)	<0 Sig: Mitchell & Hsin (1997) NS: Useem & Mitchell (2000)
Management practices			
SpecTax	NS: Mitchell & Hsin (1997)	NS: Mitchell & Hsin (1997)	
Portable	<0 Sig: Mitchell & Hsin (1997)		
AmortPer		NS: Mitchell & Hsin (1997)	
Reporting practices			
Disclose	NS: Mitchell & Hsin (1997)	NS: Mitchell & Hsin (1997)	
IndPerf			NS: Useem & Mitchell (2000); Mitchell & Hsin (1997)
Investment practices			
InState			<0 Sig: Mitchell & Hsin (1997) NS: Munnell & Sunden (2001); Coronado, Engen & Knight (2003)

Table 8.2 (continued)

	StockFund	FlowFund	ROR
InvstIns	>0; Mitchell & Hsin (1997)		
Other controls			
Fiscal stress	<0 Sig: Mitchell & Hsin (1997); Chaney, Copley & Stone (2002);[c] Johnson (1997) NS: Mark (1997)[d]	NS: Mitchell & Hsin (1997)	
Nocarry	<0 Sig: Chaney, Copley & Stone (2002) NS: Mitchell & Hsin (1997); Bohn & Inman (1996)[e]	NS: Bohn & Inman (1996); Mitchell & Hsin (1997) <0 Sig: Mitchell & Smith (1994)	
SP500	>0 Sig: Mark (1997)		

NS = not significant; Sig = significant at least at the 10 per cent level.
a   See Appendix A8.1 for variable definitions.
b   Mitchell and Hsin (1997) use the proportion of board members elected by active and retired members, while we use the proportion of board members who are themselves active or retired plan participants. Useem and Mitchell (2000) and Coronado, Engen and Knight (2003) use the total number of board members elected by members.
c   Chaney, Copley and Stone (2002) use the current year's general fund surplus to measure fiscal distress.
d   Mark (1997) uses plan unfunded liabilities divided by plan income rather than a more conventional stock or flow funding measure.
e   Bohn and Inman (1996) summarize unreported regression results in the text.

not investigate the role of governance. Neither did Chaney, Copley and Stone (2002), who used 1994–95 data in a single-equation study to revisit the relationship between underfunding and fiscal stress as well as the balanced budget restrictions of some states. They concluded that public plan funding was worse when states were experiencing fiscal stress and when states had mandatory balanced budget requirements. Coronado, Engen and Knight (2003) explored whether the conflicts of interest inherent in public pension plans hurt their investment performance. Employing cross-sectional PENDAT data for 2000, they found some evidence that economically targeted investments and country/industry restrictions were associated with lower investment returns, and that public plans achieved significantly lower rates of return than private plans.

Only three previous studies have used multiple-equation models to evaluate public plan funding and investment behaviour, allowing for the possibility that plan funding may be endogenously determined with other plan characteristics. The earliest of these studies, by Inman (1982), was not concerned with funding *per se*; rather, the author investigated whether public pension funding affected public employee earnings and labour supply, and also whether taxpayers might flee a locality to avoid being taxed to cover unfunded public pension liabilities. He used data for 60 large US police and firefighter plans in 1970–73 to estimate a three-equation model determining public employee wages, employment levels and pensions. The analysis concluded that higher wages could offset pension underfunding and that taxpayer migration to avoid public plan underfunding might occur. A later analysis (Johnson 1997) explored the question of why pension plans in the public sector are more generous than those in the private sector, using a two-equation recursive model. The author showed that the relative generosity of a public pension plan was related to the ability to underfund the plan, which in turn was constrained by outmigration. The third previous multi-equation study, by Mitchell and Smith (1994), analysed the interactions between required pension contributions, actual contributions and public sector wage levels. It used cross-sectional data from the late 1980s to show that pension funding practices tend to be perpetuated over time, and that underfunding grows in times of fiscal pressure.

To summarize, then, the majority of previous public pension studies did not focus on the interaction between funding and investment performance. Those that did tended to confirm, using single-equation models, that public plan funding and investment performance were influenced by governance and investment practice. They did not take into account the possibility that plan funding and investment performance may be determined endogenously, or that funding results in one year may be related to lagged funding measures. In the next section, we explore both possibilities using a new panel dataset from PENDAT.

3. EMPIRICAL METHODOLOGY

We build on past research on public plans in two ways. First, our focus is on public plan funding and investment performance, using a decade of data on US public pension plans. With the exception of Mitchell and Smith (1994), previous authors have not examined the extent to which funding status persists over time for public plans and what leads to this outcome.[10] In the present study, therefore, we investigate in more detail the links between past and current funding ratios. Second, our particular interest is in examining the links between plan funding and governance structure, taking into account investment performance. Our panel dataset offers an insight into behaviour through time, enriching findings from the predominately cross-sectional studies in the literature.

The econometric model posits that three dependent variables are of most interest: a plan's stock funding ratio, its flow funding ratio and its investment performance. The key relationships between the variables are as follows. At time t, usually in mid-year, a public pension plan asks in-house or outside actuaries to conduct an actuarial evaluation on plan assets (A) and liabilities (L). From these data, both the stock funding ratio (A/L) in year t and the required contribution (RC) for year $t+1$ are calculated. Then, between time t and $t+1$, the plan sponsor must make actual contributions (AC) according to its policy. At the end of year $t+1$, the flow funding ratio (AC/RC) for that year can be calculated from the actual and required contributions.

We hypothesize that investment performance in year t (ROR_t) has a positive effect on a public pension plan's stock funding ratio in year t ($StockFund_t$), and this in turn will affect its flow funding ratio in year $t+1$ ($FlowFund_{t+1}$). The specific empirical framework we estimate with the PENDAT information may be stipulated as follows:

$$StockFund_t = \alpha_0 + \alpha_1 ROR_t + \alpha_2 StockFund_{t-1} + \alpha_3 Composition_t$$
$$+ \alpha_4 Management_t + \alpha_5 Reporting_t + \alpha_6 X_t + e_1 \qquad (1)$$

$$FlowFund_{t+1} = \beta_0 + \beta_1 StockFund_t + \beta_2 ROR_t + \beta_3 Composition_t$$
$$+ \beta_4 Management_t + \beta_5 Reporting_t + \beta_6 X_t + e_2 \qquad (2)$$

$$ROR_t = \gamma_0 + \gamma_1 StockFund_{t-1} + \gamma_2 Composition_t + \gamma_3 Management_t$$
$$+ \gamma_4 Reporting_t + \gamma_5 Investment_t + \gamma_6 X_t + e_3 \qquad (3)$$

We also hypothesize that the dependent variables are influenced by three types of factors: lagged dependent variables, factors representing plan governance and indicators of plan investment practices. Specifically, $Composition_t$, $Management_t$, $Reporting_t$ and $Investment_t$ respectively reflect pension board composition, management practice, reporting practice and investment practice; the X_t vector refers to other control variables.

The pension liability measures used here involve the actuarial accrued liability (AAL) concept, which differs from other liability measures used in past public pension studies.[11] Of course, the choice of the discount rate used to compute liabilities plays an important role in funding models.[12] In the PENDAT files, the nominal discount rates reported range from 4.5 to 11.2 per cent, with the real discount rate ranging from –0.22 to 7.67 per cent. We follow Winkelvoss (1993) in adjusting liabilities to a common economic discount rate.[13] Required contributions are adjusted using the same approach. Since we postulate that the stock funding ratio affects future flow funding ratios, the model is recursive and may be estimated using pooled OLS with robust standard errors.[14]

Endogenous Dependent Variables

As noted above, the stock funding ratio represents the ratio of plan assets to plan liabilities. It reflects the accumulated effects of plan contributions plus investment performance on plan assets, as well as changes in plan liabilities. In the corporate sector, federal regulations require plan sponsors to maintain full funding and to boost contributions if the stock funding ratio goes below a certain level. No such regulation is nationally mandated in the public sector; therefore, state and local governments have less incentive to fully fund their public sector pension plans. Also, in most cases public sector pension plans are able to amortize their unfunded pension liabilities over future years. Hence, we hypothesize that the stock funding ratio in year *t* will be positively correlated with a plan's past stock funding ratio, which we capture through the use of a lagged dependent variable.

In addition, when modelling stock funding patterns, we must recognize the role of investment returns in influencing plan funding levels. State and local governments have historically tended to prohibit managers from investing in what were perceived to be 'risky' assets, including equity, venture capital and foreign holdings. In the early 1990s, for instance, public plans were still found to hold more conservative assets than private plans, and hence earned returns below the market indices (Mitchell and Hsin 1997). But as the PENDAT data files reveal, during the 1990s public plans gradually increased their equity holdings, from around 35 per cent in 1990 to 55 per cent in 2000. Naturally, holding more equities means that the plans are subject to more volatile investment returns, making public pension plan funding levels more sensitive to investment returns today than they were decades ago. Nevertheless, previous studies on public sector pension plan funding have stressed the willingness and capacity of state and local governments to make enough contributions, while neglecting the increasingly important role played by plan investment performance (Epple and Schipper 1981; Mitchell and Smith 1994; Chaney, Copley and Stone 2002). Our empirical model allows investment returns to be determinative of pension funding status, in the expectation that this relationship will be positive.

The second dependent variable of interest is the flow funding ratio, which reflects how well a plan meets its annual contribution requirements as determined by plan actuaries. One would anticipate a positive link between flow and stock funding if a government jurisdiction had a persistent political climate or 'culture'; in such cases one might expect 'behavioural persistence' with respect to funding, with a positive and possibly unitary relationship between flow and stock funding measures. An alternative hypothesis would be that state and local governments seek to balance actual and required contributions, but not necessarily over a period as short as one year. In such cases, the long-term relationship between stock and flow funding would reflect 'mean reversion'; that is, a period of flow underfunding would be followed by one of overfunding. Mitchell and Smith (1994) sought to differentiate between these hypotheses using cross-sectional data for 42 plans in 1989. They concluded that behavioural persistence dominates, that is, that there is a positive relationship between stock and flow funding. We also test this hypothesis using our larger and longitudinal dataset.

The third dependent variable of interest is a plan's investment performance, measured here by rates of return on pension investments. Clearly high investment returns are preferred, other things being equal, since they enable plans to maintain funding while avoiding the need for extra contributions. In addition, we are aware that past funding behaviour may also affect a pension plan's investment strategy. For one thing, a well-funded pension plan may be better able to bear investment risk than a poorly funded plan, since the stronger plan has more of a buffer to withstand a bear market. From this logic, one might expect a positive link between a plan's lagged funding ratio and its current investment return. Alternatively, an underfunded pension plan might invest in a riskier portfolio, in the hope of improving its asset base. In this latter case, we would expect lagged stock funding to be inversely related to current investment returns. Below, we explore which prediction is supported empirically.

Explanatory Variables

Because public plans are responsible for so many participants and such a large pool of investment funds, analysts have recently become interested in how they are governed. Governance refers to:

> the systems and processes by which a company or government manages its affairs
> with the objective of maximizing the welfare of and resolving the conflicts of interest among its stakeholders (Carmichael and Palacios 2003: 7).

In practice, state and local retirement systems are run by a retirement board that has authority over investments, actuarial valuations, system operations and often plan benefits as well. Day-to-day administration is usually managed by the retirement system's staff (Mitchell et al. 2000). In the United States, public plans exhibit great diversity in their governance structures: some have employee representatives on the board while others have only appointed board members; some are subject to annual reporting requirements while others are not; and some are subject to statutory investment restrictions while others have more freedom. In our empirical models, we measure plan governance along three dimensions: board composition, management practices and reporting practices.

Board composition is proxied by the percentage of employees on public pension boards, which previous analysis has suggested may reduce stock funding and investment performance (Mitchell and Hsin 1997). Here we disaggregate further to ask whether having active versus retired members on the board has a differential impact. Most likely, plan participants will be more concerned with benefits, and push for better funding, than politically affiliated members such as appointed and *ex officio* representatives. On the other hand, Mitchell (1988) suggests that board members who are not financially expert (such as ordinary employees) may find it difficult to monitor plan performance, in which case having a greater number of active or retired members on the board may result in lower funding. Which effect dominates is an empirical matter to be explored. The composition of the board may also influence investment performance. Previous studies have obtained mixed results on this point, with Useem and Mitchell (2000) discerning no statistically significant effect in cross-sectional data but Mitchell and Hsin (1997) finding that retiree board members had a negative effect on returns. We hypothesize that having more plan participants on the board will lead to lower returns, due to their more conservative approach to investment.[15]

To evaluate management practices in public pension plans, we control on expense ratios, defined as the sum of administrative and investment costs over total plan assets; these would be expected to have a negative effect on stock funding. Some 43 per cent of plans in the sample have reciprocal agreements with other retirement systems, permitting the transfer of service credits earned elsewhere. Such portability would be anticipated to have a negative influence on public plan stock funding, as indicated by Mitchell and Hsin (1997). Another factor that distinguishes plans is where the funds come from to cover contributions; for a quarter of our sample, states or cities have dedicated taxes to cover plan contributions. It is possible that this approach enhances funding, since the plan enjoys a stable income source rather than being influenced by variable state or local government revenues. In this case, having a special tax may be positively tied to better funding. On the other hand, a state or local government may fail to fill a contribution gap if it depends on a dedicated income stream to meet its contribution requirements. Our analysis investigates empirically the links between special taxes and plan funding ratios. Additionally, in many public pension plans, the board of trustees influences the actuarial assumptions used to set plan funding levels. One key factor is the amortization period for past service liabilities; having a longer amortization period reduces the level of required contributions, thus making it easier for employers to meet their annual contribution requirements. We hypothesize a positive link between the assumed amortization period and flow funding levels.

States and localities have developed several approaches to solving the principal–agent problem arising from the fact that a plan's board of trustees acts as the agent for the principals, who are taxpayers and plan participants. One concern mentioned by Hess and Impavido (2003) is that trustees may act in their own self-interest or simply shirk their duties. Another is that public sector trustees may seek to use fund assets to further the social or political goals of the party in power. Clearly it is critical to monitor plan trustees effectively and efficiently; this is likely to be facilitated if pension plans provide annual reports containing financial, actuarial, statistical and investment information. For this reason, we hypothesize that annual reporting practices should positively influence both funding ratios and investment performance. We also find it useful to consider whether trustees are covered by liability insurance, since private insurers may monitor plan investment behaviour in lieu of effective oversight and reporting. Nevertheless, we acknowledge that having liability insurance may increase the possibility of moral hazard if trustees feel they can invest less prudently because they are covered. Which effect dominates empirically is explored below.

Reporting practices can be very important to pension plan investment outcomes. This is evident in cases where plans engage independent entities to evaluate their investment performance. The argument is that, when done well, independent performance evaluation improves investment performance by introducing best-practice management techniques. Additionally, outside evaluation may boost information flows to taxpayers and plan participants, enabling them to better monitor board behaviour. While independent performance evaluations are expected to enhance pension investment returns, previous literature provides little hard evidence to support this supposition: neither Mitchell and Hsin (1997) nor Useem and Mitchell (2000) found a link between performance reviews and pension plan investment returns. We revisit these findings using our decade-long sample of pension plan performance and structure.

We also take note of the critical role of investment practices in influencing pension plan outcomes. One aspect of note is socially targeted investments, where social development targets are included in a plan's investment strategy alongside its risk and return policies. Such investments can be expected to have a negative effect on plan investment performance if they reduce the level of portfolio diversification. Some previous studies have reported a negative link between in-state investment and one-year investment returns (Mitchell and Hsin 1997), although others argue that such policies do not hurt investment performance (Munnell and Sunden 2001). Coronado, Engen and Knight (2003) found some evidence that in-state investment and country/industry restrictions have a negative effect on public sector plan investment performance, although the results are relatively weak. In our study, we hypothesize that the higher the fraction of plan assets directed in-state, the lower will be the plan's investment returns. Because markets rose substantially during the 1990s, the regressions also control on both stock market performance (proxied by S&P 500 returns) and plan asset allocation (proxied by the proportion of assets invested in stocks and international assets) to measure accurately how plan governance influences investment performance.

In addition to the variables described above, we control on several other factors, following previous studies. For instance, facing a budget shortfall may produce fiscal distress, and this in turn may translate into lower pension plan contributions.[16] Three studies have proxied fiscal distress by measuring the deviation between a state's recent unemployment rate and its long-term average (Mitchell and Smith 1994; Mitchell and Hsin 1997; Johnson 1997); their results show that above average unemployment is associated with lower public pension funding. Using a different measure of stress, Chaney, Copley and Stone (2002) found that state budget deficits reduce pension funding outcomes. Below, we predict that fiscal distress will negatively affect funding ratios. This may be aggravated if a state has a balanced budget requirement, as Mitchell and Hsin (1997) and Chaney, Copley and Stone (2002) found. That is, the funding status of a state pension plan may be inversely related to the existence of a balanced budget requirement, because such a requirement tends to enhance borrowing from trust funds (USGAO 1985). We also examine the balanced budget requirements of states and, because scale economies are important in the public pension system, pension plan size (Mitchell and Andrews 1981).

4. EMPIRICAL RESULTS

Most of the variables we use are drawn directly from the PENDAT survey files, which report public retirement system and plan practices related to administration, membership, benefits, contributions, funding and investments. An additional three variables are derived from outside sources: fiscal stress, budget carry-over practice and stock market returns. The deviation of the local unemployment rate from the long-term average (Unempd) measures fiscal distress. An indicator for states that are not permitted to carry over budget surpluses across years (Nocarry) is used to measure budget carry-over practice. The aggregate S&P 500 level (SP500) is used as a proxy for stock market performance.[17] Table 8.3 presents our main empirical results, pooling data on all available plans over the period 1990–2000.[18] Column 1 focuses on the stock funding ratio, where we see that higher investment returns are positively related to stock funding outcomes. Specifically, if investment returns rise by 1 percentage point, stock funding rises by 0.42 percentage points. This positive and large association explains why public plan funding in the 1990s was so

Table 8.3   *United States: Determinants of Public Pension Plan Funding*
Status and Investment Performance (pooled OLS with robust
standard errors)[a]

	StockFund	FlowFund	ROR
DEPENDENT VARIABLES			
StockFund		? 0.45** (0.15)	
FlowFund			
ROR	+ 0.42** (0.12)	+ 0.01 (0.27)	
EXPLANATORY VARIABLES			
Lagged dependent variable			
StockFund	+ 0.76** (0.05)		? −0.01 (0.01)
Governance structure			
Board composition			
Active	? −0.06** (0.03)	? 0.02 (0.05)	? −0.002 (0.01)
Retired	? −0.16** (0.06)	? −0.21* (0.13)	? −0.03* (0.02)
Management practices			
Spectax	? −4.17** (1.23)	? −7.60** (3.96)	
TotalCost	− −1.17 (1.88)		
Portable	− 1.98 (1.17)		
AmortPer		+ 0.37** (0.17)	
Reporting practices			
Disclose	+ 0.79 (2.41)	+ 3.95 (4.87)	+ 2.13** (1.08)
IndPerf			+ 0.14 (0.60)
Investment practices			
InvstIns			? −0.56 (0.41)
InState			− −0.89 (0.76)
Stock			+ 0.08** (0.02)
Intl			+ −0.07** (0.03)

Table 8.3 (continued)

	StockFund	FlowFund	ROR
Control variables			
Unempd	− −0.02	− −0.71	
	(0.21)	(0.44)	
Nocarry	− −1.85	− −4.45	
	(1.85)	(4.40)	
SP500			+ 0.42**
			(0.02)
lnAssets	+ 0.12	+ 0.24	+ 0.17*
	(0.32)	(0.77)	(0.09)
Number of plans	566	566	566
R^2	0.72	0.16	0.54

** = significant at the 5 per cent level; * = significant at the 10 per cent level.
a   Standard errors are in parentheses; hypothesized signs are at the left of the column results. See Appendix A8.1 for variable definitions.

Source: Authors' computations using PENDAT 1990–2000.

strong, but it also helps explain why public plan funding rates declined when the market turned down in 2000.

We also find that stock funding patterns are positively correlated over time, confirming the behavioural persistence hypothesis. This is partly due to the fact that there is no uniform public plan funding regulation, as there is for private pension plans under the Employee Retirement Income Security Act (ERISA). Nevertheless, stock funding ratios across years are not perfectly correlated, so that a 1 percentage point increase in stock funding in one year is associated with a 0.76 percentage point increase in funding in the following year. In other words, on average, public plans do make an effort to fill an underfunding gap over time, though not fully from one year to the next.

Governance variables such as board composition are also found to play an important role in determining plan funding status. The results suggest that, other things being equal, a greater number of plan participants on the board, whether retired or active, is associated with lower levels of public plan stock funding. The coefficients are strong and negative: the point estimates indicate that adding one more active plan member to a board decreases stock funding by 0.7 percentage points, while adding one more retired member decreases stock funding by 1.7 percentage points. These findings are consistent with the magnitudes reported by Mitchell and Hsin (1997).

Management practices are also influential; having a dedicated tax for contributions appears to reduce, rather than enhance, funding. This may be because state and local governments assume that such taxes will cover contributions, so that they do not need to fill gaps as they arise. In contrast, Mitchell and Hsin (1997) found that funding did not respond to having a dedicated tax; however, their data were cross-sectional and did not control on lagged dependent variables. We find no evidence that fiscal distress due to unusually high unemployment rates prompts public employers to underfund their pension promises. This result is consistent with Mark (1997), which also finds no direct link, but not with Mitchell and Hsin (1997), Johnson (1997) or Chaney, Copley and Stone (2002), which all report a negative link between government fiscal distress and pension underfunding. Moreover, the data reveal no significant effect of budget non-carry-over requirements on stock funding, consistent with Bohn and Inman (1996) and Mitchell and Hsin (1997). Our results are in contrast to those of Chaney, Copley and Stone (2002), whose research is cross-sectional and does not control on the endogenous effect of investment performance and governance practice as ours does.

Column 2 explores the determinants of flow funding, where we see a positive association between current flow funding and past stock funding patterns. Nevertheless, this relationship is not one to one; when the stock funding ratio increases by 1 percentage point, the flow funding ratio rises only by about half a percentage point. Hence, like Mitchell and Hsin (1997), we find that the behavioural persistence hypothesis cannot be rejected; the point estimates suggest that this persistence is attenuated by mean reversion effects. Since there is no additional tie between investment performance and flow funding, we conclude that flow funding responds to stock funding rather than current investment performance. It is interesting that having more retirees on the board is associated with lower flow funding patterns, but having more active participants is not statistically significant. Once again, having a special tax dedicated to contributions reduces flow funding, as was the case for stock funding. While many of the other control variables are not statistically significant (fiscal stress, plan size and budget carry-over policy), we do find that plans reporting a longer amortization period are more likely to report higher flow funding, as is consistent with our earlier discussion.

Column 3 focuses on the determinants of investment performance. Here we see that the lagged funding ratio is not statistically significant, if the portfolio mix and other factors are held constant. On the other hand, the composition of the pension board does have an effect on pension investment performance. Specifically, yields are significantly lower when retiree representation increases, confirming the findings of Mitchell and Hsin (1997). This could be due to the lack of expertise in investment decision making of retired participants. We also find that pension reporting practices have a potent effect on investment returns. For instance, having an annual report is positively and significantly associated with investment returns, and the effect is large; annual returns are

Table 8.4   United States: Estimated Responsiveness of Key Explanatory Variables (percentage points)

	Stock Funding Ratio	Flow Funding Ratio	One-year Investment Return
Capital market and performance factors			
30 percentage point fall in S&P 500 index			−12.0
20 percentage point fall in one-year plan investment return	−8.0		
24 percentage point fall in plan stock funding ratio		−11.0	
Governance factors			
One more active board member	−0.7		
One more retired board member	−1.7	−2.3	−0.4
Annual report issued			+2.1

Source: Authors' computations using PENDAT 1990–2000.

2.1 percentage points higher for plans that provide annual reports containing financial, actuarial, statistical and investment information. This may be due to the mitigation of information asymmetry, which helps stakeholders monitor trustees more effectively.

Our study also confirms that some pension investment practices are influential in plan performance. There is a negative link between economically targeted investments (where assets must be directed in-state) and plan investment returns, but statistically the effect is not significantly different from zero. This result is consistent with analysis by Munnell and Sunden (2001) but not with earlier analysis by Mitchell and Hsin (1997). A greater concentration of the portfolio in stocks (international equity) had a positive (negative) association with pension investment returns, holding market performance constant (proxied by S&P 500 returns). A rise in the S&P 500 of 1 percentage point was associated with a 0.42 percentage point increase in public pension annual investment returns.

Table 8.4 summarizes our main empirical results, focusing only on statistically significant and interesting relationships in the context of economic conditions around 2000–02. All estimates hold other factors constant at their mean values. One provocative finding is that a 30 per cent drop in the S&P 500 index, as was experienced during 2000–02, would be predicted to cut public pension investment returns by 12 percentage points. Given that the real annual return over the previous decade averaged less than 8 percentage points, this is a substantial impact. A large drop in investment returns would also depress stock funding: a 20 percentage point fall in one-year returns would cut the stock funding ratio by 8 percentage points. Turning to the stock funding ratio, Nesbitt (2003) reported a 24 percentage point drop between 2000 and 2002; according to our model, this would decrease the flow funding ratio by 11 percentage points. Governance changes could also have an important effect. For example, adding one more active plan member to a board would be predicted to lower a plan's stock funding ratio by 0.7 percentage points. Adding a retired member would decrease the stock funding ratio by 1.7 percentage points, reduce flow funding by 2.3 percentage points and cut annual investment returns by 0.4 percentage points. Finally, holding all else equal, issuing an annual report with financial, actuarial, statistical and investment information would boost a plan's annual investment returns by 2.1 percentage points.[19]

6. DISCUSSION AND CONCLUSIONS

Previous studies of the performance of public sector employee pension plans did not take into account the possibility that pension funding and investment performance may be endogenously determined, and that funding patterns may be linked over time. This study has explored both possibilities, and examined the links between plan funding and governance structure, taking into account investment performance. Our longitudinal dataset offers a view of behaviour across years, enriching findings from what until now have been mainly cross-sectional analyses.

The results suggest that investment performance positively influences stock funding ratios in public sector pension plans, and stock funding ratios in turn positively affect flow funding ratios. In addition, plan funding status tends to be positively correlated over time, confirming that there is persistence in pension managers' behaviour. Like previous researchers, we find that public plan governance has an important impact on plan investment performance and funding status. Having more retired employees on the board depresses investment performance, stock funding and flow funding, while having more active employees on the board depresses stock funding. We confirm that having a dedicated tax to cover plan contributions does not enhance funding. Investment practices have a major impact on plan investment performance, as does plan transparency. A plan that reports its financial, actuarial, statistical and investment information is more likely to have higher investment returns.

To make public plans more resilient to adverse financial shocks such as those that occurred in 2000–02, plan governance structures should be enhanced to boost investment performance and funding status. One way of doing this would be to increase the number of experts on the board; another might be to provide better training for board representatives, especially if they are active or retired employees.

There is reason to believe that these findings are also relevant for pension plans in the corporate pension sector. For instance, corporate accounting standards have come under heavy scrutiny of late (Fore 2005), partly as a result of the extraordinary drops in funding of private sector defined benefit plans, driven by some of the same phenomena as were apparent in the public sector. In fact, the abrupt global downturn in the funding levels of defined benefit plans is raising questions about whether pension plan reporting and transparency in all sectors should be required to conform to new and more comprehensive international standards. Recent experience with public pensions does suggest that greater transparency would enhance both funding and investment results. Pension stakeholders of all stripes could be expected to benefit from more detailed and timely financial, actuarial, statistical and investment information. What the costs of such additional transparency might be is a topic for future research.

NOTES

* Funding for this research was provided by the Pension Research Council and the Boettner Center for Pensions and Retirement Research, both at the Wharton School of the University of Pennsylvania, and by a Bradley Foundation Fellowship for Tongxuan (Stella) Yang. We thank Chris Allen, Nick Greifer, Robert Inman, Karl Johnson, Marie-Eve Lachance, Steven Nesbitt, John Piggott and Perry Young for their helpful assistance and suggestions. Opinions and any errors remain the authors' responsibility.
1. The severe underfunding of state pension systems has attracted media interest. See, for instance, Edwards and Gokhale (2006), Turque (2006) and Walsh (2006).
2. For example, the State Teachers' Retirement System for Ohio's public school teachers and administrators required retired teachers who had taught for less than 15 years to pay their full health care premiums. In addition, retirees were unable to salvage the subsidies that had traditionally been paid to teachers' spouses and dependents (Warsmith 2003).
3. Past research has shown that public employees require compensating wage differentials in times of more severe underfunding, which in turn drives salary pressure (Inman 1982; Mitchell and Smith 1994).
4. Young (2003) notes that inadequately funded pension plans can drag down sponsor credit quality.
5. The PENDAT surveys are quite reflective of the national public plan universe. In fiscal year 2000, they represented approximately 58 per cent of all public retirement plans, 67 per cent of active plan participants and 68 per cent of all state and local retirement system assets (PPCC 2002). Data available in machine-readable format cover the years 1990, 1991, 1992, 1994, 1996, 1998 and 2000.
6. Governmental Accounting Standards Board Statement (GASB) No. 27 requires public pension plans to report actuarial accrued liabilities (AAL), with a cost method selected from a menu (for example, entry age normal, projected unit credit, frozen entry age normal, attained age, frozen attained age, aggregate and so on). On average, 47 per cent of the public plans

examined here used the entry age normal cost method and 15 per cent the projected unit credit method; the rest used other methods.

7. The analysis omits six PENDAT observations with stock or flow funding ratios greater than 500 per cent; detailed evaluation of these cases suggests that such high funding ratios represent input error.

8. See, for instance, Bahl and Jump (1974), Testin (1984, 1986), Taylor (1986), Testin and Snell (1989) and Turner and Beller (1989). Dulebohn (1995), who evaluated 205 plans in 1988 and 1992, concluded that public plans had improved their funding status over time. More recent descriptive studies include Mitchell et al. (2000).

9. Here we focus only on empirical studies of public pension plan funding; the theoretical studies include Mumy (1978), Epple and Schipper (1981) and D'Arcy, Dulebohn and Oh (1999).

10. Mitchell and Smith (1994) evaluated the influence of stock funding ratios on flow funding ratios using only a single survey year (1989). They found a positive, strong relationship between the two ratios, supporting the hypothesis of behavioural persistence.

11. Before 1996, GASB No. 5 required public plans to report both the AAL and the projected benefit obligation (PBO), where the latter is a standardized measure calculated using projected benefit methods. From 1997 on, GASB Statement No. 27 required plans to report the AAL only. Mitchell and Hsin (1997) used the PBO for PENDAT information before 1996. We obtained similar results from both methods for the period 1990–96.

12. For instance, Winkelvoss (1993) concluded that a 1 per cent increase in the discount rate reduced the AAL by 16 per cent; a similar point was made by the US General Accounting Office (USGAO 1993).

13. Following Winkelvoss (1993), pension actuarial liabilities as well as normal costs are measured using the AAL method altered by 4 per cent for each 0.25 per cent change in the interest rate. To adjust liabilities to a common discount rate, we first calculate $q =$ (reported discount rate – standard discount rate)/0.25, where the standard discount rate is the mean discount rate for each year in our sample, and then multiply the reported AAL by 1.04^q. Hence, if the plan's reported discount rate is larger than the standard discount rate, the adjusted AAL will be larger than the reported one, and vice versa. In unreported regressions, we also estimate two alternative models: one without adjusting the discount rate, and the other with the discount rate decided simultaneously with the stock funding ratio. The estimated coefficients are similar in sign and significance to those reported here.

14. It is also possible that the flow funding ratio influences stock funding ratios; that is, stock funding may be larger when flow funding ratios are higher. We experimented with this question by including lagged flow funding ratios in the stock funding regressions, but the coefficients were not statistically significant. In results not reported in detail here, we also re-estimated the model using 3SLS and 2SLS. The coefficients were similar in sign and magnitude to those reported here, so in this study we simply present the pooled OLS results. As there were lagged variables in the equations, we tested the serial correlation in the error terms after doing a pooled OLS regression on the panel data, as Wooldridge (2002) recommends. Since the error was a first-order auto-regressive process, we used a robust variance matrix estimator.

15. The educational level of board members may be positively related to their financial sophistication, but PENDAT contains no direct information on this point. We tested the hypothesis that boards representing teachers are more financially sophisticated than other boards by interacting board composition with a teacher plan variable; however, the interactions were generally not statistically significant.

16. For instance, North Carolina's governor suspended contributions to the state retirement system when faced with an impending budget shortfall in 2001 (Chaney, Copley and Stone 2002).

17. Unemployment rates are drawn from the Bureau of Labor Statistics website at <www.bls.gov>. Indicators of budget carry-over practice are taken from Bohn and Inman (1996). Annual S&P 500 returns are derived from indices compiled by the Center for Research in Securities Prices (CRSP).

18. The conclusions are similar if we limit the analysis to those plans included in all years.

19. It is possible that there is some reverse causality here, with only well-managed funds that also perform better issuing reports. However, since 96 per cent of funds do issue reports, such self-censoring is likely to be relatively unimportant.

APPENDIX A8.1: DESCRIPTIVE STATISTICS AND VARIABLE DEFINITIONS

		Mean	Standard Deviation
DEPENDENT VARIABLES			
StockFund	Stock funding ratio (%)	88.07	26.42
FlowFund	Flow funding ratio (%)	97.96	31.69
ROR	Annual investment return (%)	7.90	6.93
EXPLANATORY VARIABLES			
Lags			
StockFund	Lag of stock funding ratio (%)	84.77	29.09
Governance structure			
Board composition			
Active	% of active members	51.92	24.08
Retired	% of retired members	11.49	11.54
Management practices			
Spectax	Dedicated tax (0/1)	0.25	0.43
TotalCost	(Administration + investment costs)/plan assets (%)	0.48	0.61
Portable	Employees may switch plans and take accruals (0/1)	0.44	0.50
AmortPer	Amortization period for past service liabilities (no.)	22.19	12.64
Reporting practices			
Disclose	Annual report containing financial, actuarial, statistical and investment information (0/1)	0.96	0.20
IndPerf	Independent investment performance evaluation (0/1)	0.86	0.35
Investment practices			
InvstIns	Investment decision makers covered by liability insurance (0/1)	0.49	0.50
InState	% of pension investment directed in-state	0.08	0.27
Stock	% of assets invested in stocks	49.75	14.96
Intl	% of assets invested in international equities and bonds	8.21	8.25
Control variables			
Unempd	Current unemployment rate – average past decade's unemployment rate (%)	1.14	2.80
Nocarry	State law disallows carry-over of state budget deficit (0/1)	0.77	0.42
SP500	S&P 500 return (%)	14.57	11.71
lnAssets	Natural log of plan assets (US$)	12.98	2.40
Number of observations: 566			

Source: Authors' computations using PENDAT 1990–2000.

9. How Do Australian Superannuation Fund Trustees Perceive Their Role and Effectiveness?

Vrinda Gupta, Henry Jin, Michael Orszag and John Piggott*

1. INTRODUCTION

The collapse of WorldCom and Enron highlighted several failings of US corporate governance. Subsequent scrutiny has revealed that while some of the circumstances surrounding the collapses were specific to the companies themselves, systemic failures of corporate governance also played a part. Excessive executive pay and deficiencies in the settlement of mutual fund charges are just two examples of systemic failures that have come to the forefront recently. Governance failures are also apparent globally, with examples ranging from the failure of Equitable Life in the United Kingdom to the collapse of Parmalat in Italy.

Pension funds deliver a significant component of retirement income in many countries, but their governance has attracted much less attention than the governance of corporations. In many cases, decision making in pension funds is in the hands of a relatively small number of individuals who are subject to relatively little oversight. While regulation is quite stringent in some countries, in others it is often inconsistent or nonexistent. Clark (2000) reviews private pension fund governance in detail in an international context.

Analyses of public pension funds find underperformance relative to benchmarks. Governance, especially with respect to portfolio management, has significant implications for the investment performance of funds, and deserves attention for this reason alone. Iglesias and Palacios (2000) find that public pension funds in countries with poor governance structures significantly underperform the wider market. Mitchell and Hsin (1999) find that, in general, the poor investment performance of US state pension funds is due to their inadequate governance structures. There is thus ample evidence to suggest that in the public sector, pension investments underperform at least in part because of weak governance. Weak governance and poor performance are by no means universal in the public sector, however. For example, the US Federal Thrift Savings Plan is a clear example of a public sector entity with a strong governance structure which has performed well relative to its peers.

In a private setting, the most significant issue seems to be how decision makers make their investment decisions. These individuals do not exhibit high degrees of financial literacy and their investment behaviour tends to gravitate towards default options (Choi et al. 2001; Iyengar and Jiang 2003). If the trust structures for corporate pension fund governance rely on individuals who are not required to have high levels of expertise, then there is clearly a need for more oversight of pension fund decision making.

In 2000, the British Treasury commissioned Paul Myners to conduct a review of institutional investment in the United Kingdom (HM Treasury 2001). Myners focused in particular on pension fund investment governance. At the time, there was concern that pension fund trustees were excessively conservative and unwilling to consider investments (such as private equity) deemed necessary to develop British industry. The review found that although UK trustees in aggregate were managing assets worth over £600 billion on behalf of members, most had received only a few days of investment training. This is of concern, because there are complex factors involved in overseeing defined benefit pension fund assets, ranging from the interpretation of powers in the trust deed to careful attention to the risk profile of the sponsor. Slow decision making, especially in asset allocation, can be a problem, as can conflict-of-interest issues arising from the lack of separation of some trustee boards from their corporate parents.

The situation is somewhat simpler for trustees in Australia in that most funds are defined contribution funds. This means that there is less need to worry about the strength of the sponsoring company or to understand in detail the implicit options embedded in trust deeds and covenants. Defined contribution funds also offer less scope for discretionary adjustments to redistribute benefits across generations. Nevertheless, in any setting with directed investment decision making, there is still an important burden in selecting investments on behalf of members. And, as Bateman and Mitchell (2004) show, the range of defined contribution funds in Australia in terms of costs and structures is quite broad, thereby complicating analysis.

This chapter reviews the results of a survey of pension fund governance in Australia conducted by the authors in 2004–05. It is a modification of a 2001 survey of 106 large British pension funds developed by Professor A. Kakabadse of the Cranfield School of Management in conjunction with Watson Wyatt.[1] The British survey confirmed many of the key findings of the Myners review, including the lack of specific expertise of many pension fund trustees.

On the whole trustees did not view this as an impediment, however, because they saw themselves not as technical experts but as a body *to select* technical experts. Most trustees had held their positions for some time, felt that the board of trustees functioned cohesively as a group and found their work enjoyable and rewarding.

We begin in section 2 by discussing the main features of the Australian survey and summarizing the results on trustee demographics. Section 3 reviews the expertise of trustees and section 4 examines their beliefs, attitudes and working relationships. Section 5 focuses specifically on trustee decision making and section 6 discusses issues for the future. Our conclusions are presented in section 7.

2. SURVEY INSTRUMENT AND TRUSTEE DEMOGRAPHICS

Data collection began with a pilot survey administered in May 2004. This involved mailing questionnaires to approximately 1,000 trustees from funds in the Australian Prudential Regulation Authority (APRA) database. Of the surveys mailed out, a substantial number (about 100) were returned because they were incorrectly addressed, and in the end we received only 48 completed surveys. About half of these were from corporate funds, with the remainder split among master trusts, industry funds, public funds and self-managed funds.

The pilot survey was followed by a more structured survey of the top 200 funds in Australia. Conducted in late 2004 and early 2005, it generated responses from 131 trustees at 54 funds (Table 9.1). About 53 per cent of the trustees who responded were from industry funds and 37 per cent from corporate funds. Another 8 per cent were from public sector funds, with other categories occupying negligible proportions. In aggregate, the 54 funds managed about A$103 billion in assets and hence represented about 17 per cent of total funds under management in Australia.

In Australian terminology, corporate funds are superannuation funds established for the benefit of employees of a particular company, group of companies or group of employers. Industry funds are multi-employer superannuation funds. An industry fund may cover a specific industry or a range of industries, either nationally or within a state. The trustees of industry funds are generally appointed by trade unions or employer associations. Public sector funds are superannuation funds (often referred to as 'schemes') that provide benefits for federal, state, territory or local government employees. A master trust allows individual investors to pool their funds so as to obtain wholesale prices and rates unavailable to regular investors. Wholesale arrangements can sometimes be negotiated by employers.

Table 9.1 Australia: Distribution of Funds and Trustees

Fund Type	Distribution of Funds		Distribution of Trustees	
	(no.)	(%)	(no.)	(%)
No answer	1	1.85	1	0.76
Master trust	1	1.85	1	0.76
Industry fund	25	46.30	70	53.43
Public sector fund	5	9.26	11	8.40
Corporate fund	22	40.74	48	36.64
Self-managed fund	0	0.00	0	0.00
Total	**54**	**100.00**	**131**	**100.00**

Source: Authors' survey of Australian superannuation funds.

Only about 5 per cent of the trustees in our sample were under the age of 40 (Table 9.2). Over 40 per cent had more than five years' experience on their current board and over half reported an average length of service across all the boards on which they had served of more than five years. Most trustees were sitting on only one board at the time of the survey. Altruism and loyalty did not feature prominently among their reasons for becoming a trustee. Some had to do it as part of their job or had been invited to join the board. About a third viewed it as an opportunity to either acquire new skills or learn more about superannuation.

A substantial minority of the trustees surveyed (about 40 per cent) had a background in finance. Almost all trustees considered their fellow trustees to be financially proficient. These results are consistent with those of Robinson and Kakabadse (2002) for the United Kingdom, where not a single trustee admitted to poor financial expertise and very few thought this was true of their trustee group as a whole.

3. EXPERTISE

While believing themselves to be financially proficient, many trustees lacked formal investment qualifications (Table 9.3). Indeed, 13.7 per cent said they had no relevant qualifications and a further 12.2 per cent reported a trustee designation only. A similar result was evident in the United Kingdom, where 23.9 per cent of trustees reported having no relevant qualifications (Robinson and Kakabadse 2002). As in the United Kingdom, the share of trustees with an

Table 9.2   Australia: Background of Trustees

	No. of Responses	%
Age		
No answer	2	1.53
Under 40	7	5.34
40–44	14	10.69
45–49	13	9.92
50–54	28	21.37
55–59	28	21.37
60–64	19	14.50
Over 65	20	15.27
Total	**131**	**100.00**
Group membership		
No answer	5	3.82
Chair	18	13.74
Member nominated	33	25.20
Company nominated	43	32.82
Union nominated	19	14.50
Government nominated	2	1.53
Other	11	8.40
Total	**131**	**100.00**
No. of boards trustee is working on		
No answer	22	16.79
1	95	72.52
More than 1	14	10.69
Total	**131**	**100.00**
No. of trustees working as independent persons or employees		
No answer	2	1.53
Independent	63	48.09
Employee	66	50.38
Total	**131**	**100.00**
Years spent on current board		
No answer	3	2.29
Less than 1	11	8.40
1–2	10	7.63
3–5	51	38.93
6–10	26	19.85
11–20	28	21.37
More than 20	2	1.53
Total	**131**	**100.00**
Average years of service on current and past boards		
No answer	1	0.76
Less than 1	10	7.63
1–2	10	7.63
3–5	38	29.01
6–10	32	24.43
11–20	35	26.72
More than 20	5	3.82
Total	**131**	**100.00**

Table 9.2 (continued)

	No. of Responses	%
No. of members on board		
No answer	2	3.70
1–3	2	3.70
4–6	11	20.37
7–9	24	44.44
10–12	10	18.52
More than 12	5	9.26
Total	**54**	**100.00**
Reasons for becoming a trustee		
(multiple responses allowed)		
Loyalty to company	7	5.34
Altruism	15	11.45
Part of job	18	13.74
Was invited	39	29.77
Workforce representative	44	33.59
Control over own benefit	4	3.05
Union representative	16	12.21
Pensioner/retired	0	0.00
Consultant	8	6.11
Trade	1	0.76
Learn more about superannuation	24	18.32
Acquire new skills	19	14.50
Other	11	8.40
Work background		
(multiple responses allowed)		
Engineer	7	5.34
Human resources	25	19.08
Marketing	6	4.58
Sales	7	5.34
Information technology	2	1.53
Finance	52	39.69
General management	35	26.72
Executive or non-executive director	24	18.32
Clerical	1	0.76
Own financial expertise		
No answer	3	2.29
High	50	38.17
Proficient	74	56.49
Poor	4	3.05
Total	**131**	**100.00**
Financial expertise of trustee group		
No answer	6	4.58
High	56	42.75
Proficient	66	50.38
Poor	3	2.29
Total	**131**	**100.00**

Source: Authors' survey of Australian superannuation funds.

Table 9.3   Australia: Expertise of Trustees

	No. of Responses	Average Response
Knowledge of key areas *(average response, 1 = good, 2 = satisfactory, 3 = poor)*		
Liability-linked benchmarks	130	2.10
Risk budgeting	130	1.78
Investment language	130	1.48
Asset–liability modelling	130	2.00
Performance measurement reporting	130	1.39
Qualifications of trustees (%)		
No answer	1	0.76
Trustee designation	16	12.21
Other superannuation qualification	15	11.45
Investment or finance qualification	19	14.50
Professional accounting qualification	29	22.14
Other relevant qualification	33	25.19
No relevant qualification	18	13.74
Total	**131**	**100.00**
Training programmes offered by fund (%)		
No answer	4	3.05
Fund specific	61	46.56
Ad hoc, as requested	66	50.38
Total	**131**	**100.00**
Days of training in first 12 months (%)		
No answer	2	1.53
None	22	16.79
Less than 1	22	16.79
1–2	25	19.08
2–3	26	19.85
More than 3	34	25.95
Total	**131**	**100.00**
Investment decisions taken principally by consultants *(multiple responses allowed)* (%)		
Mission and governance	60	45.80
Risk budgeting	71	54.20
Strategic asset allocation	94	71.76

Table 9.3 (continued)

	No. of Responses	Average Response
Benchmark design	91	69.47
Managerial structure	81	61.83
Selection of managers	84	64.12
Performance monitoring	85	64.89
How often trustee effectiveness is assessed (%)		
No answer	2	1.53
Assessed regularly at set intervals	49	37.40
Ad hoc	80	61.07
Total	**131**	**100.00**

Source: Authors' survey of Australian superannuation funds.

investment or finance qualification was low in the Australian sample, at 14.5 per cent.

About half of the funds in the Australian survey had regular training programmes in place, with most others relying on *ad hoc* training as required.[2] Only 26.0 per cent of trustees received more than three days of training within 12 months of becoming a trustee and 17.0 per cent received none. Despite their lack of training, most trustees considered they had a good knowledge of investment language and performance management reporting. They also felt they had a satisfactory understanding of asset–liability modelling, risk budgeting and liability-linked benchmarks. They tended to delegate important areas of decision making to consultants, from strategic asset allocation and performance monitoring through to managerial structures and benchmark design.[3] More than 60 per cent of trustees said there were no regular measures in place to assess their effectiveness.

4. BELIEFS, ATTITUDES AND WORKING RELATIONSHIPS

A majority of the trustees surveyed found their work challenging and reported having excellent working relationships with their fellow trustees (Table 9.4). This was especially evident in the answers to the questions about the functioning of the board of trustees. On a scale of 1 (strongly disagree) to 7 (strongly

Table 9.4   Australia: Beliefs, Attitudes and Working Relationships of Trustees

	No. of Responses	Mean	Standard Deviation	Minimum[a]	Maximum[a]
Role of trustee					
I find my role challenging	131	5.83	0.87	3	7
I see my role as a trustee changing significantly in the future	130	4.95	1.41	1	7
I feel sufficiently rewarded for the work I undertake	127	4.81	1.59	1	7
I find I face a heavy regulatory burden as a trustee	131	5.37	1.45	1	7
My role and responsibilities are clearly defined	129	5.52	1.03	3	7
I have enough freedom to perform effectively in my role	130	5.75	1.03	2	7
I want to effect change on the board but feel there are obstacles	131	3.02	1.66	1	7
Trustees should be paid for their role	130	5.05	2.07	1	7
I am paid (other than my normal employee remuneration) for being a trustee	129	3.85	2.77	1	7
I enjoy my role as a trustee	131	6.28	0.85	3	7
Working relationships					
There is a good working relationship between the chair and the board	131	6.25	0.96	3	7
The board is pulling in the same direction	131	5.95	1.12	1	7
There is a good team spirit on the board	130	6.04	1.04	2	7
There are one or two individuals on the board who are not suited to the role	131	3.10	1.98	1	7
It takes time for people to get to know each other	130	5.22	1.35	1	7

Table 9.4 (continued)

	No. of Responses	Mean	Standard Deviation	Mini-mum[a]	Maxi-mum[a]
Individuals on the board could be more tolerant of each other	131	2.97	1.52	1	7
The quality of board meetings is high	131	5.92	1.02	1	7
Board members have a good understanding of each other	131	5.58	1.03	2	7
Skills and capabilities					
I have the appropriate financial and investment skills necessary to undertake the role	131	5.56	1.05	3	7
If there is a financial matter I do not understand, I know where to get advice/training	131	6.31	0.81	3	7
I have received the technical training I asked for or desired	131	6.11	0.87	4	7
I am very good at time management	130	5.52	1.05	3	7
It is difficult to keep pace with current changes/trends	131	4.71	1.62	1	7
The role is becoming too complex to cope with	130	3.41	1.56	1	7
The experience I bring is invaluable to the business	131	5.09	1.24	1	7
It takes time to get up to speed on certain issues	131	5.47	1.23	1	7
We need more resources to perform effectively	131	3.53	1.39	1	7
There is a good mix of skills and capabilities in the group	131	5.89	0.99	2	7
I don't feel very influential in trustee decision making	131	2.43	1.38	1	6
I am fully aware of my fiduciary responsibilities	131	6.18	0.88	2	7

a   1 = strongly disagree; 7 = strongly agree.

Source: Authors' survey of Australian superannuation funds.

Table 9.5   Logit Results: Quality of Meetings, Skill Mix and Responsibilities[a]

The quality of board meetings is high	Coefficient	Standard Error	z	P > z
There is a good mix of skills and capabilities in the group	1.22234	0.2015622	6.06	0.000
Trustees' roles and responsibilities are clearly defined	−0.903235	0.4785646	−1.89	0.059

a   When $0.10 \geq P > 0.05$, the explanatory variable is significant at the 10 per cent level of confidence; when $0.05 \geq P > 0.01$, the explanatory variable is significant at the 5 per cent level of confidence; and when $0.01 \geq P$, the explanatory variable is significant at the 1 per cent level of confidence.

Source: Authors' calculations.

agree), 37 per cent of trustees strongly agreed with the statement that there was a good working relationship between the chair and the board of trustees, and none gave this a score of less than 3. There was also a high level of agreement with the statements that 'The board of trustees is pulling in the same direction', 'There is a good team spirit on the board of trustees' and 'The quality of board meetings is high'. Trustees strongly disagreed with the statements that 'There are one or two individuals on the board of trustees who are not suited to the role' and 'Individuals on the board of trustees could be more tolerant of each other'. They strongly agreed with the statement that trustees faced a heavy regulatory burden.

Based on ordered logit regressions, Table 9.5 presents the results for the statement that 'The quality of board meetings is high'. The analysis indicates that a good mix of capabilities and skills on the board of trustees greatly improves the quality of meetings, whereas a clear statement of responsibilities for the group, if anything, works in the opposite direction.

The picture that emerges from the analysis is one of a rather contented group of individuals who dislike formality and regulation and share a common set of beliefs, as reflected in regression results exploring trustees' attitudes towards the trustee model. They indicate that the trustees of public sector and other large funds (those with more than 10,000 members) are significantly less likely to agree with the statement that the current trustee model is outmoded and needs a radical overhaul—as, surprisingly, are trustees with a finance background. They are more likely to agree that individuals on the board of trustees could be more tolerant of each other, that the trustee's role is becoming more complex and that trustees face a heavy regulatory burden.

5. DECISION MAKING

Table 9.6 summarizes the results for trustee decision making. It shows a high degree of consensus among trustees that they represent all stakeholders, that they are given adequate time to discuss issues, and that neither the chair nor outside advisers have a high degree of influence over the agenda. For example, the lowest score on a scale of 1–7 for the statement that 'The quality of decision making on the board is high' is 3 and the average almost 6. The same pattern of a high mean score of over 6 and little dissent occurrs for 'Decisions are made on a well-informed basis', 'I support most of the board's decisions' and 'Trustees follow good governance procedures in making decisions'. There is also a clear consensus among those surveyed that communication among trustees is excellent, that a minimum of jargon is used during board meetings and that there are no hidden agendas.

The ordered logit regressions reported in Table 9.7 confirm these impressions. For example, agreement with the statement that 'The board is pulling in the same direction' is positively related to the perception that roles and responsibilities are clearly defined, and that trustees are given enough time to discuss key issues on the agenda. The results for other variables also suggest strong board cohesion.

Table 9.8 indicates a good partial correlation between those who are aware of their fiduciary responsibilities and those who believe trustees follow good governance procedures.

Table 9.9 shows that the trustees who find it most difficult to grasp issues are also likely to be the ones who are less financially proficient, who believe that decision making is becoming more complex or who are finding it difficult to keep up with current trends.

6. INDUSTRY ISSUES

Table 9.10 presents some summary statistics on questions involving industry issues and Table A9.1 in Appendix A9.1 gives a breakdown of trustees' responses. There is a strong sense among trustees that they are burdened with too many regulations and that more should be done to assess advisers. There is less of a sense that the current model needs radical rethinking or that there needs to be better selection procedures for trustees. Figure 9.1 compares the answers of the Australian trustees with those of their British counterparts. As the figure shows, there is a high level of support in both Australia and the United Kingdom for a code of governance for trustees.

Table 9.6   Australia: Decision Making

	No. of Responses	Mean	Standard Deviation	Mini-mum[a]	Maxi-mum[a]
Decision making					
The quality of decision making on the board is high	130	5.95	0.82	3	7
Decisions are mainly driven by operational issues	130	3.86	1.38	1	7
Decisions are arrived at through consensus	130	5.87	1.04	2	7
Enough time is given to discuss key issues on the agenda	129	5.85	1.04	2	7
I support most of the board's decisions	130	6.24	0.73	4	7
There are too many items on the agenda	130	2.96	1.43	1	7
The board is not a risk taker when it comes to key decisions	130	4.48	1.70	1	7
The decision-making process is too slow	130	3.30	1.59	1	7
Decisions are made on a well-informed basis	129	6.02	0.86	2	7
Decision making is more complex than it used to be	129	5.58	1.32	1	7
Decision making is driven by strategic issues	128	4.96	1.18	2	7
Work is too specialized for trustees to have an impact	129	2.51	1.38	1	6
Trustees represent all key stakeholders	130	5.82	1.53	1	7
Trustees follow good governance procedures in making decisions	129	6.18	0.91	2	7
Decision-making performance					
My performance is heavily influenced by the chair	127	3.02	1.72	1	7

Table 9.6 (continued)

	No. of Responses	Mean	Standard Deviation	Mini-mum[a]	Maxi-mum[a]
My performance is heavily influenced by group dynamics	130	3.16	1.56	1	7
My performance is heavily influenced by the relationship with investment managers	131	2.72	1.48	1	7
My performance is heavily influenced by the relationship with investment consultants	131	3.18	1.72	1	7
My performance is heavily influenced by the time taken to understand issues	131	4.01	1.74	1	7
My performance is heavily influenced by continuity/turnover of members	131	2.23	1.29	1	7
Communication					
I communicate effectively with those around me	131	5.57	0.94	1	7
Too much jargon is used during meetings	129	3.19	1.46	1	7
There is a lot of email communication outside regular meetings	129	3.33	1.66	1	7
Communication among trustees is friendly	131	6.12	0.86	3	7
Trustees are encouraged to discuss issues at board level	131	6.26	0.87	3	7
Communications at board level are open and there are no hidden agendas	131	5.96	1.18	1	7
Our professional advisers communicate with us effectively	131	5.74	1.03	2	7
Our investment managers communicate with us effectively	131	5.65	0.92	3	7

a   1 = strongly disagree; 7 = strongly agree.

Source: Authors' survey of Australian superannuation funds.

Table 9.7   Logit Results: Board Cohesion, Responsibilities and Time[a]

The board of trustees is pulling in the same direction	Coefficient	Standard Error	z	P > z
Trustees' roles and responsibilities are clearly defined	0.3972554	0.1848276	2.15	0.032
Enough time is given to discuss key issues on the agenda	0.6656583	0.2077889	3.20	0.001
As a board of trustees we genuinely invest and plan for the long term	0.3277906	0.1811707	1.81	0.070

Table 9.8   Logit Results: Good Governance, Skill Mix and Awareness of Fiduciary Responsibilities[a]

Trustees follow good governance procedures in decision making	Coefficient	Standard Error	z	P > z
There is a good mix of skills and capabilities in the group	0.6752435	0.1896068	3.56	0.000
I am fully aware of my fiduciary responsibilities	1.003065	1.003065	4.29	0.000

Table 9.9   Logit Results: Time, Decision Making and Financial Proficiency[a]

Decision-making performance is strongly influenced by the time taken to understand issues	Coefficient	Standard Error	z	P > z
Financial expertise of trustee	0.8645949	0.2951041	2.93	0.003
Decision making is more complex than it used to be	0.2218122	0.1144774	1.94	0.053
It is difficult to keep up with current changes/trends	0.2649344	0.1052721	2.52	0.012

a   As for Table 9.5.

Source: Authors' survey of Australian superannuation funds.

Table 9.10   Australia: Industry Issues

	No. of Responses	Mean	Standard Deviation	Mini-mum[a]	Maxi-mum[a]
A shared philosophy exists as to the future shape and characteristics of the industry	130	4.51	1.55	1	7
The markets in which we operate are becoming increasingly more sophisticated	131	5.94	0.97	1	7
There are too many regulations in this industry at present	131	5.32	1.50	1	7
I would welcome a code of governance for the industry	131	5.03	1.41	1	7
As a board of trustees we genuinely invest and plan for the long term	131	6.09	0.95	1	7
The performance of advisers should be measured and assessed	131	6.37	0.91	1	7
Our superannuation fund is performing very well	131	5.98	0.85	3	7
Advisers should become more integrally involved in the work of superannuation fund groups	130	4.43	1.39	1	7
Better selection procedures are needed to select new trustees	130	4.32	1.74	1	7
The current trustee model is outmoded because of the burden on trustees and needs to be rethought radically	131	3.36	1.84	1	7

a   1 = strongly disagree; 7 = strongly agree.

Source: Authors' survey of Australian superannuation funds.

*Figure 9.1   Mean Response of Australian and British Trustees to Industry
            Issues*[a]

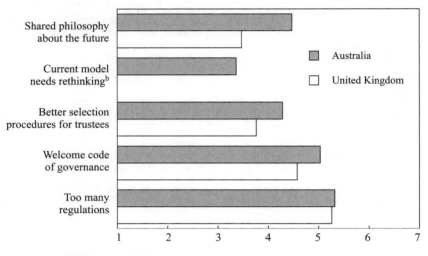

a   1 = strongly disagree; 7 = strongly agree.
b   The UK survey did not ask this question.

Source: Australia: Authors' survey; United Kingdom: Robinson and Kakabadse (2002); Kakabadse,
Kakabadse and Kouzmin (2003).

7. CONCLUSIONS

The survey described in this chapter is one of the first to be undertaken on
trustee effectiveness in Australia. Some striking conclusions emerge. Trustees
are confident about their overall level of financial skills but only a small proportion have formal training in investment or finance. Trustees tend to serve on
boards for lengthy periods of time, and most serve on only one board at a time.
They are hostile to formal regulation, and licensing in particular; most seem
to view the present system as functioning relatively efficiently. Nevertheless,
most would welcome a code of governance for trustees.

Strikingly, despite the significant differences in benefit structures between
the United Kingdom and Australia, the results of the Australian survey largely
mirror those of a similar survey conducted in the United Kingdom in 2001
(Robinson and Kakabadse 2002; Kakabadse, Kakabadse and Kouzmin 2003).
We believe this is because the structures put in place in Australia many years
ago for what were then primarily defined benefit schemes have not evolved
over time in line with the evolution towards defined contribution schemes. It
may now be time for a review of trustee governance in Australia.

NOTES

* We are grateful to Rainmaker for access to their superannuation fund database, which enabled us to locate the chief executive officers of the 200 largest Australian superannuation funds, and to the Australian Institute of Superannuation Trustees for their support of our research. We would like to thank David McCarthy for valuable discussion and comments. Any opinions expressed in this chapter are those of the individual authors and not necessarily those of their employers.
1. We are grateful to Professor Kakabadse for permission to use a modified version of the British survey. The results are reported in Robinson and Kakabadse (2002) and Kakabadse, Kakabadse and Kouzmin (2003).
2. In the pilot survey, only 20 per cent of funds had regular training programmes in place.
3. This was not the case for the smaller funds in the pilot survey.

APPENDIX A9.1: INDUSTRY ISSUES

Table A9.1   Breakdown of Trustees' Responses to Industry Issues

	No. of Responses	%
A shared philosophy exists as to the future		
shape and characteristics of the industry		
Missing	1	0.76
1	5	3.82
2	12	9.16
3	11	8.40
4	35	26.72
5	30	22.90
6	25	19.08
7	12	9.16
Total	**131**	**100.00**
The markets in which we operate are		
becoming increasingly sophisticated		
1	1	0.76
2	1	0.76
3	1	0.76
4	2	1.53
5	29	22.14
6	60	45.80
7	37	28.24
Total	**131**	**100.00**
There are too many regulations in the industry at present		
1	2	1.53
2	3	2.29
3	12	9.16
4	20	15.27
5	29	22.14
6	27	20.61
7	38	29.01
Total	**131**	**100.00**
I would welcome a code of governance for the industry		
1	3	2.29
2	6	4.58
3	5	3.82
4	27	20.61
5	39	29.77
6	31	23.66
7	20	15.27
Total	**131**	**100.00**
As a board of trustees we genuinely		
invest and plan for the long term		
1	1	0.76
2	0	0.00
3	0	0.00
4	7	5.34
5	17	12.98
6	58	44.27
7	48	36.64
Total	**131**	**100.00**

The performance of advisers should
be measured and assessed

1	2	1.53
2	0	0.00
3	0	0.00
4	0	0.00
5	9	6.87
6	52	39.69
7	68	51.91
Total	**131**	**100.00**

Our superannuation fund is
performing very well

1	0	0.00
2	0	0.00
3	1	0.76
4	7	5.34
5	21	16.03
6	66	50.38
7	36	27.48
Total	**131**	**100.00**

Advisers should become more integrally involved
in the work of superannuation fund groups

Missing	1	0.76
1	3	2.29
2	7	5.34
3	23	17.56
4	35	26.72
5	28	21.37
6	28	21.37
7	6	4.58
Total	**131**	**100.00**

Better selection procedures are
needed to select new trustees

Missing	1	0.76
1	4	3.05
2	25	19.08
3	14	10.69
4	23	17.56
5	26	19.85
6	23	17.56
7	15	11.45
Total	**131**	**100.00**

The current trustee model is outmoded
because of the burden on trustees and
needs to be rethought radically

1	19	14.50
2	40	30.53
3	15	11.45
4	19	14.50
5	19	14.50
6	8	6.11
7	11	8.40
Total	**131**	**100.00**

Source: Authors' survey of Australian superannuation funds.

PART IV

GOVERNMENT GUARANTEES

10. Pricing Defined Benefit Pension Insurance

David McCarthy and Anthony Neuberger

1. PENSION GUARANTEE FUNDS

Concern about the security of occupational defined benefit pensions when sponsoring firms default on them has led to the establishment of pension guarantee funds in several countries. The largest and best established exemplar of a guarantee fund is the Pension Benefit Guaranty Corporation (PBGC) of the United States, which was introduced with the passage of the Employee Retirement Income Security Act (ERISA) in 1974 following some highly publicized pension defaults. The United Kingdom followed suit in 2004, when public concern about the security of defined benefit pensions led to the establishment of the Pension Protection Fund (PPF), which was largely modelled on the PBGC. The purpose of this chapter is to identify and quantify some of the main policy issues involved in the establishment and management of pension guarantee funds.[1]

One key issue is the solvency of these funds, and possible claims on the public purse. For instance, after a run of years of very low claims—claims averaged US$300 million per year over the period 1980–99—the PBGC faced very large claims in the period 2000–04, amounting to some US$21 billion in total. Its 2004 accounts show a deficit of US$23.3 billion, after probable claims from currently insured plans are taken into account. The total underfunding of US pension plans covered by the PBGC increased from less than US$30 billion in 1999 to more than US$450 billion in 2004, as a result of interest rate changes and poor equity market performance (PBGC 2004). With premium income of US$1.5 billion per year and strong opposition in Congress to a substantial rise in premium levels, it is questionable whether the PBGC will be able to meet its obligations without government support. The PPF is still too new to allow any kind of financial analysis of its claims process.

In this chapter we model a generic pension guarantee fund to help analyse the extent to which these problems are inherent in any plan to protect defined benefit pensions. Recognizing that corporate pensions are similar to corporate debt obligations, we show that our generic fund is likely to face many years of low claims interspersed irregularly with periods of very large claims when prolonged weakness in equity markets coincides with widespread corporate insolvencies. We argue that our formulation is general enough to be applicable to both the PBGC and the PPF. Furthermore, we argue that it is not possible to build up sufficient surpluses in these funds in good years to pay for the bad years. It will also be difficult to raise premiums sufficiently after a run of bad years to bring these funds back to solvency. Because public pressure will prevent governments from letting guarantee funds default, the inescapable conclusion is that these funds will ultimately be underwritten by governments, whether the guarantee is formally recognized or not.

We consider, and reject, the argument that the problem can be mitigated by levying 'risk-based' premiums. Using a second model, we show that risk-based premiums will have a limited impact on moral hazard in the schemes most at risk of defaulting: those sponsored by financially weak employers who are unlikely to be able to simultaneously pay large insurance premiums and reduce the deficits in their pension plans. These schemes are precisely those that represent the bulk of the cost of pension insurance. We argue that the likely outcome of risk-based premiums is the bifurcation of pension schemes into those that are fully funded and sponsored by strong employers and those that are heavily underfunded and likely to default.

To address these issues, we develop a simple model of a pension plan. If the firm becomes insolvent, any deficit in the pension plan is picked up by the guarantee fund. The contribution of the firm to the pension plan follows a simple smoothing rule that ensures that any deficits and surpluses are amortized over a number of years, a common rule in practice. Plan solvency varies because of the mismatch between assets and liabilities; the assets are partly invested in equities while the liabilities are bond-like. The investment policy and the contribution policy are exogenous. Since a downturn in equity markets will not only increase pension fund deficits but also tend to be accompanied by an increase in insolvencies, we model the default rate stochastically using a structural model of the firm. We choose a model based on Collin-Dufresne and Goldstein (2001), where the firm's assets follow a stochastic process and the firm defaults when its leverage ratio reaches a critical level. With defaults being correlated across firms (because of the positive correlation in asset values across firms), the claims process is much more volatile than with non-stochastic default rates. With default being correlated with deficits in pension plans (because the assets of the firm are positively correlated with the assets of the pension plan), the claims level also becomes much larger.

The original paper on pension insurance was by Marcus (1987). He also used an options framework to value pension guarantee insurance, and in many respects our model builds on his work. While he computed the value of insurance on a fixed portfolio of risks that evolve with time in a non-stationary way, we compute the value of insurance for a steady-state population of firms. We choose to model firm funding policy in a way that leads to the sponsors' assumptions about the equity risk premium entering into the steady-state, risk-neutral density of firm solvency ratios. In common with other, more recent, work,[2] we assume that the pension guarantee fund does not receive the pension surplus of a bankrupt firm and does not have any claim on its assets.

None of these papers address the issue we discuss in the second half of this chapter: how the premium to the pension guarantee fund should be divided between firms with different credit ratings. We argue that for the guarantee fund to be sustainable, some degree of cross-subsidy between firms is necessary, implying that there will always be grounds for moral hazard on the part of unscrupulous pension sponsors. We conclude that any pension guarantee system cannot rely entirely on risk rating to control moral hazard, but needs to be complemented by direct regulation of scheme funding levels.

2. MODELLING THE GUARANTEE

In this section we first describe the model of the solvency ratio of an individual pension fund and then present our model of firm default.

Modelling Scheme Solvency

For simplicity, we assume that our generic pension guarantee fund guarantees all the liabilities of a pension plan, although neither the PPF nor the PBGC does so in practice. We assume that there is an infinite number of identical small firms, and focus on one representative firm. The present value of the accrued liabilities of the firm's pension plan at time t, denoted by L_t, may vary over time, but we assume that it is non-stochastic. The assets of the plan have value A_t, so if the firm becomes insolvent at time t, and if the guaranteed liabilities of the plan exceed the assets, the guarantee fund pays $L_t - A_t$.

In practice pension plan liabilities are measured in several different ways. For the purpose of this model, L_t should be interpreted as the cost at time t of buying out the guaranteed liabilities of the pension plan, and A_t as the market value of the assets of the plan, after allowing for any costs of winding up. Implicitly, we are assuming that if the firm becomes insolvent, the guarantee fund has full access to the assets of the pension plan, at least so far as they do not exceed the guaranteed liabilities, but no access to the assets of the firm itself. By topping up the pension plan's assets to equal its liabilities, the guarantee fund can ensure that it faces no further claim from that pension plan.

The assets of the pension plan comprise a riskless bond with constant interest rate r, and an equity portfolio. We assume that each plan invests in the same market index fund, which may be assumed to be the portfolio of all available equities weighted in proportion to their market capitalization. We assume that the instantaneous return on the market portfolio, dS/S, follows an Ito process:

$$dS/S = (r + \alpha)dt + \sigma_m dz_m, \tag{1}$$

where z_m is a standard Brownian process, α is the market risk premium and σ_m is the volatility of the market. The first term represents the mean instantaneous return on the portfolio, which is the risk-free rate plus the equity risk premium, while the second has zero expected value and models random variation around the mean instantaneous return.

It should already be clear from the above discussion that the claims on the guarantee fund will be stochastic, and will depend on future stock market performance. Rather than compute the expected level of future claims and take their present value by discounting back to the present at a suitably chosen discount rate that reflects the riskiness of the cash flows, we use the risk-neutral methodology that is standard in the finance literature. Where, as in our model, all risks are hedgeable,[3] present values can be obtained by projecting future outcomes using a risk-neutral pricing measure Q in place of the objective probability measure, and discounting the expected claims using the risk-free interest rate. The risk-neutral probability measure is that measure under which all the assets have an expected return equal to the risk-free rate. Hence, (1) can be rewritten as

$$dS/S = rdt + \sigma_m dz_m^Q, \tag{2}$$

where dz_m^Q is a standard Brownian motion process under measure Q. Setting the right-hand sides of (2) and (1) equal, we can derive an expression for dz_m^Q in terms of dz_m:

$$dz_m^Q = \frac{\alpha}{\sigma_m} dt + dz_m. \tag{3}$$

The expected value of dz_m^Q under measure Q is zero, so taking expectations of both sides under the risk-neutral measure Q gives

$$E^Q[dz_m] = -\frac{\alpha}{\sigma_m} dt \tag{4}$$

I_t is an indicator function that takes the value 1 if the firm is still solvent at time t, and zero otherwise. If the firm becomes insolvent, the pension plan is closed. If the firm becomes insolvent at time t (so $dI_t = -1$) and if the pension fund is in surplus at that time ($L_t \leq A_t$), then the pension plan is able to pay pensions due in full, and no liability falls on the protection fund.[4] If there is a deficit in the pension plan when the firm becomes insolvent, the protection fund takes over both the assets and the liabilities. The cost to the fund at the time the firm becomes insolvent is thus:

$$-\int_t^\infty \left[L_u - A_u\right]^+ dI_u \text{ where } \left[x\right]^+ \equiv Max(x,0). \tag{5}$$

Determining the Premium

The firm pays an insurance premium P_t to the pension guarantee fund. From the fund's perspective, insuring the plan has a present value equal to the expected value of the premiums paid by the firm when it is solvent, less the expected value of the payments that the fund will have to make if a firm defaults, both discounted at the risk-free rate. We take expectations using the risk-neutral measure Q to ensure that the value obtained takes proper account of the risk in the fund's premiums and its liabilities:

$$E^Q\left[\int_t^\infty P_u I_u e^{-r(u-t)} du + \int_t^\infty \left[L_u - A_u\right]^+ e^{-r(u-t)} dI_u\right]. \tag{6}$$

If the fund is to be able to cover the cost of claims from its premium income, then, ignoring administrative costs, the present value of premium income less claims must be zero. Hence, any premium must satisfy the condition:

$$E^Q\left[\int_t^\infty P_u I_u e^{-r(u-t)} du + \int_t^\infty \left[L_u - A_u\right]^+ e^{-r(u-t)} dI_u\right] = 0. \tag{7}$$

In principle, there are many ways of levying the premium. The PBGC uses a combination of a charge per member covered and a charge proportional to the dollar size of any deficit in the scheme. In the United Kingdom, the PPF is required to take account of other matters, including the solvency of the scheme sponsor. For the present, we assume that the premium is set as a constant proportion of the scheme's liabilities.

The Dynamics of Pension Scheme Funding

In order to evaluate the expectation in equation (7), we need to specify the dynamics of the scheme solvency ratio A_u/L_u under the risk-neutral measure Q. The dynamics of A depend on the return on the portfolio, outflows to pensioners and inflows from contributions. Again, written as an Ito process, we have:

$$dA = \left[(r + x\alpha)A + (\kappa_t - \pi_t)\right]dt + x\sigma_m A dz_m, \tag{8}$$

where x is the (fixed) proportion of the assets held as equity, κ is the contribution rate and π is the rate of pay-out to pensioners. The first component of the dt term states that the expected rate of return on the assets is the risk-free rate plus the equity risk premium on the equities held by the plan. The second component shows that the assets increase at rate κ because of contributions to the scheme and decrease at rate π because of payments to pensioners. As before, the dz term has zero expected value and models how the value of the assets changes as a result of random fluctuations in the value of the equities held by the scheme.

The firm's contribution to the pension plan has two components. The first maintains the current solvency level after allowing for payments to pensioners, any change in net liabilities, and the expected return on the assets of the plan. The second component is designed to eliminate any surplus or deficit in the plan over a specified period of T years. The lower the level of T, the faster any deficit is eliminated and the lower the potential claim on the PPF. The simplest formulation that achieves this is

$$\kappa_t = \left(\pi_t + \frac{dL_t}{dt}\frac{A_t}{L_t} - (r + x\hat{\alpha})A_t \right) + \left(\frac{L_t - A_t}{T} \right). \tag{9}$$

In this formulation, $\hat{\alpha}$ is the excess return on equities assumed by the firm in setting its contribution rate; it may be identical with the true α, but is not necessarily so. Define the solvency ratio of the scheme a as:

$$a_t = A_t / L_t. \tag{10}$$

Then, using Ito's lemma, we can calculate the stochastic differential equation governing the evolution of the solvency ratio as follows:

$$da = dA / L - adL / L$$

$$= \left[\left(r + x\alpha - \frac{dL}{Ldt} \right)a + \left(\kappa_t - \pi_t \right) / L \right]dt + x\sigma_m adz_m$$

$$= \left(\frac{1-a}{T} + x(\alpha - \hat{\alpha})a \right)dt + x\sigma_m adz_m. \tag{11}$$

We can express this equation in terms of the risk-neutral probability measure Q by substituting equation (3) to give:

$$da = \left(\frac{1-a}{T} - \hat{\alpha}ax \right)dt + x\sigma_m adz_m^Q. \tag{12}$$

Given the investment policy and the contribution policy, the solvency ratio follows a stationary stochastic process that is independent of the behaviour of liabilities. We can derive the unconditional distribution of a at time t under the risk-neutral measure, $g^Q(a)$, by stating the condition that the distribution is stationary and using equation (12) to derive a differential equation.[5]

Assume for the moment that sponsor default is a random Poisson event that occurs with probability δ per year. Formula (7) then gives the fair premium rate p (expressed as a proportion of the liabilities of the pension plan) as:

$$p = \delta \int_0^1 (1-a)g^Q(a)da. \tag{13}$$

Note that the true equity risk premium, α, does not enter into equation (12), and hence will not affect the risk-neutral density function g^Q or the premium rate p. A higher equity premium raises the expected future solvency level of pension schemes, but this is offset by the increase in the discount rate used to value the guarantee fund's liabilities. However the equity premium assumed by the scheme ($\hat{\alpha}$) does enter into the premium; the higher the assumed premium, the lower the contribution rate and the greater the expected claim on the fund.

The premium can be compared with the unconditional objective expectation of the rate of claims as a proportion of liabilities, c, which we calculate in a similar way, using equation (11) instead of equation (12).[6]

Extending the Model

One unrealistic element of our model is that the solvency ratio of the pension fund is not bounded above. There are limits on the degree to which the pension fund can hold assets in excess of its liabilities, imposed largely to prevent the sponsor company from using the pension fund as a tax avoidance device. We can readily impose the condition in our model that a is not permitted to exceed some limit a^*. Whenever a does exceed the limit, the contribution rate is constrained to force a below the limit; a^* acts as a reflecting barrier.

We assume that firms are able to reclaim investment surpluses from their pension plans over the same time horizon over which deficits are amortized. In practice firms may struggle to reclaim investment surpluses, either because they face pressure to improve benefits or because they do not wish to be seen to be 'raiding' the pension plans of their employees.

We also assume that the liabilities that are guaranteed by the guarantee fund are the same as those used to determine the firm's pension contributions. In practice these two measures of liability may well differ substantially, and in either direction. First, not all accrued liabilities may be guaranteed by the fund, as in the case of the PBGC and the PPF. In addition, the definition of liabilities used by actuaries when they report funding levels generally takes account of future wage growth in computing the pension liability arising from past service. Finally, the actuarial valuation may also use a higher discount rate in valuing liabilities than the rate at which the liabilities can be bought out in the market. The model can easily be adjusted to take some of these factors into account, but this issue is not explored further here.

Choosing a Model of Firm Default

In this subsection, we model the default of the firm sponsoring the pension plan whose solvency ratio we modelled above. From empirical evidence that we discuss below, it is clear that firm default rates vary considerably over time, are correlated across firms and are negatively correlated with the equity market. This has three important implications.

1. A falling equity market increases both the probability of sponsor firms becoming insolvent and the size of pension plan deficits. So stochastic default induces a positive correlation between the probability of a claim on the guarantee fund and the size of the claim. This increases the fair premium.
2. The correlation between default risk and equity returns means that default risk is priced. This will further increase the difference between the (objective) expected rate of claims on the fund and the fair premium.
3. The correlation of default risk across firms increases the skewness of the claims process.

To explore the practical significance of these issues, we need a model of default that captures correlations across firms as well as correlations with the equity market. We explore three possible strategies for modelling default: fitting the empirical evidence on default directly; fitting the behaviour of corporate debt spreads; and using a structural model of the firm. We explain why we choose to follow the structural model approach, and why we choose the structural model with mean-reverting leverage of Collin-Dufresne and Goldstein (2001). Based on this model, we then present premium calculations and claim simulations.

The simplest strategy for modelling default is to take historical default rates, postulate some functional form for their time-series behaviour and estimate a relationship. The problem with this is the paucity of data. Defaults are rare; there are fewer than 1,500 defaulted issuers in Moody's database between 1970 and 2003. As shown in Figure 10.1, default rates are highly auto-correlated over time. This is obviously important for modelling the PPF. But basing a model purely on the limited empirical data would be hard to do with any reliability. The peaks in 1990–91 and 2000–02 would drive any analysis.

An alternative approach is to use information on the behaviour of credit spreads. The empirical evidence does strongly support correlations in changes in credit spread across firms and a strong negative correlation between credit spreads and the equity market. Pedrosa and Roll (1998) document the existence of strong common factors in credit spreads for portfolios of credit, where the 60 portfolios in question are characterized by broad industry group, credit

*Figure 10.1   Historical Default Rates of Global Bond Issuers,
                1970–2003*

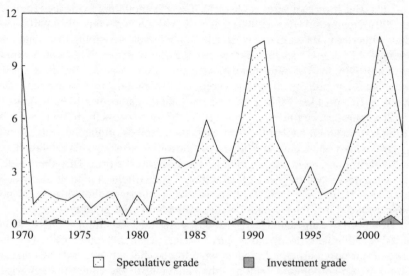

Speculative grade   Investment grade

Source: Hamilton et al. (2004).

rating category and maturity. A more detailed analysis of the spreads on individual US industrial bonds is given by Collin-Dufresne, Goldstein and Martin
(2001). They look at weekly changes in spreads against comparable Treasury
bonds on a universe of 688 straight (not callable or convertible) bonds from
261 different issuers over the period 1988–97. They regress the changes on
changes in a number of factors suggested by theory, including the firm leverage ratio, the level and slope of the government yield curve, the level and
slope of implied volatility on the equity market, and the level of the equity
market. They find that a 1 per cent increase in the S&P 500 index is associated with a credit spread decrease of about 1.6 basis points. Their regressions
explain about 25 per cent of spread changes; by examining the residuals from
the regression, they show that 75 per cent of the unexplained change can be
ascribed to a common factor that they fail to identify with any other macroeconomic variable.

    While these results are based on US data, Manzoni (2002) obtains similar
results for the sterling Eurobond market, where daily changes in the spread of
the yield on the market index to UK Treasury yields are negatively correlated
with returns on the UK stock market. Over the period 1991–99, a 1 per cent
increase in the FTSE 100 index is associated with a credit spread decrease of
2.1–3.5 basis points depending on the specification.

Building a model of default that is calibrated to bond prices is attractive because of the large amount of high-quality data on the behaviour of bond yield spreads. But it faces a serious obstacle. There is mounting evidence (Elton et al. 2001; Huang and Huang 2003) that credit risk accounts for only a part—less than a quarter in the case of investment grade bonds, according to Huang and Huang—of the yield spread. In the absence of any generally accepted explanation of why the risk-adjusted expected return on corporate bonds is higher than that on default-free bonds, the credibility of a model that incorporates the whole yield spread in valuing the pension fund guarantee would be in doubt.

The approach we follow is to model the default process from fundamentals, using a structural model of the firm. Structural models originated with Merton (1974), who modelled a risky bond as a portfolio consisting of a riskless bond and a short position in a put option on the assets of the firm. This simple idea has been developed by many other authors,[7] and structural models are widely used as a basis for pricing credit-sensitive instruments, though they do not appear to capture yield spreads on corporate bonds with great accuracy.

However, Huang and Huang (2003) show that structural models, when suitably calibrated, do fit the empirical data on default rather well. For our specific purpose, structural models have three other advantages: the correlation between corporate default and the behaviour of the equity market arises naturally within the model; the correlation in default rates across firms arises naturally in the model from the correlation in firms' asset values; and, unlike models based on the yield spread, the price of default risk can be computed within the model, without the need to make any assumptions about the behaviour of recovery rates.

In the previous subsection we had a stationary process for pension plan deficits that allowed us to compute an unconditionally fair insurance premium that was a constant proportion of the value of insured liabilities. To retain this feature, we need a structural model of default that is also stationary. The natural candidate is Collin-Dufresne and Goldstein (2001), who have a model with mean-reverting leverage ratios. As in other structural models based on Merton (1974), debt is a claim on the firm's assets V. The assets follow a diffusion process with constant volatility σ_v, and the firm's leverage varies accordingly. But Collin-Dufresne and Goldstein argue that firms tend to adjust their leverage over time through their financing strategy. This causes the leverage ratio to revert to some target level.

The key variable in their model is the log leverage ratio of the firm, l. The leverage ratio is defined as the ratio of the critical asset level at which default will occur to the current asset level. Collin-Dufresne and Goldstein model the dynamics of l as a first-order auto-regressive process:

$$dl = \kappa\left(\overline{l} - l\right)dt + \sigma_v dz_v. \qquad (14)$$

If $l > \bar{l}$, then the dt term in equation (14) is negative, causing the value of l to fall in expectation; if $l < \bar{l}$, the opposite is true. Therefore, the process reverts to the mean value $\bar{l}$. κ determines the speed of mean reversion and $\sigma_v dz_v$ is the random innovation in the log return on the firm's assets. The expected value of $\sigma_v dz_v$ is zero. We assume a constant correlation between changes in firm value and changes in the assets of the pension plan, so the two stochastic processes, z_v and z_m, have constant correlation ρ.

The log leverage ratio l is strictly negative so long as the firm is solvent; if it hits zero, the firm defaults. We have now fully specified the processes governing the claim on the PPF from an individual firm. The log leverage ratio, which determines firm solvency—and, thus, when any claim is made—follows the stochastic process in (14) above. The pension plan solvency ratio, which determines the size of any claim that is made, is governed by the stochastic process in (11).

We need two more elements to complete the specification of the model. First, we must specify the correlation structure of firms' asset returns. We assume that each firm's return is the market return plus a noise term that is identically and independently distributed across firms. So, given two firms i and j, we have:

$$dz_v^i dz_v^j = \rho^2 dt \quad \text{if } i \neq j. \tag{15}$$

Second, we assume that idiosyncratic risk is unpriced. Following a similar argument to that used to derive equation (4), we find that:

$$E^Q\left[dz_v^i\right] = -\rho \frac{\alpha}{\sigma_m} dt. \tag{16}$$

Starting with a portfolio of firms with the same leverage and the same pension funding, the pension funding level varies over time with the equity market, but remains the same across firms, while leverage ratios disperse because of firm idiosyncratic risk.

With no new firms being born, the steady-state joint probability function of a and l is $g(a,l)e^{-\delta t}$, where δ is now the steady-state default rate driven by the condition that $l = 0$ is an absorbing barrier. The results are unaltered if there is a steady entry of new firms into the portfolio, provided that their distribution in (a, l) space is the same as the steady-state distribution.

Estimating the Model

In estimating the model, we generally follow Huang and Huang (2003); their estimates are broadly consistent with those of Collin-Dufresne and Goldstein (2001). Since their estimates vary slightly according to the credit rating of the bond in question, we take their estimates for an A-rated issuer (Moody's or Standard & Poor's). In particular, we take the mean reversion parameter κ to be 0.2, the asset volatility σ_v to be 24.5 per cent and the asset risk premium to be 4.89 per cent. Huang and Huang show that these values are consistent with an equity premium for the firm of 5.99 per cent. Taking the equity beta to be 1, the market risk premium is also 5.99 per cent, and the asset beta is 0.82. Using an equity market volatility σ_m of 18 per cent, the correlation between the change in firm asset value and the equity market return is

$$\rho = \beta \frac{\sigma_m}{\sigma_v} = 0.60. \qquad (17)$$

Using Huang and Huang's estimate of the long-term average leverage ratio of 38 per cent gives a long-run average default rate of 0.75 per cent per year. This looks very high, so we have used an average leverage ratio of 31.7 per cent, which gives a long-run default rate of 0.25 per cent per year.

Rather than solving the partial differential equation directly, we compute the steady-state joint density of the solvency ratio a and the leverage ratio l using a two-dimensional binomial tree with births and deaths, and iterate forward in time until the default rate and the rate of claims on the fund converge to their limiting values. In all the iterations we use a time step of 0.1 years.

Table 10.1 shows the premium and expected claims rate for a variety of parameter values. Using the base case parameters that two-thirds of the pension fund is invested in equities, that there is a 120 per cent ceiling on over-funding and a 10-year deficit amortization period, and that 90 per cent of plan liabilities are guaranteed by the fund, the average rate of claims is £0.68 per £1,000 of liabilities per year. To illustrate the effects of the stochastic default rate, we compare the results with a non-stochastic Poisson default rate with the same expected value as the stochastic default rate. In this case, the claims rate is £0.17 per £1,000. The difference is entirely attributable to the correlation between corporate defaults and the underfunding of pension schemes in the structural model.

The impact of the structural default model on the premium is still greater. With Poisson default, the fair premium is £0.50 per £1,000. With the structural default model it is more than seven times as high at £3.90 per £1,000. The other two rows of the table show that the level of premiums, and the average rate of claim, can be reduced significantly by limiting the proportion of liabilities guaranteed (with the guarantee fund retaining first claim on all the assets of the pension fund) and by imposing stricter pension fund solvency requirements.

These figures for the fair premium level seem to be substantially higher than those first envisaged for the PPF, although direct comparison is not easy. It is more difficult to compare our calculated premiums with the actual premiums charged by the PBGC, as the latter depend on actual pension underfunding while our calculations assume a steady-state distribution of funding and firm

Table 10.1 Premium and Average Claims with Structural Default
(£ per £1,000 of liabilities per year)[a]

Model of Firm Default	Equity Proportion (x)			
	Two-thirds		100%	
	Premium	Claim	Premium	Claim
Poisson default	0.50	0.17	0.73	0.31
Structural default				
Base case	3.90	0.68	5.23	1.01
Variant 1 ($\lambda = 80\%$)	2.86	0.45	4.19	0.77
Variant 1 ($T = 4$)	2.34	0.43	3.50	0.70

a The Poisson default case is from Table 10.2. The base case of the structural default model has the same dynamics for the solvency ratio as the Poisson model; the two also have the same expected default rate (0.25 per cent). The first variant on the base case has only 80 per cent of liabilities guaranteed by the PPF, and the second has an amortization period for pension fund deficits of four rather than 10 years. The other parameters of the models are: $a^* = 120\%$, $\sigma_m = 18\%$, $\sigma_v = 24.5\%$, $\bar{l} = -1.15$, $\kappa = 0.2$ and $\rho = 0.6$.

Source: Authors' calculations.

leverage. However, the PBGC's annual report shows that in fiscal year 2004 it collected US$1,481 million in premiums on its single-employer programme (PBGC 2004). Guaranteed liabilities amounted to US$1.35 trillion in 2001— the latest date for which figures are available (PBGC 2003)—a premium of US$1.10 per US$1,000 of liability. Our premium is thus more than three times greater than the PBGC premium and our expected claims are roughly half the PBGC premium. However, it would be wrong to attach too much importance to our absolute numbers. They are very sensitive to the parameters chosen, and in particular to the assumptions concerning the long-run average leverage ratio. Using Huang and Huang's estimate of 38 per cent rather than the value we have used of 31.65 per cent would lead to fair premiums that are more than twice as high.

Simulating the Claims Distribution

The previous subsection established the average level of claims in the long run. The premium reflects the average long-run claims experience of our model guarantee fund, but the variation in the claims level is also a matter of considerable concern. To investigate the variation in the claims level, we simulate the claims process and ask how high a claims rate one can reasonably expect over a period of, say, 30 years.

Table 10.2 Simulation of Claims in Worst One-year and Five-year Period in 30 years (£ per £1,000 of liabilities per year)

	Structural Default		Poisson Default	
Fair premium	3.90		0.50	
Average claim	0.68		0.17	
	1 year	5 year	1 year	5 year
Median	4.1	6.9	0.59	2.1
Worst quartile	11.5	19.2	0.74	2.9
Worst decile	24.1	42.8	0.87	3.6

a   The table is based on 1,000 simulations of the evolution of the distribution of firm leverage and solvency level for the population of insured firms, and shows the average and peak annual claim level over each 30-year period. The parameter values for the base case are: $a^* = 120\%$, $T = 10$, $\lambda = 90\%$, $\beta = 1$, $\sigma_m = 18\%$, $\sigma_v = 24.5\%$, $\bar{l} = -1.15$, $\kappa = 0.2$ and $\rho = 0.6$. The Poisson default case is identical except that $\rho = 0$.

Source: Authors' calculations.

The simulations are carried out with the same base case as Table 10.1, using the structural default model and an equity proportion of two-thirds. As set out in Table 10.1, the fair premium is £3.90 per £1,000 of liabilities, while the expected level of claims is £0.68 per £1,000.

Table 10.2 shows the distribution of the 30-year worst case, using objective probabilities; it is based on 1,000 simulations, with a time step of one-tenth of a year. The simulations start with the steady-state distribution of firm leverage and pension fund solvency. A path for the equity market is then simulated. The liabilities of schemes grow at a constant rate that is equal to the average rate of insolvency, thus ensuring that the level of insured liabilities is stationary.

Since the pension assets of all firms are perfectly correlated, and deficits are corrected by adjusting the contribution policy, the initial dispersion in pension funding levels among firms quickly narrows. Firm asset value is subject to idiosyncratic risk, so while there is co-movement, there is also substantial dispersion.

In running the simulations, the first 70 years are used as a conditioning period; the following 30 years are then used as the sample period. The conditioning period is needed to ensure that the start of the sample period is suitably randomized. For comparison, we also show the figures for the Poisson default case. The claims are expressed as a percentage of the average size of liabilities over the 30-year period. The results are shown graphically in Figure 10.2.

Table 10.2 and Figure 10.2 show how the structural model of default not only increases the magnitude of average claims, but also greatly increases their

Figure 10.2   Distribution of Claims in Worst One-year and Five-year Period in 30 Years (simulation)

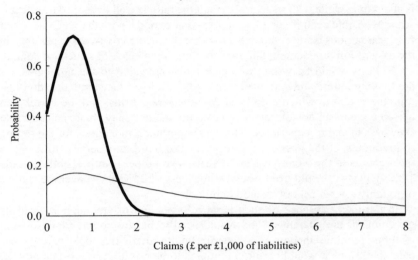

Worst One-year Period in 30 Years

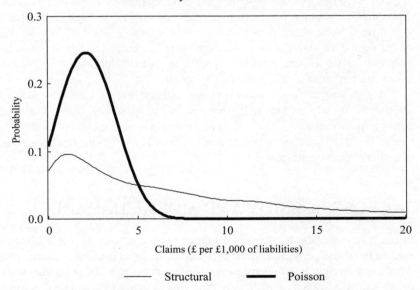

Worst Five-year Period in 30 Years

——— Structural   ▬▬▬ Poisson

Source: Authors' calculations.

skewness. In the Poisson model, the level of claims in the worst year in 30 years is just over three times the average claim level in the median case; with the structural default model, the ratio is in excess of six. In the worst decile of 30-year periods, the contrast is even more stark. With Poisson default, the ratio is about five, while with structural default the ratio is well over 30. The effect is strongly visible even if one looks at five-year periods, with the worst decile of five-year periods being comparable to twice the median five-year experience in the case of Poisson default, but over six times in the case of structural default.

While it would be wrong to attach much precision to the numbers—we are looking at rare and extreme events—the results of the simulation do illustrate the extent to which correlated defaults across firms, and the correlation between the mean default rate and the equity market, may create considerable skewness in claims experience. This has important implications for the setting of premiums. If the guarantee fund wanted to build up reserves sufficient to meet claims in the worst year in 30 years with 90 per cent probability, Table 10.2 suggests it would need reserves in excess of 24 years of average claims, or roughly 2.5 per cent of insured liabilities.

In the likely absence of such large reserves and of any support from its government, the guarantee fund would need to borrow to pay claims, using its future premium income as collateral. But this alternative looks barely more palatable, since it would require premiums to be raised very substantially. If, for example, there were claims equal to 2.5 per cent of liabilities in one year, and they were met by borrowing that had to be repaid over 10 years, then additional premiums equal to nearly four times the normal average claims level would need to be charged to repay the debt, ignoring any real interest due on the debt. This high premium would have to be charged at a time when, by assumption, the solvent firms that remain are heavily leveraged, and themselves have pension funds in substantial deficit.

If the guarantee fund cannot weather extreme events either by way of reserves or by way of borrowing backed by increased premiums, then that leaves two alternatives: default, or some form of government involvement. It is hard to avoid the conclusion that governments will be left as the final guarantor of defined benefit pensions.

3. CROSS-SUBSIDY AND MORAL HAZARD

In our base case, the breakeven insurance premium is £3.90 per £1,000 of insured liabilities per year, and the expected claim level is £0.68 per year. This is not a deadweight loss to pension plans. The total cost of the premiums to all pension plans is exactly matched by the gains to pensioners in failed pension plans. But for individual schemes the costs and benefits will not match. For pensioners of firms that are financially weak and that have significantly under-funded pension schemes, the true cost of insurance is much higher than the premium we derived for an average scheme. If all schemes are charged a premium that is a fixed proportion of insured liabilities, the weaker schemes will derive windfall gains from the pension guarantee fund. Firms can maximize the value of the windfall by changing their contributions to their pension schemes and by altering the investment mix of their pension assets. This classic moral hazard problem has plagued the PBGC since its inception (Utgoff 1993). It is often suggested that a risk-rated premium system, where funds pay the true value of their insurance in premiums each year, would solve this problem.

In this section, we use a cross-sectional model of firms with different credit ratings to assess the implications of a risk-rated premium system for a pension guarantee fund. Our conclusion is stark: pension guarantee systems must inevitably involve some degree of cross-subsidy, implying that at least some moral hazard is unavoidable. Even our simple model of risk rating is sufficient to show that pension guarantee funds cannot rely on risk-based premiums alone to ensure good behaviour from pension sponsors. Legislative requirements, such as minimum funding requirements, regular monitoring of problem schemes and giving the regulator power to intervene to protect the interests of the guarantee fund, may also be needed.

We assume that there are N credit ratings, where rating 1 is the highest possible credit rating and N is insolvency. We assume that rating transitions follow a Markov process. The probability that an employer who starts the year in class i ends the year in class j is p_{ij}. We have:

$$\sum_{j=1}^{N} p_{ij} = 1 \quad \text{for all } i;$$

$$p_{Nj} = 1 \quad \text{if } j = N, \text{ and 0 otherwise.}$$

(18)

The guarantee fund charges the scheme an annual premium equal to l_i times the deficit of the scheme, where i is the employer's current credit rating. The deficit of a particular scheme is currently (in year t) D_t. Claims arise only when the sponsor becomes insolvent, and then the guarantee fund incurs a loss equal to the deficit.

The expected net revenue that the guarantee fund will receive from the scheme over the current year is

$$(l_i - p_{iN})D_t.$$

(19)

For convenience, we assume that the premium is paid with certainty at the beginning of the year and that there is no discounting within the year.

We define V_t as the present value to the guarantee fund of the scheme; it is equal to the present value of the future stream of premium payments less the present value of any claims. The value can be defined recursively by the equations:

$$V_t = -D_t \text{ if } i = N;$$
$$V_t = (l_i - p_{iN})D_t + E_t[\delta.V_{t+1}] \text{ otherwise,} \tag{20}$$

where δ is the annual discount factor, and E_t is the expectation operator at time t.

Since credit ratings follow a Markov process, and assuming that the deficit is a random walk and uncorrelated with any future rating change, and making the additional assumption that the discount factor is independent of the scheme,[8] the value of a scheme can be expressed as a function of the size of the scheme's deficit and of the employer's credit rating:

$$V_t = v_i D_t, \tag{21}$$

where the vector $\{v_i\}$ satisfies the following recursive equation:

$$v_i = (l_i - p_{iN}) + \delta \sum_{j=1}^{N-1} [p_{ij}v_j] \text{ if } i < N;$$
$$v_N = 0 \tag{22}$$

Equation (22) can be read as defining the valuation vector given a premium vector. Alternatively it can be used the other way round, to define a premium vector to produce a desired valuation vector.

A Fair Risk-rated Premium

If the guarantee fund charges a premium that is fair between schemes, each scheme must pay its own way. Therefore $v_i = 0$ for all rating classes i apart from $i = N$. It can readily be seen that this can only be achieved by setting $l_i = p_{iN}$.

But there is a critical implicit assumption in this argument: that all schemes can actually pay the premium without any adverse effect on their funding status. If sponsors that are likely to become insolvent do not increase their contributions to the pension scheme to make up for the effect of the levy, the logic fails. The premium paid by weaker schemes is then paid, not by the sponsor, but by the guarantee fund itself. For when the employer does become insolvent, and the assets and liabilities of the pension scheme fall to the fund, the assets will be diminished by the amount of the premium paid.

Assume that there is a maximum level of premium that can be paid, and call it $\overline{l}$; then weaker employers—those with a credit rating of some level m or worse—pay the capped premium, and have negative value to the guarantee fund, while stronger employers have their premium set to ensure that they have zero value to the fund. Formally, we require that the premium be set to ensure that

$$v_i = 0 \quad \text{if} \quad i < m;$$
$$l_i = \bar{l} \quad \text{and} \quad v_i < 0 \quad \text{if} \quad i \geq m. \tag{23}$$

The lower the premium cap, the higher the risk-based premium paid by uncapped schemes. If the scheme sponsored by a strong employer is to have zero value, the premium paid must cover not only the risk of insolvency in the year, but also the risk of the employer's credit rating deteriorating to the extent that the scheme has negative value to the guarantee fund. The lower the cap, the lower the critical credit rating m at which the cap comes into force, and the greater the probability that the strong employer will become a capped employer with negative value to the guarantee fund next year. Also, the lower the cap, the greater the loss of value if the employer's credit rating does fall below the critical level.

With the cap, the recursive equation then becomes:

$$l_i = \begin{cases} p_{iN} - \delta \sum_{j=1}^{N-1} \left[p_{ij} v_j \right] & \text{if } i < m; \\ \bar{l} & \text{if } m \leq i < N; \end{cases}$$
$$v_i = \begin{cases} 0 & \text{if } i < m; \\ \bar{l} - p_{iN} + \delta \sum_{j=1}^{N-1} \left[p_{ij} v_j \right] & \text{if } m \leq i < N; \\ 0 & \text{if } i = N. \end{cases} \tag{24}$$

It is straightforward to solve this set of equations for the premium vector l, the valuation vector v and the critical rating level m for any given transition matrix, and the values of $\bar{l}$ and δ.

With this methodology, some schemes have a negative value and none have a strictly positive value. With a mixed population of schemes, the present value of the guarantee fund's aggregate income from the risk-based premium is lower than the present value of future claims. If the guarantee fund simply charged the risk-based premium computed in this way, it would in the long run become insolvent. The only way the guarantee fund can ensure that it remains solvent in the long run is to charge solvent schemes more than the pure risk-based premium so that the average scheme has zero value to the guarantee fund.

A Quantification of the Model

To illustrate the argument, we now quantify the effect on the whole premium structure of imposing a plausible ceiling on the premium rate. The main inputs needed are the transition probabilities between different credit ratings. Since they are used in a valuation context, it is correct to input risk-adjusted numbers, as used in the previous section of this chapter. Changes in both credit ratings and scheme deficits have a substantial systematic component: there are large differences between objective and risk-adjusted probabilities, and these have a large impact on the required level of the premiums. The risk-adjusted transition matrix can be estimated from the objective transition matrix by making use of market data on the credit spreads of rated bonds, and on recovery rates (Lando 2004), but this assumes that the risk-adjusted expected return on all bonds is the same. Since our concern here is less with the overall level of the premium than with illustrating the effects of its distribution between different schemes, we base our figures on historical default and transition rates, and leave the difficult question of the appropriate risk adjustments to future work.

Using the Standard & Poor's database, we estimate the transition matrix for all countries and all industries over the period 1981–2003. More specifically, we take the five-year transition matrix, recalculate it to exclude companies that were not credit rated at the end of the period, and compute the corresponding single-year transition matrix. Companies may become non-rated because they have repaid all their debt, because they have been merged or taken over, or because they cease to cooperate with the rating agency. Depending on the rating class, between 19 and 38 per cent of companies become non-rated after five years; the methodology assumes that the non-rated company and its successor are of similar average credit quality.

The use of annualized five-year transition data rather than annual transition data is intended to mitigate the problem of rating momentum—if a company has been downgraded, it is slightly more likely to suffer a further downgrade. This is inconsistent with our model in this section, which assumes that rating transitions follow a Markov process, but does not alter the conclusion. The transition matrix we use is shown in panel A of Table 10.3.

To compute the overall effect on the guarantee fund, we need to fix the distribution of schemes by rating class (more accurately, the distribution of deficits by rating class). Approximate figures for the United Kingdom are given in panel B of the table.

Assuming an annual discount factor of 0.98, with values of $\bar{l}$ of 5, 10 and 15 per cent, the figures for the premium are shown in Table 10.4.

The set of figures in the final column of Table 10.4 correspond to the pure uncapped philosophy where each scheme pays a premium on its deficit equal to the probability of the employer becoming insolvent in the year. On the quite implausible assumption that the premium is paid by all schemes without increasing their deficits, every scheme has zero value.

The table shows that as the cap is reduced, the risk-based premium rises substantially for uncapped schemes. The effect of imposing a 5 per cent cap on the rate paid means that all schemes that are not investment grade now represent a significant net cost to the guarantee fund. Because there is a chance

Table 10.3   Five-year Ratings Transition Matrix (p_{ij}) and Distribution of
UK Pension Schemes by Rating Category (%)

A. Five-year ratings transition matrix

	AAA	AA	A	*Transition to:* BBB	BB	B	CCC/C	Default
Transition from:								
AAA	92.04	7.46	0.27	0.19	0.01	0.03	0.00	0.01
AA	0.64	90.35	8.44	0.39	0.03	0.10	0.00	0.04
A	0.02	2.26	91.44	5.46	0.50	0.29	0.00	0.02
BBB	0.06	0.16	4.53	89.66	4.21	0.71	0.34	0.33
BB	0.00	0.12	0.10	7.37	81.19	7.24	1.05	2.92
B	0.02	0.01	0.28	0.02	7.66	77.87	3.83	10.31
CCC/C	0.10	0.00	0.00	1.35	0.00	12.75	55.45	30.35

B. Distribution of UK pension schemes by rating category

Rating	Proportion
AAA	2
AA	15
A	30
BBB	29
BB	17
B	6
CCC/C	1
D	0

Source: Panel A: Standard & Poor's Risk Solutions, June 2005, and authors' calculations; Panel B:
PPF (2005), Figure 6.

that investment grade-rated employers will become junk rated, their levy rate
is raised. The increases are quite substantial. It should be stressed that the reason that their premium is increased is *not* to subsidize the cap on the weaker
employers, but rather to recognize that their own credit rating may well dete-
riorate, and they would then be unable to pay the uncapped premium.

Since 25 per cent of schemes are estimated to be junk rated, the net
position of the guarantee fund (risk-rated premium less claims) is equal to
–3.56 per cent of the value of the aggregate deficit. With an annual discount

Table 10.4   Cross-subsidies under Different Premium Arrangements (%)[a]

Rating	$\bar{l} = 5\%$		$\bar{l} = 10\%$		$\bar{l} = 15\%$		No Cap	
	Premium Rate	Value	Premium Rate	Value	Premium Rate	Value	Premium Rate	Value
AAA	0.02	0	0.01	0	0.01	0	0.01	0
AA	0.08	0	0.00	0	0.04	0	0.04	0
A	0.14	0	0.00	0	0.02	0	0.02	0
BBB	1.00	0	0.00	0	0.40	0	0.33	0
BB	0.00	–	4.02	0	3.27	0	2.92	0
B	0.00	–34	10.00	–9	11.70	0	10.31	0
CCC/C	0.00	–6	10.00	–47	1.00	–34	30.30	0
Mean value		–3.6		–0.99		–0.34		0.0

a   The table shows the premium rates and net present values to the pension guarantee fund of pension schemes with different credit ratings, assuming the model described in equation (23) and the assumptions described in the text. When there is no premium cap, all funds pay premiums with a present value equal to the present value of their future claims. However, the introduction of a premium cap implies that schemes with lower-quality sponsors are unable to pay the present value of their future claims, while the premium rates for schemes with higher-quality sponsors increase to reflect the possibility that they may in future become subject to the premium cap. The mean value refers to the present value of the total subsidy that the guarantee fund will require to remain solvent in the long run.

Source: Author's calculations.

factor of 0.98, this could be neutralized by an additional annual premium of $3.56\% \times (1 - 0.98) = 0.07$ per cent on all deficits. This extra premium represents a pure subsidy from sponsors with investment grade ratings to sponsors with junk ratings, and is unavoidable due to our assumption that weaker firms cannot simultaneously pay large premiums for pension insurance and maintain the funding of their pension schemes.

Some of the assumptions we make in this simple model bias this subsidy downward significantly. For instance, we assume in the model that sponsor rating transitions are uncorrelated with changes in the scheme's deficit. In practice one would expect a fall in equity values to be associated with both a decline in ratings and an increase in deficits, as discussed earlier. Furthermore, standard finance theory suggests that a lower discount factor should be used for such situations, and that a higher discount factor should be used for more benign circumstances where rising equity markets tend to cause both a strengthening of the sponsor's condition and a reduction in scheme deficits. Finally, even idiosyncratic falls in credit ratings are probably associated with increases in pension underfunding as firms reduce or postpone pension contributions.

The assumption that there is a ceiling on the pension guarantee premiums that firms can realistically pay implies that there is necessarily a subsidy from firms with strong credit ratings to firms with weaker ones. While a risk-rated premium structure will effectively reduce moral hazard for stronger schemes, it may actually encourage moral hazard by weaker schemes, which are precisely the ones that will make most of the claims on the guarantee fund. We therefore believe that a premium structure of this type may result in the bifurcation of pension schemes between those that are well funded with financially secure sponsors and those that are poorly funded with insecure sponsors. But this outcome is not inevitable. If a risk-rated premium structure is introduced simultaneously with controls on scheme funding and investment, if there is regular monitoring of problem schemes to prevent moral hazard and if there is some degree of cross-subsidy between stronger and weaker schemes, this undesirable result may be avoided.

5. CONCLUSIONS

Our analysis does not claim to be extremely precise. However, we believe that it is broadly applicable to both the PBGC and the PPF. The way that pension schemes are funded, and the way that funds are invested, implies that a deep and prolonged decline in financial markets could readily lead to widespread failure. An inherent feature of the claims process of any pension guarantee fund is likely to be that many years of small claims will be interspersed with rare and unpredictable periods of exceedingly large claims. These periods will coincide with periods when the stability of the whole financial sector is under maximum strain. We suggest that the magnitude of the claims in these unstable periods will be so large that it is not politically feasible or economically sensible to build up reserves to meet them. When such a crisis does occur, it may well be impossible to meet claims through a steep increase in the levy on employers, since they will at the same time be facing heavy financial demands to rebuild their own depleted pension funds. This has already happened with the PBGC and we believe that it may also happen to the PPF in due course. It is hard to see any alternative to governments stepping in to rescue these funds at some point in the future.

Furthermore, we argue that any attempt to risk rate the premiums charged by these funds will not resolve the problem, because weaker schemes will be unable to simultaneously improve their funding ratios and pay large pension guarantee premiums. Risk rating will also never entirely eliminate subsidies between stronger and weaker schemes, and therefore never entirely eliminate moral hazard. Premium risk rating will therefore need to be implemented in tandem with strong minimum funding requirements, to reduce the potential cost of guarantee funds and prevent a bifurcation of pension schemes into well-funded and poorly funded groups—an outcome that would be politically and economically costly in the long run.

NOTES

1. This chapter relies on work published in McCarthy and Neuberger (2005a, 2005b).
2. See, for example, Pennacchi and Lewis (1994) and Lewis and Cooperstein (1993).
3. The level of liabilities faced by the guarantee fund is perfectly correlated with the level of the equity market. This means that the fund could in principle reduce or even get rid of credit risk by selling equities. While this hedging may not be desirable or even practicable, it does provide a price for the risks to which the fund is exposed.
4. We are implicitly assuming that the investment policy of a closed fund precludes the trustees from investing in risky assets and putting the solvency of the fund at risk.
5. The unconditional stationary distribution is $g^Q(a)$ where g^Q satisfies the differential equation:

$$\frac{1}{2}\frac{d^2}{da^2}\left(x^2\sigma_m^2 a^2 g^Q(a)\right) - \frac{d}{da}\left(\left(\frac{1-a}{T} - x\hat{\alpha}a\right)g^Q(a)\right) = 0.$$

   The equation expresses the condition that the unconditional distribution of a is stationary over time.
6. The resulting expected cost of claims is:

$$c = \delta\int_0^1 (1-a)g^P(a)da$$

   where g^P satisfies:

$$\frac{1}{2}\frac{d^2}{da^2}\left(x^2\sigma_m^2 a^2 g^P(a)\right) - \frac{d}{da}\left(\left(\frac{1-a}{T} + x(\alpha - \hat{\alpha})a\right)g^P(a)\right) = 0.$$

   The differential equation expresses the condition that the distribution of the solvency ratio is stationary.
7. See Duffie and Singleton (2003) for an overview.
8. Earlier we emphasized the importance of risk-adjusted discount rates and correlations between deficits and credit ratings. In this section of the chapter, where our concern is with the way the premium varies across schemes, we ignore the correlation between deficits and credit ratings.

References

Aghion, Philippe and Patrick Bolton (1992), 'An Incomplete Approach to Financial Contracting', *Review of Economic Studies*, 59(3): 473–94.

Agosin, R. and E. Pastén (2001), 'Corporate Governance in Chile', OECD Development Centre, Paris.

Alchian, A. (1950), 'Uncertainty, Evolution and Economic Theory', *Journal of Political Economy*, 58: 211–22.

Allen, Franklin and Douglas Gale (2000), *Comparing Financial Systems*, MIT Press, Cambridge MA.

Allen, Franklin and Douglas Gale (2002a), 'Capital Adequacy Regulation: In Search of a Rationale', Wharton Financial Institutions Center Working Paper 03-07, Pennsylvania PA, September.

Allen, Franklin and Douglas Gale (2002b), 'A Comparative Theory of Corporate Governance', Wharton Financial Institutions Center Working Paper 03-27, Pennsylvania PA, December.

Anonymous (1982), 'An Economic and Legal Analysis of Union Representation on Corporate Boards of Directors', *University of Pennsylvania Law Review*, 130: 919–56.

APRA (Australian Prudential Regulation Authority) (2001), *Half Yearly Financial Bulletin on Life Insurance*, Sydney, December.

APRA (Australian Prudential Regulation Authority) (2003), *Superannuation Trends*, Sydney, December.

APRA (Australian Prudential Regulation Authority) (2007), *Annual Superannuation Bulletin*, Sydney, March.

Arrau Pons, P. (1994), 'Fondos de Pensiones y Desarrollo del Mercado de Capitales en Chile: 1980–1993', Serie Financiamiento del Desarrollo No. 19, Comision Economica para America Latina y el Caribe (CEPAL), Santiago de Chile.

ASIC (Australian Securities and Investment Commission) (2004a), 'Revised Good Practice Model for Fee Disclosure', Sydney, July, <http://www.asic.gov.au/asic/pdflib.nsf/LookupByFileName/revised_fees_model.pdf/$file/revised_fees_model.pdf>.

ASIC (Australian Securities and Investment Commission) (2004b), 'Disclosure of Soft Dollar Benefits', Sydney, June.

Atiyah, P.S. (1979), *The Rise and Fall of Freedom of Contract*, Oxford University Press, Oxford.

Bahl, R. and B. Jump, Jr (1974), 'The Budgetary Implications of Rising Employee Retirement System Costs', *National Tax Journal*, September: 479–90.

Bateman, H. (2001), 'Disclosure of Superannuation Fees and Charges', Discussion Paper 03/04, Centre for Pensions and Superannuation, University of New South Wales, Sydney.

Bateman, H. and O. Mitchell (2004), 'New Evidence on Pension Plan Design and Administrative Expenses: The Australian Experience', *Journal of Pension Economics and Finance*, 3(1): 63–76.

Bateman, H., G. Kingston and J. Piggott (2001), *Forced Saving*, Cambridge University Press, Cambridge.

Becht, Marco, Patrick Bolton and Ailsa Röell (2003), 'Corporate Governance and Control', in George Constantinides, Milton Harris and René Stulz (eds), *Handbook of the Economics of Finance*, North-Holland, Amsterdam, pp. 1–109.

Beck, Thorsten and Ross Levine (2004), 'Legal Institutions and Financial Development', NBER Working Paper 10417, National Bureau of Economic Research, Washington DC, April, <http://www.nber.org/papers/w10417>.

Beck, Thorsten, Asli Demirguc-Kunt, Ross Levine and Vojislav Maksimovic (2000), 'Financial Structure and Economic Development: Firm, Industry, and Country Evidence', Policy Research Working Paper Series 2423, World Bank, Washington DC, 14 June.

Beim, D. and C. Calomiris (2001), *Emerging Financial Markets*, McGraw-Hill Irwin, New York NY.

Berger, A.N., J.D. Cummins and M.A. Weiss (1997), 'The Coexistence of Multiple Distribution Systems for Financial Services: The Case for Property–Liability Insurance', *Journal of Business*, 70(4): 515–46.

Berglöf, Erik and Ernst-Ludwig von Thadden (1994), 'Short-term Interests vs. Long-term Interests: Capital Structure with Multiple Investors', *Quarterly Journal of Economics*, 109(4): 1,055–84.

Bernheim, B. Douglas and Michael D. Whinston (1985), 'Common Marketing Agency as a Device for Facilitating Collusion', *RAND Journal of Economics*, 16(2): 269–81.

Bernheim, B. Douglas and Michael D. Whinston (1986), 'Common Agency', *Econometrica*, 54(4): 923–42.

Besley, Timothy and Andrea Prat (2003), 'Pension Fund Governance and the Choice between Defined Benefit and Defined Contribution Plans', CEPR Discussion Paper No. 3955, Centre for Economic Policy Research, London, June.

Bhagat, Sanjai and Bernard S. Black (1999), 'The Uncertain Relationship between Board Composition and Firm Performance', *Business Lawyer*, 54(3): 921–63.

Bhattacharya, U. and H. Daouk (2002), 'The World Price of Insider Trading', *Journal of Finance*, 57(1): 75–108.

Black, B. (1992), 'Agents Watching Agents: The Promise of Institutional Voice', *UCLA Law Review*, 39: 811–93.

Black, D. (2003), *Pension Schemes and Pension Funds in the United Kingdom*, second edition, Oxford University Press, Oxford.

Blake D. and A. Timmermann (2002), 'Performance Benchmarks for Institutional Investors: Measuring, Monitoring and Modifying Investment Behaviour', in John Knight and Stephen Satchell (eds), *Performance Measurement in Finance: Firms, Funds and Managers*, Butterworth Heinemann, Oxford, pp. 108–41.

Blake, D. and A. Timmermann (2004), 'Performance Persistence in Mutual Funds: An Independent Assessment of the Studies Prepared by Charles River Associated for the Investment Management Association', Financial Services Authority, London.

Block, S.B. and D.W. French (2002), 'The Effect of Portfolio Weighting on Investment Performance Evaluation: The Case of Actively Managed Funds', *Journal of Economics and Finance*, 26(1): 16–30.

Bohn, Henning and Robert P. Inman (1996), 'Balanced-budget Rules and Public Deficits: Evidence from the U.S. States', *Carnegie-Rochester Conference Series on Public Policy*, 45: 13–76.

Bonafede, Julia K., Steven J. Foresti and John Dashtara (2007), '2007 Wilshire Report on State Retirement Systems: Funding Levels and Asset Allocation', Wilshire Associates, Inc., Los Angeles CA, 5 March.

Bourdieu, P. (1990), *In Other Words: Essays towards a Reflexive Sociology*, Polity Press, Cambridge.

Broecker, T. (1990), 'Credit-worthiness Tests and Interbank Competition', *Econometrica*, 58(2): 429–52.

Buckley, F.H. (1999), 'Free Contracting in Bankruptcy', in F.H. Buckley (ed.), *The Fall and Rise of Freedom of Contract*, Duke University Press, Durham, pp. 301–11.

Bunt, K., M. Winterbotham and R. Williams (1998), 'The Role of Pension Scheme Trustees', Research Report 81, HM Department of Social Security, London.

Burkart, Mike (1999), 'Economics of Takeover Regulation', Stockholm School of Economics Working Paper No. 99/06, Stockholm, December.

Campbell, J. and L. Viceira (2002), *Strategic Asset Allocation: Portfolio Choice for Long-term Investors*, Oxford University Press, Oxford.

Carhart, M.M. (1997), 'On Persistence in Mutual Fund Performance', *Journal of Finance*, 52(1): 57–82.

Carmichael, Jeffrey and Robert J. Palacios (2003), 'A Framework for Public Pension Fund Management', paper presented at the Conference on Public Pension Fund Management, World Bank, Washington DC.

Carmichael, Jeffrey and Robert J. Palacios (2004), 'Managing Public Pension Funds: A Framework', in A.R. Musalem and R.J. Palacios (eds), *Public Pension Fund Management: Governance Accountability and Investment Policies*, World Bank, Washington DC, pp. 1–48.

Cartwright, J. (1991), *Unequal Bargaining: A Study of Vitiating Factors in the Formation of Contracts*, Oxford University Press, Oxford.

Chan, H.W.H. and P.F. Howard (2002), 'Additions to and Deletions from an Open Ended Market Index: Evidence from the Australian All Ordinaries', *Australian Journal of Management*, 27(1): 45–74.

Chaney, Barbara A., Paul A. Copley and Mary S. Stone (2002), 'The Effect of Fiscal Stress and Balanced Requirements on the Funding and Measurement of State Pension Obligations', *Journal of Accounting and Public Policy*, 21: 287–313.

Choi, J., D. Laibson, B. Madrian and A. Metrick (2001), 'For Better or Worse: Default Effects and 401(k) Savings Behaviour', University of Pennsylvania Working Paper, Philadelphia PA.

Clare, R. (2001), 'Are Administration and Investment Costs in the Australian Superannuation Industry Too High?', Association of Superannuation Funds of Australia (ASFA) Research Centre, Sydney, November.

Clark, G.L. (2000), *Pension Fund Capitalism*, Oxford University Press, Oxford.

Clark, G.L. (2003a), 'Twenty-first Century Pension (In)security', in G.L. Clark and N. Whiteside (eds), *Pension Security in the 21st Century*, Oxford University Press, Oxford, pp. 225–50.

Clark, G.L. (2003b), *European Pensions and Global Finance*, Oxford University Press, Oxford.

Clark, G.L. (2004), 'Pension Fund Governance: Expertise and Organizational Form', *Journal of Pension Economics and Finance*, 3: 233–53.

Clark, G.L. (2006), 'Regulation of Pension Fund Governance', in G.L. Clark, A. Munnell and M. Orszag (eds), *The Oxford Handbook of Pensions and Retirement Income*, Oxford University Press, Oxford, pp. 483–99.

Clark, G.L. (2007), 'Expertise and Representation in Financial Institutions: UK Legislation on Pension Fund Governance and US Regulation of the Mutual Fund Industry', *21st Century Society: Journal of the Academy of Social Sciences*, 2: 1–23.

Clark, G.L. and T. Hebb (2004), 'Pension Fund Corporate Engagement: The Fifth Stage of Capitalism', *Relations Industrielles/Industrial Relations*, 59: 142–70.

Clark, G.L., E. Caerlewy-Smith and J. Marshall (2006), 'Pension Fund Trustee Competence: Decision Making in Problems Relevant to Investment Practice', *Journal of Pension Economics and Finance*, 5: 91–110.

Clark, G.L., E. Caerlewy-Smith and J. Marshall (2007), 'Consistency of UK Pension Fund Trustee Decision-making', *Journal of Pension Economics and Finance*, 6: 67–86.

Coffee, J. (2006), *Gatekeepers*, Oxford University Press, Oxford.

Coleman, A.D.F., N. Esho and M. Wong (2003), 'The Investment Performance of Australian Superannuation Funds', APRA Working Paper, Australian Prudential Regulation Authority, Sydney.

Coleman, J. (1992), *Risks and Wrongs*, Cambridge University Press, Cambridge.

Collin-Dufresne, Pierre and Robert S. Goldstein (2001), 'Do Credit Spreads Reflect Stationary Leverage Ratios?', *Journal of Finance*, 56(5): 1,929–57.

Collin-Dufresne, Pierre, Robert S. Goldstein and Spencer J. Martin (2001), 'The Determinants of Credit Spread Changes', *Journal of Finance*, 56(6): 2,177–207.

Coronado, Julia L., Eric M. Engen and Brian Knight (2003), 'Public Funds and Private Capital Markets: The Investment Practices and Performance of State and Local Pension Funds', *National Tax Journal*, 56(3): 579–94.

D'Arcy, Stephen P., James H. Dulebohn and Pyungsuk Oh (1999), 'Optimal Funding of State Employee Pension Systems', *Journal of Risk and Insurance*, 6(3): 345–80.

del Guercio, D. and J. Hawkins (1999), 'The Motivation and Impact of Pension Fund Activism', *Journal of Financial Economics*, 52: 293–340.

Demarco, Gustavo, Rafael Rofman and Edward Whitehouse (1998), 'Supervising Mandatory Funded Pension Systems: Issues and Challenges', Social Protection Discussion Paper Series 9817, World Bank, Washington DC, December, <http://siteresources.worldbank.org/SOCIALPROTECTION/Resources/SP-Discussion-papers/Pensions-DP/9817.pdf>.

Dewatripont, Mathias and Jean Tirole (1994), *The Prudential Regulation of Banks*, MIT Press, Cambridge MA.

Diamond, W. Douglas (1984), 'Financial Intermediation and Delegated Monitoring', *Review of Economic Studies*, 51(3): 393–414.

Dixit, Avinash K. (1996), *The Making of Economic Policy: A Transaction Cost Politics Perspective*, Munich Lectures in Economics, MIT Press, Cambridge MA.

Dixit, Avinash K., Gene Grossman and Ethan Helpman (1997), 'Common Agency and Coordination: General Theory and Application to Government Policy Making', *Journal of Political Economy*, 105(4): 752–69.

Duffie, Darrell and Kenneth J. Singleton (2003), *Credit Risk: Pricing, Measurement and Management*, Princeton University Press, Princeton NJ.

Dulebohn, H. James (1995), 'A Longitudinal and Comparative Analysis of the Funded Status of State and Local Public Pension Plans', *Public Budgeting and Finance*, Summer: 52–72.

Edwards, Chris and Jagadeesh Gokhale (2006), 'A $2-Trillion Fiscal Hole', *Wall Street Journal*, 12 October.

Edwards, S. (1998), 'The Chilean Pension Reform: A Pioneering Program', in Martin Feldstein (ed.), *Privatizing Social Security*, University of Chicago Press, Chicago IL, pp. 33–57.

EFRP (European Federation for Retirement Provision) (2003), *European Institutions for Occupational Retirement Provision*, Brussels.

Ellison, R. (2002), *Pensions Law and Practice with Precedents*, Sweet & Maxwell, London.

Elton, Edwin, M. Gruber, D. Agrawal and C. Mann (2001), 'Explaining the Rate Spread on Corporate Bonds', *Journal of Finance*, 56(1): 247–77.

Emmerson, C. (2003), 'Pension Reform in the United Kingdom: Increasing the Role of Private Provision?', in G.L. Clark and N. Whiteside (eds), *Pension Security in the 21st Century*, Oxford University Press, Oxford, pp. 168–92.

Epple, Dennis and Katherine Schipper (1981), 'Municipal Pension Funding: A Theory and Some Evidence', *Public Choice*, 37: 141–78.

Epstein, R. (1999), 'Contracts Small and Contracts Large: Contract Law through the Lens of Laissez-faire', in F.H. Buckley (ed.), *The Fall and Rise of Freedom of Contract*, Duke University Press, Durham, pp. 25–61.

Ferson, W.E., S. Saskissian and T.T. Simin (2002), 'Spurious Regressions in Financial Economics', NBER Working Paper 9143, National Bureau of Economic Research, Washington DC.

FIEL and ASAP (Fundación de Investigaciones Económicas Latinoamericanas and Asociación de Administradoras Privadas) (1998), *La Reforma Previsional en Argentina: El Impacto Macroeconómico y la Organización del Mercado de las AFJP*, Buenos Aires.

Fisher, L. (1966), 'Some New Stock-market Indexes', *Journal of Business*, 23: 191–225.

Fore, Douglas (2005), 'Changes in Accounting Practices Will Drive Pension Paradigm Shifts', in Olivia Mitchell and Robert Clark (eds), *Re-inventing the Retirement Paradigm*, Oxford University Press, Oxford, pp. 173–87.

Frances, Jane and Brian McCulloch (2003), 'Governance of Public Pension Funds: New Zealand Superannuation Funds', paper presented to the second Public Pension Fund Management Conference, World Bank, Washington DC, May 5–7.

Gale, Douglas and Martin Hellwig (1985), 'Incentive-compatible Debt Contracts: The One-period Problem', *Review of Economic Studies*, 52(4): 647–63.

Gigerenzer, G., P.M. Todd and the ABC Research Group (1999), *Simple Heuristics that Make Us Smart*, Oxford University Press, New York NY.

Glover, J. (1995), 'Banks and Fiduciary Relationships', *Bond Law Review*, 7(1): 50–66.

Glover, J. (2002), 'Conflicts of Interest in a Corporate Context', in G. Acquaah-Gaisie (ed.), *Corporate Crime Workshop*, Department of Business Law and Taxation, Monash University, Melbourne, pp. 39–57.

Hamilton, David T., Praveen Varma, Sharon Ou and Richard Cantor (2004), 'Default and Recovery Rates of Corporate Bond Issuers', *Special Comment*, Moody's Investors Service, New York, January.

Hawley, J. and A. Williams (1999), *The Rise of Fiduciary Capitalism*, University of Pennsylvania Press, Philadelphia.

Hebb, T. (2006), 'The Economic Inefficiency of Secrets', *Journal of Business Ethics*, 63: 385–405.

Hermalin, Benjamin E. and Michael S. Weisbach (1998), 'Endogenously Chosen Boards of Directors and Their Monitoring of the CEO', *American Economic Review*, 88(1): 96–118.

Hermalin, Benjamin E. and Michael S. Weisbach (2001), 'Boards of Directors as Endogenously Determined Institution: A Survey of the Economic Literature', NBER Working Paper 8161, National Bureau of Economic Research, Washington DC, March.

Hess, David and Gregorio Impavido (2003), 'Lessons from Corporate Governance and International Evidence', paper presented at the Conference on Public Pension Fund Management, World Bank, Washington DC.

Hess, David and Gregorio Impavido (2004), 'Governance of Public Pension Funds: Lessons from Corporate Governance and International Evidence', in A.R. Musalem and R.J. Palacios (eds), *Public Pension Fund Management: Governance Accountability and Investment Policies*, World Bank, Washington DC, pp. 49–89.

Hill, R.J. (2004), 'Stock Market Indices: The Good, the Bad and the Average', University of New South Wales, Sydney, mimeo.

Hirshleifer, David (1995), 'Mergers and Acquisitions: Strategic and Informational Issues', in R.A. Jarrow, V. Maksimovic and W.T. Ziemba (eds), *Handbooks in Operations Research and Management Science, Volume 8: Finance*, Elsevier, Amsterdam.

Hirshleifer, David and Anjan V. Thakor (1994), 'Managerial Performance, Boards of Directors and Takeover Bidding', *Journal of Corporate Finance: Contracting, Governance and Organization*, 1(1): 63–90.

Hirshleifer, David and Anjan V. Thakor (1998), 'Corporate Control through Board Dismissals and Takeovers', *Journal of Economics and Management Strategy*, 7(4): 489–520.

HM Treasury (2001), 'Institutional Investment in the United Kingdom: A Review', Her Majesty's Treasury, London, March, <http://www.hm-treasury.gov.uk/media/2F9/02/31.pdf>.

HM Treasury (2004), 'Myners Review of the Governance of Life Mutuals', Her Maj-

esty's Treasury, London, December, <http://www.hm-treasury.gov.uk/independent_
reviews/myners_review/review_myners_index.cfm>.

HM Treasury (2005), 'Morris Review of the Actuarial Profession: Final Report',
Her Majesty's Treasury, London, March, <http://www.hm-treasury.gov.uk/media/
CA0/9C/morris_final.pdf>.

Holström, Bengt and Jean Tirole (1997), 'Financial Intermediation, Loanable Funds,
and the Real Sector', *Quarterly Journal of Economics*, 112(3): 663–91.

Horack, S., A. Martin and P. Young (2003), 'The Myners Principles and Occupational
Pension Schemes', Research Report 195, HM Department for Work and Pensions,
London.

Houthakker, H. and J. Williamson (1996), *The Economics of Financial Markets*, Oxford
University Press, New York NY.

Hsin, Ping-lung and Olivia S. Mitchell (1994), 'The Political Economy of Public Pensions: Pension Funding, Governance, and Fiscal Stress', *Revista de Analisis Economico*, 9(1): 151–68.

Huang, Jing-Zhi and Ming Huang (2003), 'How Much of the Corporate–Treasury Yield
Spread Is Due to Credit Risk?', Working Paper, Pennsylvania State University, University Park PA, May.

Iglesias, A. (2000), 'Pension Reform and Corporate Governance: Impact in Chile',
Revista ABANTE, 3(1): 109–41.

Iglesias, A. and R. Palacios (2000), 'Managing Public Pension Reserves, Part I: Evidence from the International Experience', Social Protection Working Paper, World
Bank, Washington DC.

Iglesias, A. and D. Vittas (1992), 'The Rationale and Performance of Personal Pension
Plans in Chile', Working Paper No. 867, World Bank, Washington DC.

Ilkiw, John (2003), 'Investment Policies, Processes and Problems in U.S. Public Sector Pension Plans: Some Observations and Solutions from a Practitioner', paper
presented at the Conference on Public Pension Fund Management, World Bank,
Washington DC.

Impavido, Gregorio (2002), 'Governance of Public Pension Fund Management: Pre-
liminary Considerations', in R. Litan, M. Pomerleano and V. Sundarajan (eds),
Financial Sector Governance: The Role of the Public and Private Sectors, Brook-
ings Press, Washington DC, pp. 371–400.

Inman, Robert P. (1982), 'Public Employee Pensions and the Local Labor Budget',
Journal of Public Economics, 19: 49–71.

Inman, Robert P. (1985), 'Appraising the Funding Status of Teacher Pensions: An
Econometric Approach', *National Tax Journal*, 39(1): 21–34.

Iyengar, S. and W. Jiang (2003), 'Choosing Not to Choose: The Effect of More Choices
on Retirement Savings Decisions', Columbia University Working Paper, New York
NY.

Jensen, M. (2000), *A Theory of the Firm*, Harvard University Press, Cambridge MA.

Johnson, C. (1991), *Moral Legislation: A Legal–Political Model for Indirect Conse-
quentialist Reasoning*, Cambridge University Press, Cambridge.

Johnson, Richard W. (1997), 'Pension Underfunding and Liberal Retirement Benefits among State and Local Government Workers', *National Tax Journal*, 50(1):
113–39.

Kakabadse, N., A. Kakabadse and A. Kouzmin (2003), 'Pension Fund Trustees: Role and Contribution', *European Management Journal*, 21(3): 376–86.

Kaufmann, Daniel, Aart Kraay and Massimo Mastruzzi (2003), 'Governance Matters III: Governance Indicators for 1996–2002', World Bank Policy Research Working Paper No. 3106, World Bank, Washington DC, 30 June.

Keneley, M. (2004), 'Adaptation and Change in the Australian Life Insurance Industry: An Historical Perspective', *Accounting, Business and Financial History*, 14(1): 91–109.

Klein, B. (1996), 'Vertical Integration as Organizational Ownership: The Fisher Body–General Motors Relationship Revisited', in S.E. Masten (ed.), *Case Studies in Contracting and Organization*, Oxford University Press, Oxford, pp. 165–78.

Krasa, Stefan and Anne P. Villamil (1992), 'Monitoring the Monitor: An Incentive Structure for a Financial Intermediary', *Journal of Economic Theory*, 57(1): 197–221.

La Porta, R., F. Lopez-de-Silanes, A. Shleifer and R. Vishny (1997), 'Legal Determinants of External Finance', *Journal of Finance*, 52: 1,131–50.

La Porta, R., F. Lopez-de-Silanes, A. Shleifer and R. Vishny (1998), 'Law and Finance', *Journal of Political Economy*, 106: 1,113–55.

La Porta, R., F. Lopez-de-Silanes, A. Shleifer and R. Vishny (2000), 'Investor Protection and Corporate Governance', *Journal of Financial Economics*, 58: 3–27.

Lando, David (2004), *Credit Risk Modeling: Theory and Applications*, Princeton University Press, Princeton NJ.

Langbein, J. (1997), 'The Secret Life of the Trust: The Trust as an Instrument of Commerce', *Yale Law Journal*, 107: 165–89.

Lefort, F. and E. Walker (2000), 'Ownership and Capital Structure of Chilean Conglomerates: Facts and Hypotheses for Governance', *Revista ABANTE*, 3(1): 3–27.

Levine, Ross, Norman Loayza and Thorsten Beck (1999), 'Financial Intermediation and Growth: Causality and Causes', World Bank Policy Research Working Paper No. 2059, World Bank, Washington DC, February.

Lewis, Christopher M. and Richard L. Cooperstein (1993), 'Estimating the Current Exposure of the Pension Benefit Guaranty Corporation to Single-employer Pension Plan Terminations', in Ray Schmitt (ed.), *The Future of Pensions in the United States*, University of Pennsylvania Press for the Pension Research Council, Philadelphia PA, pp. 247–76.

Litterman, B. et al. (2003), *Modern Investment Management*, Wiley, New York NY.

Llewellyn, David (1999), 'The Economic Rationale for Financial Regulation', Occasional Paper Series No. 1, Financial Services Authority, London, April, <http://www.fsa.gov.uk/pubs/occpapers/op01.pdf>.

Maclean, D. (2000), 'Superannuation Trustees and Conflicts of Interest', *Australian Law Journal*, 74(1): 47–57.

Majluf, N., A. Nureya, D. Rodriguez and L. Fuentes (1998), 'Governance and Ownership Structure in Chilean Economic Groups', *Revista ABANTE*, 1(1): 111–39.

Manzoni, Katiusca (2002), 'Modelling Credit Spreads: An Application to the Sterling Eurobond Market', *International Review of Financial Analysis*, 11(2): 183–218.

March, J. (1994), *A Primer on Decision Making*, Free Press, New York NY.

Marcus, Alan J. (1987), 'Corporate Pension Policy and the Value of PBGC Insurance', in Z. Bodie, J.B. Shoven and D.A. Wise (eds), *Issues in Pension Economics*, National

Bureau of Economic Research Project Report, University of Chicago Press, Chicago IL and London, pp. 49–76.

Mark, Stephen T. (1997), 'The Welfare Implications of Political and Economic Decentralization', unpublished PhD dissertation, Wharton School, University of Pennsylvania, Pennsylvania PA.

Masten, S.E. (ed.) (1996), *Case Studies in Contracting and Organization*, Oxford University Press, New York NY.

McCarthy, David G. and Anthony Neuberger (2005a), 'The Pension Protection Fund', *Fiscal Studies*, 2: 139–67.

McCarthy, David G. and Anthony Neuberger (2005b), 'Pricing Pension Insurance: The Proposed Levy Structure for the Pension Protection Fund', *Fiscal Studies*, 4: 471–89.

Merton, Robert C. (1974), 'On the Pricing of Corporate Debt: The Risk Structure of Interest Rates', *Journal of Finance*, 29(2): 449–70.

Mitchell, Olivia S. (1988), 'Worker Knowledge of Pension Provisions', *Journal of Labor Economics*, 6: 21–39.

Mitchell, Olivia S. and Emily Andrews (1981), 'Scale Economies in Private Multiemployer Pension Systems', *Industrial and Labor Relations Review*, 34(July): 522–30.

Mitchell, Olivia S. and Ping-Lung Hsin (1997), 'Public Sector Pension Governance and Performance', in Salvador Valdes Prieto (ed.), *The Economics of Pensions: Principles, Policies and International Experience*, Cambridge University Press, Cambridge, pp. 92–126.

Mitchell, Olivia and Ping-Lung Hsin (1999), 'Managing Public Sector Pensions', in J. Shoven and S. Schieber (eds), *Public Policy toward Pensions*, MIT Press, Cambridge MA, pp. 247–66.

Mitchell, Olivia S. and Robert S. Smith (1994), 'Pension Funding in the Public Sector', *Review of Economics and Statistics*, 76(5): 278–90.

Mitchell, Olivia S., David McCarthy, Stanley C. Wisniewski and Paul Zorn (2000), 'Developments in State and Local Pension Plans', in O.S. Mitchell and E. Hustead (eds), *Pensions for the Public Sector*, University of Pennsylvania Press, Philadelphia PA, pp. 11–40.

Mumy, Gene (1978), 'The Economics of Local Government Pensions and Pension Funding', *Journal of Political Economy*, 86(3): 517–27.

Munnell, A. (2003), 'Restructuring Pensions for the 21st Century: The United States' Social Security Debate', in G.L. Clark and N. Whiteside (eds), *Pension Security in the 21st Century*, Oxford University Press, Oxford, pp. 193–224.

Munnell, A.H. and A. Sunden (2001), 'Investment Practices of State and Local Pension Funds: Implications for Social Security', in Olivia S. Mitchell and Edwin C. Hustead (eds), *Pensions in the Public Sector*, University of Pennsylvania Press, Philadelphia PA, pp. 153–94.

Murphy, Kevin (1999), 'Executive Compensation', in O. Ashenfelter and D. Card (eds), *Handbook of Labor Economics*, North Holland, Amsterdam, pp. 2,485–563.

Nesbitt, Stephen L. (2003), '2003 Wilshire Report on State Retirement Systems: Funding Levels and Asset Allocation', Wilshire Associates, Inc., Los Angeles CA, 12 March.

O'Barr, W.M. and J.M. Conley (1992), *Fortune and Folly: The Wealth and Power of Institutional Investing*, Business One Irwin, Homewood IL.

O'Brien, L. (2004), 'How to Restore the Fiduciary Relationship: A Conversation with Eliot Spitzer', *Harvard Business Review*, 82(5): 70–77.

OECD (Organisation for Economic Co-operation and Development) (2002), 'Guidelines for Pension Fund Governance', Paris, July, <http://www.oecd.org/dataoecd/22/2/2767694.pdf>.

OECD (Organisation for Economic Co-operation and Development) (2004), 'Principles of Corporate Governance', Paris, <http://www.oecd.org/dataoecd/32/18/31557724.pdf>.

PBGC (Pension Benefit Guaranty Corporation) (2003), *Pension Insurance Data Book 2003*, Washington DC.

PBGC (Pension Benefit Guaranty Corporation) (2004), *2004 Annual Report*, Washington DC.

Pedrosa, Monica and Richard Roll (1998), 'Systematic Risk in Corporate Bond Credit Spreads', *Journal of Fixed Income*, 8(3): 7–26.

Pennacchi, George G. and Christopher M. Lewis (1994), 'The Value of Pension Benefit Guaranty Corporation Insurance', *Journal of Money, Credit and Banking*, 26(3): 735–53.

PPCC (Public Pension Coordinating Council) (2002), '2001 Survey of State and Local Government Employee Retirement Systems: Survey Report', March, <http://ppcc.grsnet.com/>.

PPF (Pension Protection Fund) (2005), 'The Pension Protection Fund Levy Consultation Document', Surrey, July, <http://www.pensionprotectionfund.org.uk/rbl_consultation.pdf>.

Productivity Commission (2001), 'Review of the Superannuation Industry (Supervision) Act 1993 and Certain Other Superannuation Legislation', Report No. 18, Canberra, 10 December, <http://www.pc.gov.au/inquiry/super/finalreport/>.

Rajan, R. and L. Zingales (2003), *Saving Capitalism from the Capitalists*, Random House, New York NY.

Rawls, J. (1954), 'Two Concepts of Rules', *Philosophical Review*, 64: 3–32.

Rice, M. and I. McEwin (2002), 'Superannuation Fees and Competition', Phillips Fox Actuaries and Consultants report to the Investment and Financial Services Association, Sydney.

Roberts, M. (2002), 'Self-managed Superannuation Funds: Overview', paper presented to the 10th Annual Colloquium of Superannuation Research, University of New South Wales, Sydney.

Robinson, P. and A. Kakabadse (2002), 'Trustee Decision Making: Positive Impact of Myners', Watson Wyatt, London.

Rocha, Roberto, Richard Hinz and Joaquin Gutierrez (1999), 'Improving the Regulation and Supervision of Pension Funds: Are There Lessons from the Banking Sector?', World Bank, Washington DC, December, <http://wbln0018.worldbank.org/html/FinancialSectorWeb.nsf/(attachmentweb)/spdp0002/$FILE/spdp0002.pdf>.

Runciman, D. and M. Ryan (eds) (2003), *Maitland: State, Trust and Corporation*, Cambridge University Press, Cambridge.

S&P (Standard and Poor's) (2004a), *Understanding Indices*, May, <http://www2.standardandpoors.com/spf/pdf/index/A5_CMYK_UIndices.pdf>.

S&P (Standard and Poor's) (2004b), *S&P Global Indices Methodology*, New York, May.

S&P (Standard and Poor's) (2007), *S&P Australian Indices*, July, <http://www2.standard andpoors.com/spf/pdf/index/SP_Australian_Indices_Methodology_Web.pdf>.

Shiller, R.J. (2002), 'Bubbles, Human Judgement, and Expert Opinion', *Financial Analysts Journal*, 58(3): 18–26.

Shleifer, A. and R.W. Vishny (1997), 'A Survey of Corporate Governance', *Journal of Finance*, 52(2): 737–83.

Shleifer, A. and D. Wolfenzon (2002), 'Investor Protection and Equity Markets', *Journal of Financial Economics*, 66(1): 3–27.

Simon, H. (1982), *Models of Bounded Rationality*, MIT Press, Cambridge MA.

Smith, C.W. (1991), 'Book Review: *The Soul of the Salesman: The Moral Ethos of Personal Sales*', *Social Forces*, 70(1): 287–9.

Stetson, A., A. Stolper and J.C. Hill (1999), *Latin American Capital Markets*, Juris Publishing, New York NY.

Taleb, N.N. (2001), *Fooled by Randomness: The Hidden Role of Chance in the Markets and in Life*, Texere, New York NY.

Taylor, S.S. (1986), *Public Employee Retirement Systems: The Structure and Politics of Teacher Pensions*, ILR Press, Ithaca NY.

Teele, R. (1992), 'The Necessary Reformulation of the Classic Fiduciary Duty to Avoid Conflicts of Interest or Duties', *Australian Business Law Review*, 22(2): 99–113.

Testin, Blair (1984), 'Comparative Survey of Major Public Pension Plans, State of Wisconsin Retirement Research', Committee Staff Report No. 74, Retirement Research Committee, Madison WI.

Testin, Blair (1986), 'Comparative Survey of Major Public Pension Plans, State of Wisconsin Retirement Research', Committee Staff Report No. 77, Retirement Research Committee, Madison WI.

Testin, Blair and R.K. Snell (1989), 'Comparative Statistics of Major State Retirement Systems, 1984–1988', National Conference of State Legislatures, Denver CO, May.

Thomas, A., N. Pettigrew, S. Candy and A. Hulusi (2000), 'The Changing Role of the Occupational Pension Scheme Trustee', Research Report 124, HM Department of Social Security, London.

Trebilcock, M. (1993), *The Limits of Freedom of Contract*, Harvard University Press, Cambridge MA.

Trebilcock, M. (1999), 'External Critiques of Laissez-faire Contract Values', in F.H. Buckley (ed.), *The Fall and Rise of Freedom of Contract*, Duke University Press, Durham, pp. 78–93.

Turner, John and Dan Beller (eds) (1989), *Trends in Pensions 1989*, US Government Printing Office, Washington DC.

Turque, Bill (2006), 'Costly Change Looming for Retiree Benefits', *Washington Post*, 30 January.

Useem, Michael and Olivia S. Mitchell (2000), 'Holders of the Purse Strings: Governance and Performance of Public Retirement Systems', *Social Science Quarterly*, 81(2): 491–506.

USGAO (United States General Accounting Office) (1985), *Budget Issues: State Balanced Budget Practices*, US Government Printing Office, Washington DC.

USGAO (United States General Accounting Office) (1993), *Balanced Budget Requirements: State Experiences and Implications for the Federal Government*, US Government Printing Office, Washington DC.

Utgoff, Kathleen P. (1993), 'The PBGC: A Costly Lesson in the Economics of Federal Insurance', in Mark S. Sniderman (ed.), *Government Risk-bearing: Proceedings of a Conference Held at the Federal Reserve Bank of Cleveland, May 1991*, Kluwer Academic, Norwell MA and Dordrecht, pp. 145–60.

Valdés Prieto, S. (1992), 'Ajuste Estructural en el Mercado de Capitales: La Evidencia Chilena', in D. Wisecarver (ed.), *El Modelo Economico Chileno*, Centro Internacional para el Desarrollo Economico (CINDE), pp. 403–44.

Vittas, Dimitri (1998), 'Regulatory Controversies of Private Pension Funds', World Bank, Washington DC, January, <http://www.worldbank.org/html/dec/Publications/Workpapers/WPS1800series/wps1893/wps1893.pdf>.

Wagner, R.K. (2002), 'Smart People Doing Dumb Things: The Case of Managerial Incompetence', in R.J. Sternberg (ed.), *Why Smart People Can Be So Stupid*, Yale University Press, Yale CT, pp. 42–62.

Walsh, Mary Williams (2006), 'Public Pension Plans Face Billions in Shortages', *New York Times*, 8 August.

Warsmith, Stephanie (2003), 'Ohio Teacher Benefits Cut: Loss of Subsidized Health Care for Retirees Means New or Increased Premiums in 2004', *Beacon Journal*, 16 May, <http://www.ohio.com/mld/ohio/living/education/6061408.htm>.

Watson Wyatt (2007), *Multinational Pension Governance—2007 Survey Report*, Watson Wyatt Worldwide, <http://www.watsonwyatt.com/research/resrender.asp?id=2007-US-0053&page=1>.

Williamson, O. (1984), 'Corporate Governance', *Yale Law Journal*, 93(7): 1,197–230.

Williamson, O. (1985), *The Economic Institutions of Capitalism*, Free Press, New York NY.

Williamson, O. (1996), *The Mechanisms of Governance*, Oxford University Press, Oxford.

Winkelvoss, Howard (1993), *Pension Mathematics with Numerical Illustrations*, second edition, University of Pennsylvania Press, Philadelphia PA.

Wooldridge, Jeffrey M. (2002), *Econometric Analysis of Cross Section and Panel Data*, MIT Press, Cambridge MA.

Young, Perry (2003), 'Public Pension Funds under Stress', comments at the Public Pensions in Uncertain Times Seminar, Standard & Poor's, New York, May.

Zultowski, W.H. (1979), 'The Extent of Buyer-initiated Life Insurance Sales', *Journal of Risk and Insurance*, 46(4): 707–14.

Index

accountability 13, 28, 154
accounting procedures 67
accounting standards 2, 197
accumulation funds 64, 79
accumulation (total return) indices 160,
    162, 163
active board members 151–2, 155
  governance, funding and performance
      of public pension plans 183, 189,
      192, 193, 194, 196, 199
activism, pension fund 1, 34, 57–8, 60
actuarial accrued liability (AAL) 186
Administradoras de Fondos de
    Jubilaciones y Pensiones (AFJPs)
    122
Administradoras de Fondos de Pensiones
    (AFPs) 121
Administradoras de Fondos para el
    Retiro (AFORES) 119–21
administration
  charges 87, 88–9
  functions 12–13
    and potential conflicts of interest
        79–81
adviser-linked investments 82
advisers 24
  assessment of 211, 215, 219
  more involvement in work of pension
      fund groups 215, 219
agency, law of 70–71
agency risks 70
Agosin, R. 58
Ahold 14
All Ordinaries Index 160, 174
Allen, F. 25, 100, 145
amortization period 189, 192, 194
AMP Capital Sustainable Future
    Australian Share Fund 167–8
analysis 105–6, 125, 126, 136
  Argentina 123

Australia 111
Chile 121–2
Hong Kong 125
Hungary 117–19
Ireland 114
Mexico 120
US 113
Anglo-American reactive supervisory
    style 100
Anglo-Saxon capitalism 145
approved deposit funds 62, 63
Argentina
  pension and corporate governance
      reforms 33–4, 55–6
  supervisory practice 122–3, 125–33,
      134
assessment of advisers 211, 215, 219
asset management functions 12–13, 81–2
Atiyah, P.S. 24
attitudes, trustees' 207–10
auditors 15, 24, 103
Australia 25, 61–96
  charges to fund management industry
      85–9
  costs 84–9
  functions of trustees and potential
      conflicts of interest 74–83
  funding of commissions 73, 91–3
  main forms of regulatory protection
      65–8
  market, regulatory and institutional
      failure 68–74
  performance benchmarking see
      benchmarking performance
  returns 85, 93–4
  supervisory practice 110–13, 125–33,
      134
  trustees' perception of their role and
      effectiveness see trustees
  types of pension fund 61–5

Australian Competition and Consumer
  Commission (ACCC) 69
Australian Prudential Regulation
  Authority (APRA) 61, 62, 64, 84,
  110, 111
Australian Securities and Investment
  Commission (ASIC) 69, 78
Australian Taxation Office (ATO) 63, 64
authority, supervisor's 106–7

balanced budget requirement 191
Bank for International Settlements 118
banks 78, 84, 141
Basel Committee on Banking
  Supervision 118
Bateman, H. 201
Becht, M. 139, 140, 141, 142, 143, 144,
  145
Beck, T. 101, 129, 130
behavioural persistence 187–8, 193, 194
beliefs, trustees' 207–10
benchmarking performance 4, 158–75
  Australian stock market indices 160,
    173–5
  benchmark design 163–6
  benchmarks used by Australian
    pension funds 158–60, 161
  funds, investment choices and the
    associated benchmarks 169–72
  mismatches between benchmarks and
    investment styles 166–8
  S&P/ASX 200 indices 158, 160–63,
    164, 173
benefits
  benefit adjudication functions 12–13
  discretion over 81
  structure and classification of
    Australian pension funds 64
Berger, A.N. 77
Besley, T. 150–51
Bhagat, S. 142
BHP Billiton 163
bifurcation of pension schemes 245, 246
Black, B.S. 142
Blake, D. 9, 72, 159
Block, S.B. 164
boards of directors 142–3, 144–5, 146
boards of pension funds 151–2, 153–4,
  155
  board cohesion 211, 214

composition 151, 152, 153
  funding and performance of US
    public pensions 182, 183, 186,
    189, 192, 193, 194, 196, 197,
    199
  equal representation 66–7, 74
  functioning and organization 153
  statements of investment policies 154
  transparency and accountability 154
Bohn, H. 194
Bolton, P. 139, 140, 141, 142, 143, 144,
  145
Bonafede, J.K. 179
bond prices 231–2
borrowing, by pension guarantee funds
  238
budget carry-over practice 184, 191,
  193, 194, 199
Bunt, K. 18
Burkart, M. 142
business opportunities 81–2
business plan 67–8

Caerlewy-Smith, E. 10, 18
California Public Employees' Retirement
  System (CalPERS) 1
Campbell, J. 16
Canada Pension Plan (CPP) 147
Canadian Pension Plan Investment
  Board (CPPIB) 147–8
capital markets
  development 129–30, 135, 136
  domestic 31–2, 33, 35–6, 47–8,
    48–52, 53
  international 31–2, 33, 35–6, 37–42,
    47–8, 48–52, 53
cap, premium 240–45
Carhart, M.M. 72
Carmichael, J. 154, 188
Cartwright, J. 24
ceiling on premium rate 240–45
Central and Eastern Europe 99
chained Laspeyres formula 160–62
Chan, H.W.H. 166
Chaney, B.A. 184, 191, 194
charges 85–9
  administration 87, 88–9
  distribution 86–8
  investment management 87, 89
  waiver on small accounts 68

Chile 60
  pension and corporate governance
    reforms 33–4, 56–8
  supervisory practice 121–2, 125–33,
    134
civil law tradition 130, 136, 137
claims 224, 245
  simulating distribution of 235–8
Clare, R. 69, 84
Clark, G.L. 9, 10, 11, 12, 14, 18, 19, 23,
    25, 200
codes of conduct 13–16, 26
  survey of Australian trustees 211, 215,
    216, 218
coherence principle 15
Coleman, A.D.F. 72, 85
collective action 71
collective action problem 13
  addressing for key stakeholders
    152–4, 155
  of shareholders 140–46
collective principals 144–6
Collin-Dufresne, P. 224, 230, 231, 232,
    233
Comisión Nacional del Sistema de
    Ahorro para el Retiro (CONSAR)
    119–21
commissions 73, 91–3
  present system 91–2
  previous system 91
common law tradition 130, 136, 137
communication 104–5, 125–6, 127, 136
  Argentina 123
  Australia 111
  Chile 121, 122
  Hong Kong 125
  Hungary 117
  Ireland 114, 116
  Mexico 120
  survey of Australian trustees 211, 213
  US 113, 114
comparative analysis 108–10, 125–33,
    134
compatibility principle 15
compensatory actions 108
competence of trustees 10, 19, 26
comprehensive–exception based scale
    109–10
compulsory systems
  pay-as-you-go system 32, 48, 50

supervisory practice 101, 102, 133,
    134, 135–6
concentration of ownership 140–41, 146,
    153
conflicts of interest
  Australia 3, 65–6, 70
    functions of trustees and potential
      conflicts of interest 74–83
    separation of ownership and control
      140–46
Conley, J.M. 74
consistency principle 14–15
consultants 23–4
  decision making by 206–7
contracts
  classification of Australian funds by
      contractual party 63–4
  governance through 23–5, 26–7
control, separation of ownership and
    140–46
Copley, P.A. 184, 191, 194
Coronado, J.L. 184, 190
corporate governance 1–2, 140–46, 200
corporate governance reforms 3, 30–60
  historical background 33–4
  model 34–53
    demographic structure and
      equilibrium with endogenous
      investor protection 46–8
    economy description and decisions
      of a risk-neutral individual
      34–46
    effect of a pension reform 48–53
    optimal decisions if cost of going
      public is sunk 36–42
    optimal investor protection 42–6
  pro-investor legal reforms 33–4, 55–8
corporate pensions sector 197
  Australian corporate funds 62, 63, 74,
      85, 86, 87, 202, 203
  returns 93–4
corporate trustee directors 83
Corporations Act (2001) (Australia) 77
Corporations Law
  Argentina 55
  Chile 56–7
correction 107–8, 125, 126, 136
  Argentina 123
  Australia 111
  Chile 121, 122

Hong Kong 125
Hungary 117, 119
Ireland 114
Mexico 120
US 113, 114
corrective–deterrent scale 109–10
cost efficiency 16
cost of going public 35
    optimal decisions if this cost is sunk
        36–42
credit-rating agencies 103
credit ratings 239–40
    critical credit rating 241
    and risk-rated premium 239–40,
        241–5
credit spreads 230–32
cross-subsidy 225, 238–45, 245–6
'cults', investment 71–3
Cummins, J.D. 77
current trustee model needs rethinking
    211, 215, 216, 219
Cyprus Social Security Fund 148

Dashtara, J. 179
debt 140–41, 146, 153
    see also loans
decision making 201
    model of pension and corporate
        governance reform 34–46
    optimal decisions if cost of going
        public is sunk 36–42
    rules and procedures 19–23, 26
    survey of Australian trustees 211,
        212–13, 214
default modelling 224, 230–38
    approaches to 230–32
    estimating the model 233–5
    simulating the claims distribution
        235–8
defined benefit schemes 12, 15, 23, 197
    Australia 64, 79, 95
    pension guarantee funds *see* pension
        guarantee funds
defined contribution schemes 12, 15, 23,
    201
delegation 80
demographic structure
    Australian trustees 202–3, 204–5
    pension and corporate governance
        reforms 46–8

Department of Enterprise, Trade and
    Employment (Ireland) 114
developing countries 99, 139, 147, 148
direct sales 78
directive–negotiated scale 109–10
directly invested funds 65
directors 147
    boards of 142–3, 144–5, 146
    corporate and life insurance 83
disclosure programmes 104
discretion 9, 10, 11–12
    over benefits 81
    over fees 82–3
distribution
    charges 86–8
    functions of trustees and potential
        conflicts of interest 74–9
dividends 166
domestic capital markets 31–2, 33, 35–6,
    47–8, 48–52, 53
dot.com bubble 10
Dow Jones Industrial Average 164

economic development, stage of
    100–101, 127–9, 135, 136
Edwards, S. 59
eligible rollover funds 62, 64
Ellison, R. 12
Employee Benefits Security
    Administration (EBSA) (US) 113
Employee Retirement Income Security
    Act (ERISA) (1974) (US) 115, 141,
        193, 223
employer-sponsored funds 63, 74
employers
    key stakeholder 151–2
    role of 78–9
ENDESA 60
ENERSIS 60
Engen, E.M. 184, 190
Enron 1, 14, 200
entrepreneur's wealth 39, 42
    optimal investor protection 43, 45
equal representation rules 66–7, 74
equally weighted benchmarks 164
Equitable Life 200
equities, restrictions on 148–9
Esho, N. 72, 85
executive compensation 143–4, 146, 153
executive directors 142

expense ratios 189
expertise of trustees 3, 10, 16–19, 26, 201
  Australian survey of trustees 203–7
  and decision making rules 20–21

Federal Thrift Savings Plan 201
fee-based system 92–3
fees, discretion over 82–3
Ferson, W.E. 72
fiduciary duties/responsibilities 23, 29, 56–7, 65–6, 70, 153
  survey of Australian trustees 211, 214
financial intermediation 140–41, 146, 153
financial proficiency 211, 214
firm default *see* default modelling
fiscal stress 182, 184, 191, 194
Fisher, L. 144, 166
Fisher index 165
Fisher separation theorem 144, 156
flow funding ratio 180, 181, 183–4, 186, 187–8, 192–3, 194, 195, 196, 199
Fore, D. 197
foreign investments, restrictions on 148–9
Foresti, S.J. 179
Frances, J. 148
free float 162, 163, 164
French, D.W. 164
FTSE 100 index 231
functions of pension funds 12–13
  and trustees' potential conflicts of interest 74–82
functions of supervision 102–8, 125–7, 136
  see also supervisory practices
fund managers *see* investment managers
funded scheme, change to 30–31, 33, 48–53
funding status *see* United States of America

Gale, D. 25, 100, 145
GDP per capita 127–9, 135
general mandates 147–8, 149
Ghana Social Security and National Insurance Trust (SSNIT) 148
Gigerenzer, G. 10–11, 21
Global Industry Classification Standard

(GICS) 167
Glover, J. 65–6, 78
Goldstein, R.S. 224, 230, 231, 232, 233
good governance procedures 211, 214
government
  final guarantor 238
  key stakeholder 151–2, 155
guarantee funds *see* pension guarantee funds
guidelines for pension fund governance 2, 14–16

Hamilton, D.T. 231
Hawley, J. 11
Hebb, T. 14, 24
Hermalin, B.E. 143
Hess, D. 139, 147, 148, 149, 151, 190
Hill, J.C. 58
Hill, R.J. 164, 165
Hirshleifer, D. 142, 143
historical default rates 230, 231
Honduras 149
Hong Kong 123–5, 125–33, 134
hostile takeovers 141–2, 146, 153
Howard, P.F. 166
Hsin, P.-L. 182, 183–4, 187, 189, 190, 191, 193, 194, 195, 200
Huang, J.-Z. 232, 233–4, 235
Huang, M. 232, 233–4, 235
Hungarian Financial Supervisory Authority (HFSA) 116–19
Hungary 116–19, 125–33, 134
hybrid funds 64

Iglesias, A. 57–8, 147, 149, 200
Ilkiw, J. 179
Impavido, G. 139, 147, 148, 149, 151, 154, 190
in-state investment 190–91, 192, 195
Income Tax (Assessment) Act (1936) (Australia) 66
Income Tax (Assessment) Act (1997) (Australia) 66
independent third parties 15, 24, 103
index number formulae 160–62, 165–6
Indian Employee Provident Fund 148
industry funds 62, 63, 68, 76, 85, 86, 87, 202, 203
  REST 159, 169–70
  returns 93–4

Sunsuper 159, 170–72
industry issues 211, 215, 216, 218–19
information asymmetries 69
Inman, R.P. 182, 185, 194
innovation 22–3
institutional failures 71–4
intensity scales 108–10
interest groups 30
interest rate 39–42
    optimal investor protection 43, 45
intermediation cost reductions 31–2, 59
internal contracts 24–5
Internal Revenue Service (US) 113
international capital markets 31–2, 33,
    35–6, 37–42, 47–8, 48–52, 53
intertemporal investment theory of a
    firm 144
intervention 106–7, 111, 125, 126, 136
    Argentina 123
    Australia 111
    Chile 121, 122
    Hong Kong 125
    Hungary 117, 119
    Ireland 114, 116
    Mexico 120
    US 113
investable weight factor (IWF) 162–3
investment
    choice and regulatory protection in
        Australia 67
    function 12–13
        trustees and potential conflicts of
            interest 81–2
    manner of and classification of
        Australian funds 64–5
    practices 183–4, 186, 190–91, 192,
        195, 196, 199
    regulations 148–50
investment 'cults' 71–3
investment grade ratings 242–4
investment management charges 87, 89
investment managers
    funds placed with 65
    investment style and benchmarking
        performance 166–8
    performance 72–3
investment policies 148–50
    statement of 154
investment surpluses, reclaiming 229
investor protection 31, 32

measures of 59
model of pro-investor legal reforms
    34–54
    demographic structure and
        equilibrium with endogenous
        investor protection 46–8
    effect of a pension reform 48–53
    optimal investor protection 42–6
    pro-investor legal reforms 33–4, 55–8
Ireland 114–16, 125–33, 134

Johnson, R.W. 185, 194
junk grade ratings 243–4

Kakabadse, A. 4, 201, 203, 216
Kakabadse, N. 4, 216
Kaufmann, D. 101, 131
Keneley, M. 71
key stakeholders
    addressing the collective action
        problem of 152–4, 155
    identifying for public pension plans
        150–52
Knight, B. 184, 190
Korean National Provident Fund 148
Kouzmin, A. 4, 216
Kraay, A. 101, 131

La Porta, R. 32, 59
Lando, D. 242
Langbein, J. 9, 11, 25
Laspeyres index formula 160–62, 165–6
Latin America 30, 32, 52–3, 58, 99
    proactive supervisory style 100
    see also under individual countries
law of agency 70–71
legal failures 70–71
legal systems 101, 130–32, 135–6, 137
Lend Lease 95–6
leverage ratio 232–3
Levine, R. 101, 129, 130
liability insurance 190
licensing 102–3, 111, 125, 126, 136
    Argentina 123
    Australia 110, 111
    Chile 121
    Hong Kong 125
    Hungary 117
    Ireland 114
    Mexico 120

US 113
life insurance 76–8
    directors 83
    funds held through life insurance
        companies 65
Life Insurance Act (1995) (Australia) 83
liquidity 162
Llewellyn, D. 100
Lloyd's of London 11
loans
    member loans 154
    restrictions on 148–9
Loayza, N. 101, 129, 130
log leverage ratio 232–3
London Stock Exchange 11
long term outlook 215, 218

Maitland, F.W. 11, 13, 25
management practices 183, 186, 189–90,
    192, 193–4, 199
mandatory systems *see* compulsory
    systems
Mandatory Provident Fund Authority
    (MPFA) (Hong Kong) 124–5
Manzoni, K. 231
March, J. 16
Marcus, A.J. 224–5
Mark, S.T. 182–4, 194
market capitalization 162–3
market failures 68–9
market participation costs 35–6, 46–8,
    50–52, 53–4
market trade-weighted benchmarks 164
markets, sophistication of 215, 218
Marshall, J. 10, 18
Martin, S.J. 231
master trusts 64, 202, 203
Mastruzzi, M. 101, 131
McCulloch, B. 148
McEwin, I. 69, 84
mean reversion 188, 194
    mean-reverting leverage ratios 232–3
member-initiated funds 64
member loans 154
Merton, R.C. 232
Mexico 118, 119–21, 125–33, 134
mismatches between styles and
    benchmarks 166–8
Mitchell, O.S. 180, 182, 183–4, 185,
    187, 188, 189, 190, 191, 193, 194,

195, 200, 201
monitoring 103, 126, 127, 136
    Argentina 122–3
    Australia 110–11
    by banks 141
    Chile 121–2
    Hong Kong 124
    Hungary 117
    Ireland 114, 116
    Mexico 120
    US 113
monopolistic practices 68–9
moral hazard 9–10, 12, 27–8, 190
    pension guarantee funds 224, 225,
        238–45, 245–6
moral mandate 25
Morris review 2
multi-manager asset class options 159,
    160, 161, 170, 171–2
multi-manager diversified options 159,
    160, 161, 169, 170–71
multinational corporations 2
multiple-equation models 185
Munnell, A.H. 190, 195
Murphy, K. 143, 144
Myners review 2, 10, 17, 23, 26, 80, 201

Namibian Government Institution
    Pension Fund 148
National Australia Bank group 95–6
Nesbitt, S.L. 196
Netherlands, the 25
New Zealand Superannuation Fund 148
News Corporation 163, 164–5
non-executive directors 142–3
number of pension funds 132–3, 135–6

Oakes, G. 76–7
O'Barr, W.M. 73–4
obligation 11, 28
OECD
    guidelines for pension fund
        governance 2, 14–16
    principles of corporate governance 14
opting out 28
organizational form 3, 9–29
    codes of conduct 13–16, 26
    decision making rules and procedures
        19–23, 26
    governance through contract 23–5,

26–7
pension fund form and functions
11–13
outreach and education programmes
104–5
outsourcing 80
ownership
concentration 140–41, 146, 153
dispersion 140–46
separation of control from 140–46

Paasche index formula 165–6
Palacios, R. 147, 149, 154, 188, 200
Parmalat 14, 200
past performance 72
Pastén, E. 58
pay-as-you-go system 46–8
change to funded system 30–31, 33,
48–53
compulsory 32, 48, 50
voluntary 31, 47–8, 49, 50
Pedrosa, M. 230–31
PENDAT surveys 180, 181, 191, 197
Pension Benefit Guaranty Corporation
(PBGC) (US) 223, 225, 227, 234–5,
239, 245
Pension Board (Ireland) 114–16
pension fund activism 1, 34, 57–8, 60
pension guarantee funds 4–5, 223–46
cross-subsidy and moral hazard 225,
238–45, 245–6
fair risk-rated premium 240–41
quantification of the model 241–5
modelling the guarantee 225–38
determining the premium 227
dynamics of pension scheme
funding 227–9
extending the model 229
model of firm default 224, 230–38
modelling scheme solvency 225–7
pension ombudsman 116
Pension Protection Fund (PPF) (UK) 5,
223, 225, 227, 245
pension reforms 3, 30–60
historical background 33–4
model of corporate reforms and 34–53
effect of a pension reform 48–53
performance 215, 219
benchmarking *see* benchmarking
performance

investment managers 72–3
public pension funds 146–7
public sector pensions in US *see*
United States of America
plan participants 13, 28
Poisson default model 234, 235, 236,
237, 238
political intervention 147
pooled superannuation trusts 62, 63
portfolio restrictions 33, 52
post-retirement streams 85, 86, 87
Prat, A. 150–51
pre-announcements of index
replacements 166
premium 227, 229
cross-subsidy and moral hazard
238–45, 245–6
structural default model 234–5, 238
price indices 160–62, 163
price-weighted benchmarks 164
principal-agent problem 9–10, 12, 13,
27–8, 140, 190
proactive approach to supervision 100,
109–10
proactive–reactive scale 109–10
Probability and Impact Rating System
(PAIRS) 112
problem solving 17–18
procedures, decision making 19–23, 26
productivity 39–42
optimal investor protection 43, 44
Productivity Commission 69, 71
pro-investor legal reforms *see* investor
protection
prudent person rule 114, 115
public firms, number of 43–6
public offer funds 63–4, 76
Public Pension Coordinating Council
(PPCC) 180
public pension funds 4, 139–57,
200–201
collective action problem of
shareholders 140–46
governance, funding and performance
in US *see* United States of
America
governance practices 146–50
improving governance of 150–54
public sector funds in Australia 62, 63,
74, 85, 86, 87, 202, 203

QSuper 159, 169
returns 93–4
punitive actions 107

QSuper 159, 169
qualifications 203–7
quantitative/normative standards 105

rates of return
Australia 85, 93–4
US public pensions 183–4, 186, 188,
192–3, 194–5, 199
rationality 16–17, 21
Rawls, J. 10, 20, 29
reactive approach to supervision 100,
109–10
rebalancing 163, 164–5
regulations, too many 211, 215, 216, 218
regulatory capture 71
regulatory failures 70–71
remedial actions 107–8
reporting practices 183, 186, 190, 192,
194–5, 196, 199
reserves 238
residual claimants 150–52, 155
restrictive–open scale 109–10
Retail Employees Superannuation Trust
(REST) 159, 169–70
retail funds 62, 63, 64, 68, 76–8, 79, 85,
86, 87, 89
distribution charges 86–8
returns 93–4
retired board members 183, 189, 192,
193, 194, 196, 199
retirement savings accounts 63–4
returns *see* rates of return
revenue diversion 36–7, 48
Rice, M. 69, 84
risk-based approaches 106, 111, 112
risk management planning 67–8
risk-neutral pricing measure 226, 227,
228–9
risk-rated premium 224, 239–45, 245–6
fair 240–41
Roberts, M. 88
Robinson, P. 4, 203, 216
Röell, A. 139, 140, 141, 142, 143, 144,
145
Roll, R. 230–31
rule of law 101, 130–32, 135–6

rules, decision making 19–23, 26

S&P 500 index 164, 167, 184, 191, 193,
195–6, 199, 231
S&P/ASX 20 160, 173
S&P/ASX 50 160, 173
S&P/ASX 100 160, 174
S&P/ASX 200 158, 160–63, 164, 173
broad structure of price and
accumulation indices 160–62
features of 162–3
S&P/ASX 300 160, 173
S&P/ASX Industrial and Resources
Indices 160, 174–5
S&P/ASX MidCap 50 160, 174
S&P/ASX Small Ordinaries Index 160,
174
salespeople 76–8
Sarbanes-Oxley legislation 1–2, 2–3
Saskissian, S. 72
scale 25, 26–7
Securities Law
Argentina 55
Chile 56–7
selection procedures for trustees 211,
215, 216, 219
self-investment 82
self-managed funds 62, 64, 88, 202, 203
shared philosophy about the future 215,
216, 218
shareholder value 144–6, 156
shareholders, collective action problem
of 140–46
shelf fees 81
Shiller, R.J. 10, 22
Shleifer, A. 30, 34, 35, 37, 43, 53, 139,
141
Simin, T.T. 72
Simon, H. 17
Singapore Central Provident Fund 148
single-equation studies 182–4, 185
single manager asset class options 159,
160, 161, 171–2
single manager diversified options 159,
171
size 25, 26–7
skill mix 19, 214
small accounts, waiver of charges on 68
small funds 62, 64, 85, 86, 87
Smith, R.S. 180, 185, 188

social assets 21–2
social relationships 73–4
socially targeted investments 190
Sociedad de Inversión Especializada en
    Fondos para el Retiro (SIEFORES)
    119, 121
solvency of pension plans 224
    modelling 225–7
    solvency ratio 227–9, 233
sophistication of markets 215, 218
specialization 167
Spitzer, E. 70
stakeholder capitalism 145
Stetson, A. 58
stock funding ratio 180, 181, 183–4,
    186, 187–8, 191–4, 195, 196, 199
stock participation products 143, 144
stockbroking fees 81
Stolper, A. 58
Stone, M.S. 184, 191, 194
strong theory of rules 20–21
structural model of firm default 224,
    232–8
styles
    mismatches between investment styles
        and benchmarks 166–8
    supervisory 100, 125–7, 134, 136–7
Sunden, A. 190, 195
Sunsuper 159, 170–72
Superannuation Guarantee
    (Administration) Act (1992)
    (Australia) 66
Superannuation Industry (Supervision)
    Act (SIS Act) (1993) (Australia) 66,
    67, 77
Superintendencia de Administradoras de
    Fondos de Jubilaciones y Pensiones
    (SAFJP) 122–3
Superintendencia de Administrados de
    Fondos de Pensiones (SAFP) 121–2
Supervisory, Oversight and Response
    System (SOARS) 112
supervisory practices 4, 99–138
    comparative analysis 108–10, 125–33,
        134
    cross-country evaluation 110–25
    primary elements of supervision
        102–8
    methodology 108–10
    theoretical framework 100–102

supervisory styles 100, 125–7, 134,
    136–7

takeover, threat of 141–2, 146, 153
Taleb, N.N. 73
taxes, dedicated 189, 192, 193–4, 196
taxpayers 151–2, 155
Thakor, A.V. 143
timing of twin reforms 52–3
Timmermann, A. 72, 159
training 105, 206, 207
transparency 24, 154
trust institutions 11–12, 13, 25
trustees
    Australian trustees' perception of their
        role and effectiveness 4, 200–219
    beliefs, attitudes and working
        relationships 207–10
    decision making 211, 212–13, 214
    industry issues 211, 215, 216,
        218–19
    survey instrument 202
    trustee demographics 202–3, 204–5
    classification of Australian funds 62
    competence 10, 19, 26
    discretion 9, 10, 11–12, 81, 82–3
    expertise 3, 10, 16–19, 20–21, 26,
        201, 203–7
    fitness of 67
    functions of and potential conflicts of
        interest 74–83

underfunding 179, 182–4, 197
unemployment 191, 193, 199
union directors 74
United Kingdom (UK) 29, 88
    distribution of pension schemes by
        credit rating category 242, 243
    mis-selling scandal in life insurance
        70, 77
    Morris review 2
    Myners review 2, 10, 17, 23, 26, 80,
        201
    PPF 5, 223, 225, 227, 245
    survey of large pension funds 4,
        201–2, 203, 211, 216
United States of America (US) 12, 29,
    70, 142, 200
    EBSA 113
    ERISA 115, 141, 193, 223

Federal Thrift Savings Plan 201
IRS 113
PBGC 223, 225, 227, 234–5, 239, 245
public sector pension governance,
    funding and performance 4,
    179–99
  empirical methodology 185–91
  empirical results 191–6
  endogenous dependent variables
      183, 187–8, 192, 199
  explanatory variables 183–4,
      188–91, 192–3, 199
  overview 180–82
  previous research 182–5
Sarbanes-Oxley legislation 1–2, 2–3
supervisory practice 113–14, 125–33,
    134
Useem, M. 189, 190
Utgoff, K.P. 239

value-at-risk (VAR) model 117, 118
Viceira, L. 16
Vishny, R.W. 139, 141

voluntary pension systems
  pay-as-you-go 31, 47–8, 49, 50
  supervisory practice 101, 133, 134,
      135–6

wages, public sector 185
Wagner, R.K. 17–18
Watson Wyatt 2, 201
weighting schemes 162–3, 163–4
Weisbach, M.S. 143
Weiss, M.A. 77
whistleblower requirements 103
Williams, A. 11
Williams, R. 18
Williamson, O. 16–17, 74
Winkelvoss, H. 186
Winterbotham, M. 18
Wolfenzon, D. 30, 34, 35, 37, 43, 53
Wong, M. 72, 85
working relationships 207–10
WorldCom 1, 14, 200

Zultowski, W.H. 77